MAKE
WORLD

Val Morgan

Deaths Disasters and Destinies
Anglo Norman History in Twelve Lives

© 2023 **Europe Books**| London
www.europebooks.co.uk | info@europebooks.co.uk

ISBN 9791220144056
First edition: November 2023

Deaths Disasters and Destinies
Anglo Norman History in Twelve Lives

To all the chroniclers and historians of every age.

Grateful thanks to my husband, first reader of the manuscript, to Anat who generously contributed her invaluable insights, and thanks to all who have helped with the making of this book.

"Since we have seen many strange changes in England in our days, and developments which were quite unknown in former days, I committed to writing a brief record of some of these things, lest the knowledge of them should be entirely lost to future generations."

Eadmer, opening words of The Life of St Anselm (12th century)

Table of Contents

INTRODUCTION	17
Chapter One	40
The Death of William the Conqueror	40
Chapter Two	59
Wulfnoth – A long and wearisome life	59
Chapter Three	77
The Tragic Love of Gunhild and Count Alan	77
Chapter Four	102
William Rufus – Accident or Murder?	102
Chapter Five	132
Eadmer's Dilemma	132
Chapter Six	163
Ranulf Flambard: Escape from the Tower	163
Chapter Seven	197
Edith and Matilda	197
Chapter Eight	235
The Cousins' Tragedy	235
Chapter Nine	269
Unfortunate Life and Death of Robert Curthose	269
Chapter Ten	304

The Obscure Life and Death of Edgar Aetheling..............304

Chapter Eleven 327

William Warelwast: A Double Destiny 327

Chapter Twelve 356

The Connecting Life – Anselm 356

CONCLUSION..364

INTRODUCTION

1066 is a date everyone knows, the date of the invasion and conquest of England by William, Duke of Normandy, who became the only English monarch to bear the title 'Conqueror'. People have remembered it for nearly a thousand years.

Our earliest knowledge of these events derives in large part from the first scribes and writers who remain relatively unknown. They were mainly monks keeping chronicles and cartularies for their own abbeys or monasteries. They had many reasons for writing about the conquest. Some were trying to understand it, some to celebrate it, some trying to grasp its significance, locate its causes, observe its actors and record its effects. Some wanted to understand the meaning of these events as part of the unfolding order of God's great creation because few doubted that God disposed all things. In the Western Christian world view, everything was understood to be guided by divine authority. One monk wrote at the time that the Norman victory of 1066 could be explained by "nothing else than the miraculous intervention of God."

Among the first to record the astonishing events of 1066 and its aftermath were the small group of monks who, over many years, had been writing what has become known as the *Anglo-Saxon Chronicle*. This was not a single work, as the name suggests, but rather a collection of chronicle manuscripts. They took the form of expanded annals and were written in English. The great abbeys and monasteries of England including Peterborough, Abingdon, Worcester, Canterbury and Winchester, contributed to these chronicle histories.

The church needed to know the saints' days and how to calculate a moveable date for Easter. Therefore, keeping a 'chronicle' (literally a record of events in order of time) was not only useful but vital. Just as important for the annalist, however, was to know when one year ended and another began. Some writings accept December 25th as the starting point of the calendar year. Other entries in the eleventh century begin the year on March 25, the Feast of the Annunciation. Other writers claim the Feast of the Circumcision, January 1st as the beginning of the year. These discrepancies were adjusted by later authorities to produce a uniform calendar for the purposes of stabilising the Christian year and a reliable chronology for the purposes of history writing.

A Christian calendar to order the year of observance, a chronicle to record events across successive years; these developments gave rise to an increasing sense of God's plan for his Creation, a new focus on the events that had been divinely ordered in God's universe.

Our modern sense of history sees an established area of knowledge with rules for research, presentation and analysis which is very different from the medieval view. But common ground can be found in the very human need to tell stories. A need that stretches back into the dimmest parts of human memory and comes back in vivid form as myths and fables, a need that has been answered in every age in innumerable ways and is never exhausted. We are fascinated by our own lives and the lives of others wherever and whenever they lived.

The emphasis in the twelve lives depicted in this book, therefore, is on people, on the personality of individuals, the relationships between them and on the interconnectedness of contemporaries. Most of the people in this book knew each other, very often over a long period, their lives touched in many different places in different ways; they were related, they had relationships, whether hostile or friendly -- or both – or, ranging from one to the other with sometimes astonishing speed. For example, Ranulf Flambard, who was imprisoned by Henry I for a number of crimes, was not only forgiven but subsequently employed on spying missions later in the reign. Anselm, Archbishop of Canterbury was twice exiled, then recalled; people changed sides, enemies became friends, family members fell out, war and peace were made with equal readiness. By tracking these connections, it is possible to view the characters in various modes of life, through a range of experiences that give insight into their personalities. Many of the following chapters deal not only with events but processes which happen over time. What they reveal, very often, is how these people develop and interact over the course of years, how they reach different understandings, have different priorities and so on. What the book seeks to do is to highlight the complexity of these threads. While the characters are the heroes of their own tales, they are also part players in the stories of others, they appear each time in a slightly different light, revealing different aspects of themselves, under new variations of light and colour.

Medieval recordists and chroniclers, perhaps with a few honourable exceptions, habitually offer us the record of outward actions and events. Personality is often missed. But the subtle undercurrents of historical causes are sometimes irreducible to anything but personality, the inestimable conflux of what makes an individual at a particular time. The very idea of an 'individual' when applied to the Middle Ages, often comes under challenge. We tend to think of people as stamped with 'sameness' by the church that created their belief structure and controlled their behaviour. This is a stereotype, of course, and does an injustice to the diversity of the personalities and temperaments at play. From William Rufus's sardonic humour and penchant for bad jokes, to Edith/Matilda's sharp intelligence, to Anselm's scrupulosity which sometimes caused debilitating inertia, to Henry I's political savvy and Robert Curthoses's unfortunate penchant for wrong choices, not to mention the bright frenetic span of Ranulf Flambard's active years as a political fixer to the powerful - there are many clues to personality which give insight into the common threads of these interconnected life stories.

What we most often mean by 'history' is 'historiography' - written histories. But the written narratives of the Anglo-Norman period are often unreliable, partisan and fraught with interpretive hazards. The chronicler, even though he may be living very close to the time about which he is writing, often has to rely on earlier works whose veracity cannot be established. In this way he is in a similar situation to the modern historical novelist, but the novelist is in the happy position of being able to fill in the blank spaces with imaginative invention. Yet the difference hasn't always been well-established. To the writing monks and chroniclers of that period, the differences between history and fable, myth, sacred legend and other forms of imaginative writing were not strongly defined. This was particularly so in the case of the hagiographies. Writing the biography of a saint or holy person was a common undertaking of the monks. But it was not always pleasant or easy. Sometimes it was an onerous obligation. Chapter Five examines the difficulties and drama that Eadmer underwent in trying to complete such a task and how this apparently anodyne activity involved him in great personal anguish.

In general, though, the 'Lives of Saints' were concerned to give an account of the special blessedness of the saint in question. They often combined factual details with anecdote and miraculous story. They were religious works rather than 'History'. These forms of writing were all concerned with telling memorable stories – and this, too, is the main focus of the historical novelist. It might even be the case that the modern historical novelist is at more pains to 'get the facts right' than the early historians. For example, Geoffrey of Monmouth's, *Historia Regum Britanniae*, or *History of the Kings of Britain*, written in Latin and finished about 1136, although called a 'History', is rather a compilation of legend, fabulous tale, and imaginative invention. This supposed 'history' traces the story of the Kings of Britain from mythological beginnings in ancient Troy and portrays figures such as King Lear, Cymbeline, King Arthur and Merlin. It has little veracity as 'history' but has remained a powerful source of romantic stories, used by many later writers including Thomas Malory, Shakespeare, Dryden and Tennyson. But it is worth noting that Geoffrey of Monmouth claims that he **translated** the book out of an 'ancient British language' as though he felt the need to connect his book with some 'original' in order to give it an authentic status. As this was not the 'original' of historical fact, he claimed that it derived from the original of a 'native' language (probably Welsh), which is also doubtful. The idea implicit here is that you need to anchor your historical narrative in some 'original,' or ultimate truth.

***

Who wrote the first Histories?
More reliable than Geoffrey of Monmouth are the great history writers of the time, the best sources for this period: Eadmer, Orderic Vitalis, William of Malmesbury and Henry of Huntingdon. They write in Latin not English; they may be of mixed parentage or have English and Continental connections. But these writers, along with their contemporaries, offer us a paradoxical state of affairs – an extensive legacy of written texts of uncertain reliability.

Eadmer of Canterbury was born about 1060 and brought up by the monks of Canterbury from about the age of six and became a monk there. When Anselm became Archbishop in 1093, Eadmer devoted himself to writing about his life. The resulting work, the *Vita Sancti Anselmi*, is an invaluable source about the later years of William II. Eadmer's *Historia Novorum in Anglia (Recent Events in England)* sets Anselm's dealings in a wider context and is a vividly observed record of the times. Although he travelled widely, in England, Normandy, Lyons and Rome, among other places, Eadmer was devoted to Canterbury. He was deeply attached to the English traditions of Canterbury, to the old saints and old liturgy that had been swept aside by the increasing Normanisation of the English church. Although he felt that Anselm could have done more to defend the ancient practices of the English church, Eadmer was a partisan of Anselm and remained loyal throughout his life.

His writing conveys the immediacy of reportage, because, unlike most of the chroniclers, he was present at many of the occasions he describes and lived for many years as companion, secretary and disciple in Anselm's household. He records some of Anselm's memories and dreams which, one assumes, were told to him in the privacy of a close acquaintance; he includes certain of Anselm's letters and their replies, using them to make a point about his character or to illustrate his dealings; equally he records the 'miracles' but tells us he did not ever observe any miraculous events himself. In any other age Eadmer would have been widely read; he had imagination and a feeling for the dramatic moment. His style is vivid and at times goes beyond the traditional hagiography. While striving to give us the public face of the saint, Eadmer also gives glimpses of the private man. Sometimes we can overhear Anselm's conversation through Eadmer's gift for recording natural dialogue. Without Eadmer's writings our understanding of the period and of Anselm's motivation and character would be greatly impoverished. Understanding Eadmer himself, however, is a much more difficult task. An attempt is made in Chapter Five.

Orderic Vitalis was born in or near Shrewsbury in 1075 and was sent to Normandy in 1085 to become a child oblate at the Benedictine Abbey of Saint-Évroult in Normandy where he remained for the rest of his life. This Norman monastery was his home until he died around 1142. His work, *Historia ecclesiastica* is generally considered the most valuable for Norman, English, and French history in the period 1082–1141.

William of Malmesbury's *Gesta Regum Anglorum*, 'Deeds of the English Kings', was completed in 1125. William was born of mixed parentage about 1095 and entered the monastery at Malmesbury. At that time the abbot was a Norman monk from the abbey of Jumièges, which produced the national historian, William of Jumièges. So, in a community of mainly English monks led by a Norman abbot, William of Malmesbury got first-hand experience of living the integrated life in an Anglo-Norman community. How this may have affected his views, we do not know.

Henry of Huntingdon (1088-1157) is the third of the trio of major Anglo-Norman historians. Again, he was of mixed parentage. But perhaps more importantly, he was the first of the great historians who was not a monk. He was a secular priest and was married, as many priests at that time still were. His great work, *Historia Anglorum*, commissioned by the Bishop of Lincoln, carried the Norman story up to 1154 when King Stephen died, making way for Henry II, the first of the Plantagenets.

Hériman de Tournai (after 1090 - 1147) Abbot of Tournai (then in Flanders, now in Belgium). Wrote what might be called a town chronicle in Latin prose. The third abbot of Saint Martin of Tournai, he was a chronicler of his abbey and, in many anecdotal accounts connected with St Martin's, a social historian, giving a view from the perspective of his abbey which was an important ecclesiastical centre at the crossroads of Europe.

William of Jumièges

Perhaps the foremost chronicler from the Norman point of view was the Benedictine monk who wrote the *'Gesta Normannorum Ducum'* or 'Deeds of the Norman Dukes' between the 1050s and 1070. We know very little about his personal life beyond his association with Jumièges, a monastery of ancient foundation and great prestige. It is thought he was born about the year 1000 and he died some time after 1070 when he finished the Gesta. He has the distinction of giving us the first prose account of the conquest of England in 1066, although he was not an eyewitness to these events and was probably writing at the request of William the Conqueror, to provide a first blast of positive publicity.

The purposes of history

All these historians, with the exception of the last two, identified themselves as English in some way and showed a strong attachment to the country. But unlike the Anglo-Saxon Chroniclers they did not write in English and all of them, except possibly Eadmer, had Continental ancestors. Divided allegiances meant that their judgements and evaluations could be complex and nuanced. They might, for example, be writing in celebration of a particular individual –a saint, a king, an abbot, or commissioned to write from a particular point of view. But, as Christian historians, they were shaped by the historical understanding that God played the dominating role in history. The purpose of history was to teach moral lessons. We still talk loosely about 'lessons from history' but the chronicling monks were more actively concerned with the didactic power of history. History, they believed, teaches people about what happened, what can happen, what God allows and what he forbids.

A useful example of this practice can be seen in Orderic Vitalis's account of the death of William the Conqueror. Orderic emulates classical historians by putting detailed and dramatic speeches in the mouths of protagonists. Thus, the Conqueror is given a moving death-bed speech of contrition, lamenting his manifold sins and the cruelty of his conquest. There is no prior reference to such a speech, though other chroniclers seem to borrow it from Orderic. This is a moral story designed to show the necessity of penance even among the highest. Similarly, the death-chamber scene describes how the king's faithless hangers-on proceed to ransack his treasures, helping themselves to whatever they can find: arms, vessels, clothing, silks and embroideries, the royal furnishings. Orderic alleges that they left the royal corpse 'almost naked on the floor of the house.' Another moral story, this time to show that even the greatest may be reduced to nothing if God so disposes. No evidence exists for these stories and there is no corroborating version. Like so many of the chroniclers, Orderic was not present at the events he was describing and was writing decades afterwards. He was not a witness and the nearest he could get to a first-hand account was perhaps to question a few elderly persons long afterwards.

With the honourable exception of a few writers, this was a time when no critical analysis of the historical process, no sophisticated sense of historical detachment, no real commitment to check facts, question sources, collect data, travel to interviews and so on, was made. History was largely written from the perspective of God's unfolding plan, historians were, in a sense, trying to record the events that had been ordered in God's universe. To record was not to explain. God could not be called on to explain.

Constructing the Conquest

Another important influence on the way historians constructed their versions of the Conquest was bound up with the art of literature itself. After all, history was considered to be a part of grammar or rhetoric. History wasn't a *'disciplina'* in its own right but a branch of the trivium - grammar, logic and rhetoric. Literary effects such as tropes, metaphors, symbols, allegory, *imitatio*, were used as techniques of narrative rather than as real attempts to reflect living people or genuine dialogue. All the contemporary or near-contemporary historians of the conquest were using the events of the conquest to provide a framework for their own preoccupations. They would be influenced by their allegiances, their political and religious affiliations, or they were concerned to celebrate a patron. In addition, these historians would be influenced by whichever classical models they were using for their own practice.

There was, in other words, no attempt to analyse the dynamic of history. Thus, many factors converge in these writings – not simply the matter of laying bare 'historical truth'. In fact, they can be considered complex texts, inscribed with much more than the 'history' they purport to tell. Bound up in these writings are other stories of the writers themselves and their world. And it is to the gifted writers of these early texts that we are indebted for our first vision of the Anglo-Norman period.

Normandy not France

The importance of this era in the development of a distinctively Anglo-Norman culture cannot be overstated. On the world stage, too, great changes were happening. What follows is an attempt at scene-setting to illustrate the background against which the lives of our twelve characters play out.

In this era 'Normandy' must be distinguished from the 'France' of which it is now a part. Normandy was a duchy held by a duke who nominally paid homage to the French king but was in fact often more powerful. 'France' was at this time only a little remnant of the great empire of Francia and consisted mostly of the territories around the 'Ile de France.' Areas of present-day France such as Blois, Maine, Brittany were in various degrees of relationship to the French king but were not part of a homogenous nation called 'France.' After the conquest of England, the power of Normandy increased dramatically and led to constant battles with the French kings who struggled to maintain or increase their borders.

The Feudal System

The first two decades after the Norman Conquest saw a tremendous shift in the pattern of landownership and the imposition of what the historian Michael Woods calls 'a true feudal system.' Feudal is a word deriving from the Late Latin *feudum* and refers to the system of land tenure based on the 'fief' where a tenant or vassal holds land on the condition of military service. It is connected with the word 'fee' or the expression 'to hold in fee' which implies a heritable right to the property held. The system functioned not so much through bureaucracy and written contracts as by oath-swearing and verbal contracts, thus personal loyalty from vassal to overlord played a huge part. Where this failed, we come, of course, to the 'feud' which is a word derived from the same root and is what happened when the system broke down.

Last Conquest

This period saw the last time England was conquered by an invading power. Attacks were made from time to time but never a complete conquest in the Norman style. At the time of King John and the Barons' War the French king's son, Louis, invaded England, captured Winchester and had himself proclaimed king in London. But all of this was doomed to failure, and, after a wasteful and destructive series of sieges and battles, Louis was forced to negotiate. He gave up his claim to the throne and acknowledged that he had never been king of England. Invasions from France often occurred but they were made mainly by dynastic claimants during the Wars of the Roses and later. Henry Bolingbroke and Henry Tudor 'invaded' at different times and made themselves kings but there was never any incursion into England on the scale of the Norman Invasion which changed the nature of English life and the English language permanently or marked a date so crucially central to the English imagination as 1066. In the Raid on the Medway the Dutch famously attacked the fleet at Chatham and Gillingham in 1667; sporadic raiding parties occurred in coastal towns, one of the worst during the American War of Independence when

Captain John Paul Jones landed and looted in Whitehaven in 1778. Other invasion attempts were made by the Spanish in 1588 (Armada) and the Nazis in 1940 (Operation Sealion). But as is well-known, there was never a successful invasion of England after 1066, certainly never one that changed the country permanently.

Holy War

In this period occurred the first appeal for a Christian war against the non-Christians of the East, later termed the 'First Crusade.' Originally an appeal from the Pope to help Emperor Alexios Komnenos of Constantinople who was in the unenviable position of having to defend Constantinople against growing forces of Seljuk Turks. Pope Urban appealed to Christian knights in the West to volunteer their aid, a task which was touted as so holy that God would forgive all sins for all participants. The defence of Constantinople then morphed into a war against the occupying forces of the Holy Land and resulted in the so-called 'liberation' of the Holy Sepulchre.

The Great Schism

Pope Urban's support of Constantinople was particularly noteworthy because of the Great Schism between the churches of the East and the West that had occurred in 1054. This never-healed rift between the churches occurred over intractable theological, doctrinal and liturgical differences. The Western Roman Catholic Church adopted a creed, a liturgy, a calendar, Feast and Holy days, and other customs and practices that did not please the older, Greek-speaking churches of the East. Differences between the two leaders, the Pope and Patriarch, mounted over the preceding decades until, in 1054, the Christian Church split apart. The result was a permanent division of the Christian Church into the Roman Catholic West and the Orthodox Churches of the East.

Pre-Conquest Norman soft power

In the years leading up to the Conquest, England already had substantial links to the European mainland. This was partly because of the widespread intermarriage of Norman families, who then settled in England, and partly because of the recruitment of high church officials from continental monasteries. Therefore, it is a mistake to think that the Conquest somehow imposed an entirely alien and unknown culture and language on the country. Normans had long been at the court of King Edward the Confessor, who was himself half-Norman. In royal circles, not English but Norman French was spoken. The complexity of this pre-Conquest period is illustrated through a single life in Chapter Two and touched on from a contrasting perspective in Chapter Ten.

It is probably better to think in terms of a Norman-dominated English Court. It was Norman-speaking and had a long acquaintance with the culture. Equally many of the abbeys and monasteries had historical connections with the continental church and had been dealing with the Pope in Rome for centuries. In contrast to these Norman-penetrated institutions around the court, the mass of inhabitants was thoroughly English in culture and customs. The majority of the population lived in rural areas and spoke English. To them the Conquest was something of a shock but probably did not change the labouring lives of the poor as much as one might imagine. They still laboured for someone else, they were still taxed, they were still poor. But the conquest transformed the lives of the English aristocracy, both secular and clerical. Something of this situation can be found in Chapter Ten which illustrates the pressure of these complexities in operation on a single individual.

Post Conquest, Immediate Aftermath

After the single successful encounter known as the Battle of Hastings, the Norman conquest proceeded with speed. This battle, which occurred some distance from the place which bears its name, took place on October 14th. William burned and hacked his way to London and was crowned king on Christmas Day at Westminster, the traditional coronation venue of English Kings. Total subjection of the country followed and, except for the northern borderlands, was accomplished within the next twenty years. Violent suppression in the north, often called the Harrying of the North, caused ruination of the land for a generation and thousands were slaughtered. In other areas of the country the takeover proceeded with less bloodshed. It is clear from the survey of 1086 that a wholesale transference of land had taken place in two decades. The church, too, underwent a mass change of personnel.

By 1075 only one English bishop was left in post, Bishop Wulfstan of Worcester. He was the last surviving pre-Conquest bishop, having been appointed in 1062. He was something of a social reformer and earned a saintly reputation for interesting himself in poor relief in his diocese. Installations of bishops and archbishops proceeded apace after 1066 with monks and priests from prestigious Norman houses, most notably the Abbey of Our Lady at Bec, being placed in key English dioceses. Many of the new appointees were of Italian birth, such as Lanfranc in 1070 and Anselm in 1093. Both these men who became Archbishops of Canterbury were former Abbots of Bec.

In regard to secular society, during these twenty years many dispossessed English women whose menfolk had been killed in battle fled to holy houses, monasteries and nunneries. The nunnery at Wilton in Witshire gave sanctuary to the relatives of the defeated King Harold. One of these was his daughter, Gunhild, who spent many years at Wilton and received a superior education there as we can tell from the letters she later wrote to Anselm. Her story, including her remarkable and tragic love affair with the great Norman magnate, Count Alan Rufus, is the subject of Chapter Three.

Why the church mattered and why it was 'political'

As in most pre-modern ages, religion was important both as a practice of belief and as a means of social organisation. Throughout this period there was a struggle between the church and the monarch to establish the limits of secular power. One of the hottest issues of the Norman period was Investiture. Not for nothing was its worst phase called the 'Investiture Crisis.' This long-running crisis made life difficult for kings, sent churchmen into exile and provoked fierce arguments. It was an issue of burning importance which for many years seemed irresolvable. By a mixture of long custom, lazy habits and lack of reform, kings and other laymen had acquired the power to appoint churchmen to high office. Thus, for example, William the Conqueror appointed

Lanfranc of Bec as Archbishop of Canterbury in 1070. Part of the reason was because Lanfranc would largely go along with the king's policies. In a similar move, William II, known as 'Rufus' appointed Anselm of Bec as Lanfranc's successor.

But this partnership did not work quite so well as Anselm was not always conformable to the king's wishes. A movement towards reform of this practice became stronger after the death of the Conqueror and, from 1099, Pope Paschal began to make serious noises of discontent, including threats of excommunication. He encouraged bishops to dispute the right of any king, or any layman whatsoever, to appoint men to holy office. Essentially, the dispute was about two contrasting things: money and spirituality. If a king or layman could appoint a bishop to receive the revenue of the episcopal lands, he would to some extent, have a say over the receipt of those monies. Many thought this weakened the church by siphoning off money and authority. But there was a deeper question. Could laymen, whose hands were regularly bloodied by warfare, have the right to appoint men to spiritual office?

The protracted and bitter disputes of the Investiture Crisis form the background to Chapter Four.

Alternatives to War

In the archival records there is evidence of a large number of negotiations and treaties from this time. It suggests that although battles were constantly fought by princes and magnates jostling for power, on occasion more peaceful solutions were sought. Where concessions could be made, they were often to be preferred: treaties, truces, compromises, negotiations, marriages were other means to achieve one's aims. Kings such as Henry I, who were successful war-leaders and ready peacemakers, were widely respected. Though he did not fail to make war, when necessary, he was often ready to compromise and to that end astutely surrounded himself with good negotiators and advisers. It is most unfortunate that his largely peaceful reign was followed by the Anarchy, a violent and destructive period which threw a shadow over the previous few decades. Some of the events leading to the Anarchy, and the personalities involved, are the subject of Chapter Eight.

Property transmission

During this period, habits of property transmission began to change. Marriage, as always, remained an essential means of property transfer and, even before the conquest, intermarriage between English and Norman families was not unusual. In due course, the youngest son of the Conqueror, Henry, married a lady of the English royal line, Edith, in 1101. Her story is the subject of Chapter Seven. 'Primogeniture' (sole succession by eldest son) concentrated lands and power in the hands of a few. Property was not dispersed successively down the generations, but rather retained or augmented by one inheriting branch of the family. The Normans operated this practice but did not impose it all at once. In the course of time, however, it became widely adopted as the primary means of property transference in England. Ironically, this was a problem for William the Conqueror since neither his dukedom of Normandy nor his kingdom of England transferred smoothly on his death. The devastating consequences for his sons, particularly the eldest, Robert, is the theme of Chapter Nine.

The Great Survey of 1086

Perhaps most famously William the Conqueror is associated with what became called in common parlance the Domesday Book but was originally known, among other titles, as the Great Description. In fact, it was, in the words of the historian Michael Woods 'a tax or geld inquest', in other words a comprehensive land survey of his English territory. It was the most thorough and extensive survey of its kind, but not a totally new innovation as some may think. As Michael Woods points out: "Domesday inevitably raises the questions as to how detailed such records were before 1066." It seems that from the later 10th century at least, fairly accurate records were kept by the great monastic foundations about their estates, including some records and genealogies of the peasantry and lists of the animals that lived on abbey land. Also, when you look at the Domesday Book with its endlessly repeated letters TRE you are given a brief glimpse into an even earlier age: *Tempus Regis Edwardi*, the time of Edward (1042-1066). These letters occur after the entries recording the property details of 1086 and introduce the corresponding amounts for Edward's reign. For example, that such-and-such a place is held by so-and-so and comprises 10 pigs, a mill, 5 ploughs and is worth 8 shillings. The entry might then go on to read: 'TRE 10 shillings,' meaning that its value in King Edward's time had been two shillings more. This raises the question: where did the details about King Edward's time come from? Historians suggest that before the Conquest the country had an efficient system of local and central government with trained officials, systematic tax levies and record keeping. The Domesday Book is therefore making use of a fact-finding structure already in place. It not only records the state of the country as it was in 1086 but also tells the conquerors what its valuation was at an earlier time.

Interestingly, the Domesday Book is not actually a book but rather a collection of manuscripts. Its historic text consists of two volumes known as 'Great Domesday', now bound in two parts, and 'Little Domesday', now bound in three. 'Little Domesday' is not a supplement to the 'Great Domesday' but rather: "an undigested remnant of an intermediate stage of the survey," as Professor G. H. Martin puts it in the Introduction to the Penguin edition of the complete translation. A closely connected collection of manuscripts, known as the 'Exon Domesday,' covers the five counties of Cornwall, Devon, Dorset, Somerset and Wiltshire. London is treated separately.

Wider context

The Norman Conquest will probably always inhabit the public mind as a great schismatic event when everything in England changed. As we have seen, that was not exactly the case. Norman influence had been felt for years, not only in England but in the Mediterranean, Sicily, Calabria, Apulia, even as far as Constantinople. How did that happen?

Beginning in the ninth century Norse immigrants from Denmark, Norway and Sweden started landing in the north of France. In a short span of years their descendants had established themselves in the Northern French mainland. Their story begins in 911 when their leader, Rollo, swore fealty to Charles III of West Francia and established a territory later to become the Dukedom of Normandy. The Norsemen adopted the Gallo-Roman language of the Frankish people which they then hammered into shape as Norman French and began to produce the effects and artifacts of culture: manuscripts, poetry, artworks, letters. By the time they invaded and subdued the neighbouring kingdom of England they were thoroughly Christianised, had developed a form of architecture known as Romanesque, and had acquired or invented musical and literary traditions. They were also formidable warriors. The Norman dynasty had a major political, cultural and military impact in many parts of Europe and the Middle East. Some of this story is told in Chapter Nine.

The Conqueror

The presiding spirit of England's early Norman years is, of course, William, the illegitimate son of Duke Robert of Normandy. He is known by one title only, having swopped the dismissive 'bastard' for the enduring and never-to-be-repeated 'Conqueror.' Chapter One sets the scene of the period with an intense focus on this magnificent ego. Injured and dying, he lies contemplating his own personal mortality at the moment he is about to pass into the immortality of enduring fame. In this first chapter I wanted to get inside the mind of William the Conqueror, sitting in his brain as the fever burns during his agonising death. Who and what was this phenomenal man? A giant figure on the historical landscape even now, almost a thousand years after his death. While the 'facts' in this chapter are well established and can be found in authoritative histories by noted authors, I was tempted to tell the story of this cruel and tortured death in an intensely modern and personal style, dedicating it, in a spirit of thanks, appreciation and respect to the early chroniclers.

Finally, and inevitably, the question will be asked: "Is another such book really needed?" Every time a new work on Churchill or Wellington, Queen Elizabeth I or some other prominent historical person comes out, that question is asked. And the answer is always 'yes.' There is always more to say and another way of saying it. New facts emerge through archaeology, archival research, memoirs or new insights into old material. Historiography is rarely unpoliticised but has become increasingly politicised today. We cannot help but bring present day interests and perceptions to our treatments of the past. That is why there is always room for another history book.

Chapter One
The Death of William the Conqueror

The man in the bed was about sixty years old, big-framed and corpulent. He had been in reasonable health until a few weeks ago. He had not caught a disease. No-one had attacked him or plotted to kill him, although plenty of people would have been ready to try. In his life he had made enemies. Many had cause to bear a grudge against him, including members of his own family. But this man was a king. Who would risk God's punishment by striking down a king? Who could get near enough, who would dare try?

But it wasn't revenge or sudden illness that brought him down. On the contrary, it was a trivial incident, a banal piece of bad luck. Malign or whimsical, luck will play its sly little tricks, even around the mighty. And so it happened to the King of England, the man who was called the Conqueror.

In July 1087 King William was leading an expedition against French incursions in the Vexin region of Normandy. His own renegade son Robert, in league with Philip of France had dared to make war against him. So William had seized Mantes, burned the town, sacked the monastery and filled the surrounding roads with fleeing townsfolk and monks.

On the way back from Mantes, his horse had suddenly taken fright and reared up. Many times, in his half century of furious riding he had experienced exactly the same response from a spooked horse and instantly regained control, barely shifting in the saddle. But this time he had fallen forward on the stout pommel, and it had dug into his belly, scrunched under the rib cage, broken through the skin and ruptured his innards. It felt like an explosion in his belly. Gasping in pain while trying to hide the seriousness of his injury and bringing his horse under control, he was at length eased from the saddle by his escort and carried to a nearby house. It soon became clear that he was in a condition far beyond serious. Decisions would have to be made by those close to him, quickly.

His knights and nobles grew alarmed and began to argue over what was to be done. A king could not be allowed to die just anywhere, he must get to holy ground. He must receive the viaticum, be shriven, be absolved. Kings have more sins than other men, they reasoned, and without the proper ministrations he would be doomed to the torments of hell. But any monks in Mantes who might have prayed for him a week ago, certainly would not do so now. He must be taken to a monastery or priory elsewhere.

The choice fell on the priory of Saint Gervase. A litter was brought from somewhere and William was carried out to begin the journey to Rouen, nearly fifty miles away. It was not at all certain that he would arrive as a living king and Duke of Normandy. The journey was tedious because the litter went slowly so as to spare the injured man suffering. But suffering could not be spared, so serious was his condition. Sometimes he raged at his attendants. Still believing himself in command, he sent orders to his nobles to withdraw their forces from the Vexin. At other times he lay quiet, or had his chaplain walk alongside to speak consoling words.

At length St Gervase was reached. He was transferred to a hurriedly prepared bedchamber in the abbot's house, hung with fleabane and pungent with the smell of burning herbs which later mingled with the incense of the monks who came to say mass. Physicians came and discussed among themselves what cures to apply, spoke of Aristotle and Galen, of humours and sutures and what could be done to allay the pain. Various remedies were applied with varying degrees of failure, but no success. Except when sleeping, he was conscious and sometimes alert. He was used to keeping watch, used to hardship, used to being in command of himself. In his long life of battles, pain was just another enemy to be overcome. He thought of his son, Robert, sometimes in rage and sometimes with regret.

'Why, Robert? Why? What made you a renegade and rebel? Have I ever treated you unkindly?

The answer to this last question, he knew very well, was yes.

***

St Gervase was an abbey dependent on the great monastery of Fécamp, founded by another Duke of Normandy, the king's grandfather, Richard. Like all Norman dukes, he had been in need of the church's rites of forgiveness. Fécamp had become very famous because it boasted a relic of the real blood of Christ preserved in the church. But if the relic was brought out to perform a healing after the ordeal of his journey, it failed. William lay in agony for days with suppurating intestines while outside the roads buzzed with messengers. Then, bishops, abbots, monks and physicians with their hangers-on and servants, swarmed into the precincts.

But the people who should have been there weren't there. His brother, Odo, Bishop of Bayeux, was in prison for treason. His eldest son, Robert, had been in the midst of active treachery at the time of the accident and was a positive embarrassment to the whole court. William, his second son, was there, hanging about, itching for the old man to die. Henry, the youngest son, turned up with unseemly haste in the hope of securing a property inheritance, land and fiefs of his own. But the old man dwelt confusedly among the shades of the past.

'No land to the youngest, that was my motto. Let him go into the church. What use has he for land? Didn't I give him an education? What else for but that he would enter the church? I let Bishop Osmund take him, teach him Latin, writing, teach him how the interests of the church are best served by obeying kings. Good man, Osmund. And young Henry is an apt pupil. A capable youth, I admit. But sly, like a cat. Always was.'

Dimly aware that Henry was in the room, the old man caught snatches of conversation. Names he knew well were moving from mouth to mouth in excited whispers among the clerics. Lanfranc and Osmund.

William heard them. It was like being given two crutches to lean on. 'So, Osmund and Lanfranc are on their way. It must be serious then. Osmund, Bishop of Winchester, my old friend, my son's tutor. Lanfranc, Archbishop of Canterbury, the ablest minister in the realm. A man of probity and honour. I must tell Lanfranc to support young William for the throne, but even with Lanfranc to look out for him, there will be trouble.'

He still had a grasp of events. He foresaw difficulties. For instance, if William did establish himself on the throne, what would Robert do? And which of his brothers would Henry support?

'Well, his support won't count for much if he has no land and no knights. I still say, no land for Henry. But I will be generous.'

In the end Henry got five thousand pounds in silver, in large part from his mother's dowry. When it was withdrawn from the strong box a few days later, Henry weighed it out to the last ounce.

In fact, the matter of inheritance had been in a state of ambiguity for some time. But certain assumptions were made. Robert, as eldest son, was always expected to get Normandy, the dukedom, the title and all the appanages. If the second son, Richard, had not met an unfortunate end in a hunting accident in the New Forest, he would have inherited the English crown. On Richard's death, the next brother, another William, had stepped into the role of second son and expected to be named as heir. But he wasn't. And the expectation, continually put off, bit into him. All the Conqueror's sons were dissatisfied, in one way or another. There were no good relations either between themselves, or with their father. Henry, perhaps, as the youngest son, hungered for the recognition he had not received in childhood. If that hunger could be satisfied by lands: estates, a comté, an earldom, would it not be wise to give him a chance?

'No! I say it was wise to keep him waiting. Keep him on his toes. Well, he never rebelled like his brother, did he? though he had more aptitude for it. Denial sharpened him. So much for Henry. What shall I say of William? By the way, why do they call him Rufus? He's not choleric or florid or splenetic. Last time I saw him his hair was brown. Why *Rufus*? No matter. By God, though, the boy is well-humoured, convivial, generous, even. He didn't get that from me. Or his grandfather. Matilda's side, perhaps. He stayed loyal while Robert turned traitor. Yes, William will make a good enough king.

This last thought, however, was somehow never formulated, never formally declared or put in writing.

***

It was as if a shard of pain was lying in the bed, raw and bloody, with a man wrapped around it. He lay for days at a time, sometimes awake and breathing heavily, sometimes in a quasi-dream state where thoughts and memories brought the past close, the smells, the colours, the brutish fears, the tenuous joys, going right back to the old days in Falaise where he was born. Given his birth and family he could never have been a tender man. Yet once, he remembered clearly, he had loved someone, his old tutor, Ralph. Perhaps at the moment Ralph was killed, slaughtered in front of his child-eyes for reasons his child-understanding could not fathom, seeing the swift, brutish, finality of the act, he had let go of tenderness and love. Matilda, Matilda, though? Dead these four years. Peerless Matilda! Had it been love?

'I married a fierce woman, a Flanders countess, a strong, loyal woman who did not demand love but a share of power. Oh, what a couple we made! I could not have done it without her. I respected, I trusted, I adored her. I gave her nine children, or was it ten? But did I ever love her?

Love was not what he felt for his sons. His daughters, perhaps, or at least the thought of them. They had been no trouble. They were faceless, indistinct creatures, although, at a pinch, he could remember their names.

Agatha, Adela, Cecilia, Constance, was it? Adeliza. Oh God, so many! I gave two to the church and married off the others. Well, what would you? Adeliza took the veil, willingly. I say it was willingly. Cecilia though, was it wrong to give her to the church so young? An oblate child, gifted to Holy Trinity in Caen. Shall I send for her? Would she come to me if I did?

It was the boys, the squabbling boys, that wore us down. Even Matilda grew tired of their bickering. She always encouraged Robert, though, always her favourite. Their cursed fallings-out got worse as they grew, often drawing blood. Their flares of anger filled our lives with constant disturbances, shouting, brawling, puerile name calling. Alright, I was at fault, too, I admit. But what was I to do with Robert? Hopeless from the start: plump, short, the butt of grooms and ostlers. They called him 'Gambaron', 'Fat Legs' 'Curthose' and, instead of stopping it, I took it up. Trivial though this seems when measured against all his adult years, it is, I see now, the wounded core of Robert's character.

***

In the way of fevered men whose sleep is fitful and intermittent, William sometimes spoke and seemed lucid, giving orders to ministers or household servants. Sometimes he lay for hours in hectic sleep, peopled with dreams and loud with voices.

'If your father had ever made a proper Christian marriage,' said the voice in his head, 'you would not have stood a chance. Legitimate sons would have taken all the prizes. You would have been at best a menial, at worst a fatality. Bastard sons like you were put out of the way, often as not, or else consigned to the church. Your father, Duke Robert, never got the sons he wanted, sons sanctioned by the church, born in wedlock with a noble lady. Justice perhaps. He was an old-fashioned warlord. A semi-brute. How I adored him!

And in his rambling William would answer the voices that came and went, weaving into consciousness and out again as he held conversations with himself.

'And whatever you say of me, you out there in the darkness, hovering by my bed, whatever you say, I was worthy of more than a dukedom, as proved when God gave me victory in England. Cruel, we all were, had to be or else lose power, weaken, become prey. But I was never rapacious, or wanton. No, never.'

At the end of such ravings, he would be calm and descend into fitful sleep, during which time his physicians might come and replace the dressings on his wound, talking in low voices and shaking their heads. They tried poultices of marshmallow and mustard, pigeon innards, pastes of aromatic herbs, and infusions of meadowsweet to ease the pain. Nothing brought relief for more than a blessed hour of slumber.

Then one day a holy monk turned up and proved so importunate that he was allowed to speak to the king's physicians. It turned out that he had not always been a monk but was once a soldier serving as a Norman mercenary under the Byzantine Duke of Antioch. In his travels he had encountered many wonders and was bringing one of them to the king. He drew forth from his habit a small wooden box and opened it. He took out a stoppered clay jar. 'Put some drops in honeyed water and let him drink,' he said. 'It will take away the pain.' It was, he explained, poppy juice, a soporific used to great effect among the peoples of the east. The chief physician took the jar, intending to advocate its use since he was ready to try anything by that time. But others disagreed and, in the general squabble about the risk of using an unknown substance sourced by a stranger, it was put aside. It could be poison.

When the king's condition worsened and he was in such agony that he could not sleep, when he started to writhe and thrash, ripping away his dressings, when he began to claw at his wound as if to tear out the pain, calling on God or the devil, whoever would listen, spare me, spare me – when it got as bad as this, medical opinion shifted. After all, his condition was so grave what was to be lost? Why not try the stranger's remedy? So the little jar was brought out and some drops of its contents, diluted in honeyed water, given to the agonised man. After this he slept so profoundly that a new alarm arose. Perhaps it was poison, after all.

As the hours passed it was seen that this was an altogether different kind of sleep: peaceful, calm, a restorative sleep of the body, easy, free from pain and fever, a healing sleep such as they had not seen before. Then the physicians wondered just what sort of poppy juice the stranger had brought. But when they sent to ask him, they found he had gone. Rumours started up about a miraculous apparition. St Gervase himself had brought the blessed juice, not a simple monk. Surely this was a sign.

All that night the sick king lay in the abbot's bed, in a sleep so profound that the physicians grew anxious. Was he slipping into death? No-one guessed that an alert mind, loud with thoughts, busy with memories, regrets and insights was awake and active at some deep level in the profoundly sleeping body.

'I named my second son Richard after my grandfather, but he came to nothing. Even before he died in that wretched accident, catching his neck in a forked branch as he was hunting, (couldn't you have been more careful, you foolish boy?) I could see he had an impractical streak. He was careless of money, of people, of himself. A youth of looks, but no mettle. And William, what shall I say of William? Oh, so much promise! He has qualities, he can lead in the field, he has energy and focus. He can be shrewd. I can't say he's educated. He is easily distracted, letting his pleasures lead him. At leisure he dresses like a girl in soft drapes and bright colours and lies on swansdown. It wasn't so when Matilda was alive. When he looks at me, I see him challenging, saying - Well? What of it? What do you care? What have you ever cared?

Oh God have mercy!'

Sometimes he cried out like this, calling for mercy and the monks would come and pray for him. But he didn't always know when he was raving in his speech or only in his head. And he didn't know if any of it was true, or if he was just making it up out of the rags of guilt and the terror of death.

At such moments a physician might come and pull back his eyelids, looking down into the glittering yellow eyes.

'I know what you see there. I know. I look back and I see you looking at death.'

During the day there was a semi-permanent consultation going on around him. Physicians, monks and holy men reputed in the arts of healing would come and hold counsel together, talking in a huddle of whispers. There were comings and goings with bowls and jugs, phials and poultices, powders and infusions. Disputes might occur about the treatment, though all were agreed on the seriousness of the case.

As the days passed and the poppy juice was all used up, it became obvious that he was getting no better. William knew it and began to plan. Where should it be? It would become a matter of immense prestige so he must confer it with care. But there was really only one choice. One place. The monastery his grandfather had founded at Caen, the Abbaye aux Hommes, a prestigious Benedictine house. 'Where else should I lie? Have I not been generous over the years, with money, gifts and the immense benefit of my patronage? How marvellous of Matilda, with her usual spirit, her pragmatism and religious devotion, to found a twin establishment, the Abbaye aux Dames, the community of Holy Trinity. There I buried her, in the choir. And there she lies.'

A monk, bringing fresh herbs to his bedside, felt a grip pulling at his habit. He bent down and saw the lips move but heard no sound. A little closer and he heard a fierce rasping order. 'Get me a clerk.'

When the clerk came, William told him to write. I will be buried at Caen, in the Abbaye aux Hommes. The clerk wrote out the formal command to the Bishop of Caen. It was typical of William, everyone agreed, to wish to control everything right to the end. But they were disturbed because it seemed that the king had given up hope for himself and was allowing death to enter and undermine his will. That will, that *voluntas*, that resolution, that iron self-belief, had carried him through the many difficulties and dangers of a life exposed to injury, vengeance and accident. In the end, an accident had got him. And now he was giving up. Then his attendants decided to send for the relic, the phial of Christ's blood from Holy Trinity Church at Fécamp which had been brought to Rouen some time ago. When everyone was assembled, a mass was held in the bedchamber to bless the phial, then it was proffered to William who pressed his lips to the holy object with all the fervour of a penitent who does not really believe he has done much wrong.

***

At night he would have torches and brands around the chamber, filling it with smoke as if deliberately to stifle himself. He hated the dark. He hated being alone. He called for priests to pray or brothers to read from holy books or councillors to bring him word from outside. None of it meant anything anymore. Once he had been great enough to conquer a realm and seize a crown. He had subdued all opposition and imposed his will across half of Europe. He had contended with popes and kings, negotiated treaties, made war. But in the dark nights he wished he had not made war on Robert. He wished his sons were about him.

'William's here, Henry's here,' he thought, 'I suppose that's something. But not much. I know what they're here for.' William Rufus, having just supported his father against rebellious Robert, wanted to be named heir to the throne of England. But there were certain legalistic difficulties in the process. The difference between *patrimony* and *acquisition*. Normandy was the patrimony of the Dukes. England was merely an acquisition for which no precedent yet obtained. This inherent division in the heritage was repugnant to the Conqueror who had fought for the last twenty years to hold the territories together. At his death, he knew, they would split apart. Robert and William would tear them apart. But he could not bring himself to have it set down in writing. He could not conspire to shape such a future by having it inscribed on parchment or sworn as an oath. He delayed, prevaricated, hesitated. Besides, he could not be sure what Henry would do.

Of his fourth son, Henry, the third still living, he knew hardly anything except that he was better educated than any of them and was therefore clever and not to be trusted. But the truth was he had never given Henry the chance to prove that he was trustworthy. The issue of trust had menaced every single agreement ever made between himself and his sons. And now it was too late. He was too far gone to see this or ever to become aware that his third son had the qualities that would one day propel him onto the throne of England and into a long reign of peace and prosperity.

'I learned not to trust when Ralph was murdered. My faithful tutor, murdered. I was only a boy. After that I trusted no-one. Well, Matilda, yes. I trusted her, I could leave her to run my affairs with complete faith, but only her. No-one else.

Certainly not my own sons. Robert betrayed me. Odo, betrayed me, my own brother. Half-brother, if you like. Odo, who made his fortune from my success. That scheming, covetous, grasping earl. Earl of Kent wasn't enough for him. His eyes were on a bishopric. Bishop of Bayeux. Then he plots and schemes to become pope. He wanted to be pope, he wanted to succeed me as king. Vanity, envy, extravagance. We shared nothing but the same mother. How long has he been in prison? I forget when I had him locked up in Rouen. Is he penitent yet? No matter. I dare say it's time I let him out. Bring me a scribe. Let me dictate a writ. In the midst of death, I am in life. Though I do not forgive him, I shall set him free.'

***

The physicians, as if they had something to prove, issued pronouncements on the Conqueror's condition and when he might be expected to relinquish his soul.

At the beginning of August they had said three weeks. At the end of August they said two weeks.

They were nearly right. At the beginning of September 1087, a general flurry in the sick chamber, the comings and goings of soft-footed prelates speaking in urgent whispers proclaimed the imminent demise. A few prominent nobles, foreseeing the end, left to defend their own estates. More followed in the next few days. On the 7th of September William Rufus suddenly left in great haste with a small party and headed to the coast. Assuming he had gone to set about making a bid for the throne, Henry stayed on, still trying to secure land and titles.

Sometime later that morning the Abbot of Fécamp entered the royal chamber with a suite of followers carrying the paraphenalia of a mass. It was time for confession and absolution. William must take the host; the viaticum's holy words must fill his ear. Stain must be wiped away. He must go to the heavenly court as befits a king, full of contrition and with a prayer on his lips. And so it proved. William made himself amenable to the ministrations of the clergy and all the proper ceremonies were performed. But then he said something that astounded them all. In a last assertion of his will, in a voice dredged up from a pleuritic chest, the Conqueror formally declared that he was bequeathing his kingdom not to any of his sons, not to any individual, but to God. It was tantamount to saying, in the most direct terms possible: 'Let them fight for it.' Then, hitting the precise note of provocative hurt that he used so often with his sons, he consigned all the symbols and regalia of his reign: the sceptre and rod, a cup of rock crystal, a golden candelabra, the crown itself, to the Abbey of Saint-Etienne at Caen. The challenge was laid down. Let whoever wins the kingdom come in search of them.

From now on, priests and clerks went regularly into his chamber with pens and parchment. Writs and edicts came out. Money was gifted to various holy houses, to Mantes to rebuild what he had a few weeks before burned down, donations to chantries, requests for prayers.

'Whether I seek to atone or not, it must be said of me: 'He sought atonement.' I'll make gifts to the poor, I'll set things right with Mantes, I'll declare an amnesty for all, including Odo. Surely that will redeem my soul. But Odo will be a great inconvenience to Robert. Look out, foolish boy, or Uncle Odo will play you false like he did me.'

One night as William lay burning in his fever, he became aware of the sound of a distant bell. Or was it? A dull thud, a clunk, not musical at all but like the broken bell of some cashless provincial minster. The thud came again. Not distant. It was in the room. Someone was there. Of course, he was never alone.

A monk, no bigger than a boy, stood over him with two books in his hand, bound tomes of illustrated parchment.

'My lord king, forgive me. I dropped a book. When I bent down to pick it up, I dropped the other one.'

When no answer came back from the bed, the monk went away.

'Careless boy, don't you know how expensive they are? Well, scurry away with your books. No, don't. I'd rather you stand in the shadows and pray for me. We are all wretched on earth.'

On that thought there came to him the slow onset of a great accounting. Scenes and people from the past jostled and crowded to pass before him, glimpses merely, snatches and blurs of vision. Why did he feel suddenly empowered, invincible? A book –yes - it was a book, surely. Not a psalter, not a holy book. No, no. A book of deep meaning. Or rather, it was meant to be a book. A ledger. His masterpiece. In the end it was a just a giant pile of manuscripts, a survey, heaps and heaps of figures and names collected from all parts of the conquered realm. A rare Biblical quotation came into his head. A line replete with meaning. Meaning again. More meaning. Does meaning pile up at the end when it's too late to fathom it out and nothing signifies? But what was the line? From Proverbs, was it?

'It is the glory of God to conceal a thing: but the honour of kings to search out a matter.'

Oh, glorious God, how I searched out matters! Nothing was hidden from me. All God's concealments scattered through the realm were noted by my surveyors. I ordered them to make an inventory of the kingdom. I called it the Great Description. Everything was counted, measured and valued. Down to the last sheep and pig. The cattle in byres, the villeins in cottages, the barns, households, fields, denes, meadows. How many free landholders. The rents and revenues, the mills and fishponds. Who owned what. What every acre was worth. What land was held by my tenants and under-tenants, what by the Crown, what by the abbots, archbishops and bishops. How many ploughs, cattle, sheep, oxen, pigs in every place, how many sokemen, slaves, cottagers and villagers. The whole realm conquered again, subdued by figures, numerals and names. But it was more than a dossier of my possessions, more than a catalogue to calculate my revenue. It was the epitome of my power, a means of controlling every noble and castellan who held land in my realm. The full extent of my patronage was set down and I could hold everyone to account at the perusal of a column. Wasn't that extraordinary?

What's that, you say? They are calling it Domesday? Well, let them call it what they will, it was my great achievement. Now, go away, all of you. Leave me in peace.'

When they looked at the king, his physicians assumed he was unconscious. That evening he barely stirred. His mouth was open, and his breathing rasped in shallow breaths. It was the evening of September 9th. He was sunk deep into his mind, as if trying to get beyond the pain, but still functioning, still remembering. Was it true, then, that your memories come dancing out at death to parade before you. That the past assembles in mad snatches to lead you to the grave? Then, for the first time, he thought of Harold.

'We were so alike when you examine the thing closely, weren't we, Harold? Evenly matched in everything. It could have gone either way. But your luck ran out. And mine held. Well, it does no harm to have the Pope on your side. And you perjured yourself. I always maintained that. I started the rumour, I tricked you into that oath. But it didn't matter because you didn't keep your word any more than I did. We were at evens for everything until the last hour of that day.'

He lay still, eyes closed, listening. The last sense to leave the body, a wise old monk once told him, was hearing. He saw nothing, he felt nothing, but he could hear sounds coming to him through the darkness, a muffled singing, but close, very close.

Monks were psalming in the depths of the bedchamber, standing in shadows. The battens were up at the windows. Candles burned. Holy water was being sprinkled, prayers were being offered, people were assembling.

'Listen to them, getting ready to see me off. But, truly, truly, I am contrite, I am penitent. Dear God forgive my manifold sins and grant me grace. On the other hand, I would stay around just to spite them. What would you say to that Henry? William, eh? Robert? My dear sons, my boys. Why do I spend so much time thinking about you? It's too late now. Matilda and I made you men fit for the times, that's all to be said. The times are harsh, the world is cruel, men are greedy, weak or brutish. Amen.

At length, summoned by the royal physicians, the Bishop of Rouen came forward to the bed and stared at the king. He bent forward and put his ear to the open royal mouth. No sound came. He anointed the forehead with holy oil. Then he turned and signalled to the monks that the body of the man who, in death as in life would always be called Conqueror, was now theirs. They came forward and began to prepare for the vigil service.

***

King William 1st of England, Duke of Normandy, Conqueror, departed this life on 9th September 1087. But his journey was not yet over. His declared wish to be buried in the *Abbaye aux Hommes*, had to be honoured. So the monks of Rouen made plans for the transfer to Caen and another long journey by land and river lasting several weeks was arranged. Eventually he was brought, with great dignity and pomp, to the vault of his ancestors. His interment, with all due rites, was followed by a collapse of order in Normandy and, within a few months, war had broken out between his sons. It was his legacy. Let them fight for it.

Chapter Two

Wulfnoth – A long and wearisome life

One evening in August 1093, in the royal city of Winchester, four people gathered by chance at the same location. But they were not together. Indeed they did not all meet, since they were part of a larger gathering. They shared no bond. They did not belong to the same world or even, in a strange way, to the same span of time. The differences between them were immeasurable and, for one of them at least, incomprehensible. Yet they coincided in the same orbit of power for a few remarkable hours, circling darkly like unmapped planets. It was perhaps the last possible moment of conjunction between them. No such occasion would, or could, ever come again.

The event took place in Wolvesey Palace, the home of Walkelin, Bishop of Winchester. That evening Bishop Walkelin found himself receiving an unexpected visitor, a royal visitor. William, King of England, son of the Conqueror. With barely any time to prepare, Walkelin found himself playing host to the king and his small suite of attendants, astonished by their presence and not knowing why they were there. Wolvesey Palace was a building of some prestige but not yet fully functional nor finished in stone. However, in spite of this state of unreadiness, the good bishop was not flustered. He was familiar with William's character and knew how to navigate his stormy nature. A Norman by birth himself and connected to the Conqueror's family, Walkelin had known the king from boyhood. In those days, it had seemed unlikely that William, a mere third son of the Conqueror, would ever succeed to the throne, having two elder brothers standing in his way. Fate and a willingness to fight for what he wanted, secured the throne after his father's death and during the last few years he had established his reign to such an extent that he now felt able to go journeying through the countryside on what many viewed as a frivolous private quest. Travelling incognito with only a small retinue, William was amused at having surprised the old bishop and was boyishly delighted by the whole idea of experiencing an *ad hoc*, informal idyll, if only for a short time. Recently recovered from a serious illness, William was eager to snatch again at life. He felt buoyant with energy, charged with the bounding zest of renewed youth. All of this throbbing energy had propelled him to Winchester on his way to claim a bride. At least that was what he told himself. But it was the journey itself, the romantic quest, the knightly excursion that delighted him more than the naked prospect of marriage, for which, at the age of thirty-three, he still did not feel ready. That evening, when Bishop Walkelin received the king in the great chamber of Wolvesey Palace, he had no idea why his royal guest had come or how long he intended to stay. An extended sojourn would impose an unexpected drain on his resources which had already been greatly reduced by his grandiose building project. As it turned out, the king only wanted a one-night stay. In the morning the royal entourage would be gone, leaving the bishop bemused and short of a cask or two of the best wine from his cellars.

    Walkelin had been in his post since 1070 when he was appointed by the Conqueror, whose chaplain he had been. Having known the present king for much of that time, he was well aware that William had an appetite for levity, a mocking wit and a flippant manner. Having some experience of the king's foibles, he could, for the most part, handle them with amused calm. He was rarely at the rough end of one of William's rages. Bishop Walkelin was advanced in years, being now in his mid-sixties and had spent the last fourteen years on a massive and costly building project, a new Minster. This glorious work, lofty and magnificent and very, very expensive, had been consecrated that spring, with Walkelin giving thanks that he had lived long enough to see it completed. Immensely learned in theology and an expert in administration, he had guided the ecclesiastical estates of Winchester with a sure hand for twenty-three years. He oversaw the royal treasury and mint with scrupulous honesty and was a loyal supporter of the king. All this William knew full well. He liked and respected the old man, but there was something in William's nature that compelled him to find virtue tedious. Especially in the elderly. He revelled in the dash and spirit he was showing by undertaking this journey, believing it to be his own idea. In fact, it had come from his chief adviser, Ranulf Flambard. Flambard had recommended marriage as a way of gaining popularity among the people. The English, it was said, liked their kings to marry. And so William had set out on a romantic adventure in quest of a bride. And that was how he came to Winchester, a self-invited guest at Bishop Walkelin's table. Tomorrow, he would be off on the road towards Salisbury and then to the nearby nunnery at Wilton, where the prospective bride awaited. The plan was infinitely flawed, not least because the object of William's attention, thirteen-year-old Edith, had no idea of his imminent arrival nor any indication that she was the intended royal bride. She was kept under seclusion in the nunnery by her Aunt Christina who had no liking for the king and was certain to do her utmost to destroy William's ill-conceived plan for matrimony.

That night, sitting at ease with his attendants at the dais table in the bishop's hall, feeling himself free from the restraints of kingship, having just enjoyed a summer's day on the road, William was unaware that somewhere in that hall, not seated at his table, but some way off among the minor functionaries of the Minster, sat the last victim of the Conqueror.

***

Ranulf Flambard's plans were not usually so poorly laid or so badly carried out. The whole thing was the result of the king's convalescent energy, a strong desire for distraction, a perpetual need of popularity and his boyish sense of adventure. The king's first minister, you might think, would have a strong purchase on all the titles, securities and rights of high office, but this was not the case for Flambard. His position was, in fact, totally precarious and wholly dependent on the king's goodwill. So far, the king's goodwill was blowing nicely in his direction and had been doing so for the last few years. But there were factions against Flambard at court, primarily those nobles who scoffed at his low birth. He was also far from popular among the clergy. Monks wrote defamatory falsehoods in their chronicles against him. He suffered the fate of all political advisers: jealousy, mistrust and misrepresentation. The major offence laid to his charge was one that he would readily accept, however, since it was quite true. He kept churches vacant. This was a huge controversy which caused tremendous battles over money. When a church was vacant it meant that no incumbent was appointed as bishop or abbot or prior. It meant that the monies usually raised from rents, tithes and fees, as well as all other sources of income which belonged of right to the incumbent went instead straight into the royal coffers. The clergy saw a vacant abbey or bishopric as a scandal equivalent to robbing the church, a wholesale siphoning of funds. The royal coffers would benefit by considerable sums, but the church would suffer extensive losses. To deprive holy houses, bishoprics, priories and churches of a consecrated head, to drain away their resources, to hand them over to rapacious ministers, was wicked in itself and an outrage to all good Christians. And the worst offender in this deplorable practice, so the allegation went, was Ranulf Flambard.

In spite of this and many other detractions, Flambard was the second most powerful man in the realm, after the king. As long as he retained William's favour, he would remain so. For this he relied on his wits, his political cunning, his suave amiability and his talent for not making serious enemies; qualities that enabled him to avoid some of the pitfalls of advancement. Perhaps because he was of lowly birth, being the son of an illiterate Bayeux priest, courtiers and noblemen were inclined to either snub or underestimate him. They were foolish to do so. On this summer night in 1093, he was at the beginning of a spectacular career.

To spare the king any risk of tedious conversation, Flambard was seated next to the good prelate whom he was distracting with some flattering praise about the finished Minster, of which Bishop Walkelin was touchingly proud.

'Fourteen years it has taken, but God has blessed our labours. The brothers consecrated the nave and precincts in April. I must tell you, Flambard, that without the king's generosity we could not have finished it.'

'Really?' replied Flambard, feigning surprise.

'The king made a grant of land in the Isle of Wight, to supply stone from quarries and timber from the forest. Without that grant, we would not have finished it for many years more.'

Flambard, who had advised the king in this course of action, nodded and smiled. He was a little bored and looking forward to tomorrow when they would all be off to Salisbury. He wanted to get the whole embarrassing adventure over with as soon as possible. Why had he advised it? Was William really going to marry this girl, this little Edith? No doubt she was suitable, the daughter of the King of Scotland, no less. But it was possible that Malcolm, that malcontent, that buzzard of the north with whom relations had been mostly bad for thirty years, might be brought at last under the yoke of Norman rule by a marital alliance. The plan was good, Flambard knew it, but it was also at the mercy of William's mercurial temperament. It all depended on what would happen at Wilton.

In spite of the passing of twenty-seven years since the Conquest, there were still many detractors of the new regime and one of them was King Malcolm. Scotland, with its royal ties to the pre-conquest kings through the female line, possessed in little Edith a valuable commodity in the marriage market. Scotland, with its fierce clans and wild territories, still resisted Norman dominance while England had almost nothing left to resist with. All the senior appointments in the church and at court, all the great noble estates and baronies, were in the hands of Normans. Even Bishop Walkelin, who tried to be fair-minded and unbiassed and fostered many English careers in his diocese, was Norman by birth and by appointment. Wherever you looked, Normans were in all the positions of power. One notable exception was Wulfstan, Bishop of Worcester, the only English-born bishop left in the thoroughly Normanised church hierarchy. Admirable though Wulfstan was, thought Flambard, his bishopric was minor and counted for little alongside Canterbury. Even Winchester was less important than Canterbury in the sense that the latter had always been accepted as the premier archdiocese of England, making its incumbent an important ally of the king and a key player in policymaking. But there, Flambard's spirits began to sink.

What had they done this spring while Walkelin was finishing his Minster? They had appointed the Abbot of Bec, Anselm of Aosta, as the new Archbishop of Canterbury. Already Flambard thought it was a mistake, a bad miscalculation doomed to failure. At first Anselm rejected the post; he was sixty-three, he was a monk who liked being a monk, he hated administration, he did not want the job. But at that time William had been very ill, they had despaired of his life, they did not want the scandal of the four-year vacancy of Canterbury to continue. They thought if the vacancy was quickly filled with a holy man, God would look favourably on the act. So they had filled it with Anselm. Since then he had done nothing but complain and make difficulties and was still not consecrated. Canterbury was thus in a state of lapse. The vacancy had been filled but there was still no genuinely functioning primate to lead the English church.

Unless, thought Flambard, as he looked at the old man seated next to him, unless you place Walkelin in that role. And why not? He's a man of probity and trusted by all. In all his years of service, both to the Conqueror as chaplain and to young William as supporter, adviser and overseer of the mint, he has given the most faithful service. He is immensely learned in theology, he is a builder of some distinction. Let's say then, that he's the most senior churchman in the country. That makes the three of us at this feast: the king, Walkelin and me, the beating heart of England. And here we are together, quite by chance. The Norman hierarchy.

Flambard was quite entertained by the sudden illuminating invention of this fact. He felt it held significance, though he did not know why. An unplanned, unofficial journey, the result of a whimsical piece of advice to the king, had trapped Flambard in this madcap trip to Wilton. The king's boyish spirit of adventure in embracing it and his meanness in wanting to do it on the cheap by sponging off Walkelin, had brought them together this August night. And they were sharing a feast that no-one had even thought of the day before. The whole affair was casual, impromptu and completely unlikely. It shouldn't be happening. William was travelling incognito with only a few knights and servants. His intention had been to surprise Walkelin by turning up uninvited. Flambard had forestalled such gratuitous embarrassment by sending messengers ahead to alert the bishop to the unfolding situation. It was the least he could do. Ranulf Flambard often found himself covering for the king's schemes. But this was worse because he himself had devised the scheme. It was his fault that they were all there. He had engineered the whole thing: the trip, the visit and the significant thing that was about to happen and which was giving him a mysteriously bad feeling. Though he did not know it yet, one other figure was needed to bring about, at almost the last moment it could occur, a final encounter of the Norman hierarchy with its own haunted past.

***

Although it was not really an encounter. It should have been. There should have been a public acknowledgement, the exchange of grave words, pardon and penitence, apologies and absolution for harm inflicted, wrongs done. But there wasn't. It merely happened that, during the evening, looking about boredly at the diners while his mind was running on Wilton and the likely outcome of their current escapade, Flambard's eye was drawn to a figure seated at the far end of one of the last tables in the great hall. It was a small, thin figure, hunched into his monk's habit from which two thin white arms and a bowed head protruded. His face was obscured, but Flambard could see he was looking down at his food which he was pushing around on the wooden platter with his fingers. He bent forward, elbows on table, saying nothing to his companion whom Flambard recognised as Godfrey of Cambrai, the Prior of Winchester Abbey. Flambard was at once curious. Who was this starving boy and why was he seated next to the illustrious prior? What was he doing at such an occasion, in such company?

Godfrey was about 40 years old and had been prior for the last twelve years. Flambard knew him well since they had often met at court. He had the reputation of a fair-minded and generous man, who governed his monks with a sure hand yet was forgiving of human frailty. He was also something of a poet who wrote Latin epigrams and little polished epitaphs on those who died well. Flambard had read some of them and could not for the life of him see how anyone could compare him with the Roman poet, Martial, as some did. Godfrey was not a city sophisticate like Martial, nor was he a cynical observer or ironist. On the contrary, his verses were simple, slight and ingenuous. His poems were mild, full of conventional morality, sweet natured. Godfrey was a charitable person, a prayerful monk and a good teacher, that much Flambard knew. So then, was the boy at his side one of his pupils? A favoured oblate, a relative, perhaps? Godfrey bent towards him closely from time to time, as if straining to hear what he said, then he might nod or shake his head and lay a hand upon his arm in a gesture of sympathy.

Flambard watched them for some time, idly speculating on the strange figure who seemed so out of place, looking like a menial who had mistakenly sat down at the master's table. And yet Godfrey seemed to be treating him with gentleness, concern, indulgence. Flambard was so absorbed in the scene and his own speculations that he was slow to notice that the king had addressed a remark to him. He rejoined the conversation and returned a witty reply, making William laugh. In a good mood, the king laughed readily. Afterwards he embarked on some of his old hunting stories and drank a great deal as if trying to nerve himself for the morrow.

When Flambard looked again, he saw Prior Godfrey and the boy still sitting together as though they were alone in a quiet place, waiting for something. Unable to retain his curiosity any longer, Flambard took his goblet and drifted down the table, greeting people as he went, making slow progress so as not to draw attention to himself. Eventually he sidled into the empty seat opposite Godfrey, next to the unknown figure in the habit of a monk.

'Good evening, Prior.'

Godfrey looked up startled. Then, recognising Flambard, his face settled into the look of someone who welcomes good company.

'Good evening Ranulf Flambard. I did not know you were here, but of course I should have guessed. Wherever the king is -'

'You will find Flambard. Alas, it's true, Prior, and I am not only here, I arranged this whole embarrassing affair. Do you think the good bishop will ever forgive me?'

Godfrey laughed and shook his head. Their acquaintance was longstanding and stable enough to ride out a joke.

'But seriously,' said Flambard, turning to the figure alongside who had not moved or raised his head, 'who is your companion? Please introduce me.'

And Prior Godfrey of Cambrai said the words that were to change the nature of Flambard's evening: 'This is Wulfnoth.'

Godfrey shook his elbow. 'Wulfnoth,' he said, 'this is Ranulf Flambard, the king's minister.'

At that the figure raised his head and turned his face, slowly, as if coming back from some far distance. His expression was striking. It was empty. His face was both old and young at the same time, the face of an old man who had never experienced the world, of a youth trapped in an unfamiliar place and grown old while looking for a way out. Flambard felt curiously moved by the immense sadness of that pitiable, vague, empty face.

'You are in good health, I trust.' Flambard was thinking he looked far from well.

Wulfnoth sent a glance to Godfrey, like a pupil looking to a master for encouragement or guidance. He seemed surprised that someone had spoken to him, at having to make a reply, at being the focus of someone's attention.

'I am well,' he said after some hesitation, 'but, a little tired.'

'He attends all the offices,' said Godfrey as if in explanation. 'He rises for matins at midnight and goes to all the canonical offices through the day. He is indeed an example to all the monks.'

Flambard was not sure what that meant. Was Wulfnoth a monk or not? And what, in the name of God, would explain that expression, that old-young look, that apparent lack of engagement that made him seem like an innocent and simple-minded child? Who was he and what had happened to him?

Reading Flambard's expression, Prior Godfrey said: 'Would you like an explanation?'

Flambard indicated that he would.

'Well, to understand his story you have to cast your mind back many years to a far-off time, to a legendary time, it seems now, when many things were different. There was a lad, a boy no more than ten or twelve years old who was caught up in things he did not understand then and cannot understand now. You see how he is, his mind is gone, his memory blasted, God alone sustains him, his faith in Christ brings solace.' Godfrey paused, searching for a phrase. 'How shall I put it? Wulfnoth is the last remnant of the English royal house. He is the younger brother of that King Harold who died at Hastings. He was one of the sons of Godwin. Perhaps you have heard of them? They were a turbulent family, the old Earl Godwin of Kent and his numerous fighting sons. He caused endless trouble to the saintly King Edward who, as reassurance for Godwin's good behaviour, received Wulfnoth as a hostage along with his nephew, Hakon, the son of Sweyn, the eldest son of Godwin. These two boys, uncle and nephew, so very close in age, were held as hostages in England until an attack by Godwin of Kent caused them to be taken to Normandy where they were handed over to Duke William. They were hostages, you understand, not prisoners. They were not incarcerated or treated badly, but put into the care of Robert of Jumièges, who even did something for their education. But those were the early days. Later that changed.

When Earl Godwin died, in 1065, his son Harold asked permission from King Edward to go to Normandy to petition the release of his brother and nephew who had now spent nearly ten years in captivity.'

Flambard interrupted. 'Well, that shows a decent sense of family duty, wouldn't you say?'

'Perhaps. The king gave permission but warned that the undertaking would probably end badly.'

'Which it did?'

'It was partly successful, but mostly a disaster. First of all, Harold's ship, which had been loaded with treasure-bribes to ease his path, was overtaken by a storm and driven off course. It came to shore not in Normandy but in Ponthieu, then ruled by the greedy Count Guy. So now it was Harold who was held prisoner. But he managed to bribe a servant and got word to Duke William who ordered that Harold and his men be sent to him. Once Guy had stripped them of all their bribe money, they were handed over. But surely, you have heard all this before? It is a well-told story. Indeed, it is becoming something of a legend.'

'Yes, I've heard it. It changes in the telling, so you never know what version you'll get. But, Prior Godfrey, it is of your guest here that I want to hear,' and he nodded towards Wulfnoth who was sitting all this time alongside them, then added in a low voice: 'Should he be listening to this?'

'Alas, he does not listen. He hears but he does not listen. His mind wanders. God puts many thoughts into his mind, harmless thoughts that help him sustain a world to live in. It does not matter that his world is not quite real. It harms no-one.'

'How long has he been like this?'

'I do not know when it began. Perhaps at the time of Harold's visit. More likely afterwards. A slow onset of despair, a sustained outflow of hope. You see, Harold tried to get him released, along with Hakon, the nephew. That's when Duke William forced the oath on him, you know, not to seek the English crown when Edward died. Made him swear on the relics of a saint, that he would not contest the throne but give his support to William. At least that was Duke William's story, which he maintained until his death, though others dispute it. What is not in doubt is that Harold was faced with the cruellest choice imaginable. Only one hostage would be released. He had to choose.'

'I see, and he chose Hakon. And Wulfnoth stayed a prisoner.'

'Exactly. William promised to bring Wulfnoth with him and deliver him to freedom when he arrived in England to accede to the throne, which Harold, he believed, was going to obligingly concede to him.'

'And he never did.'

'And Wulfnoth remained a hostage, then a prisoner, then a forgotten remnant of another time.'

'I begin to see,' Flambard turned again to where Wulfnoth was still sitting over his untouched plate. But now he seemed to be alert, as if expecting something.

'It is almost time for evening prayers,' explained Godfrey. 'He will not eat until after compline. Then he will have some roasted eels which Brother John will prepare for him in the priory kitchen.'

'So when did William get around to releasing him?' asked Flambard.

'He never did. Some tried to include him in the general amnesty at William's death in 1087, but he was never released. By then he had been in captivity for thirty-six years. What was he to be released to? He has no family, save one niece he has never seen, shut away in a nunnery. He has no skills, no calling, little education. Strictly speaking, he was, and is, Earl of Kent, but what does that mean? He has no standing, no followers, no deeds on which to found a reputation. Everything was stolen from him.'

'Thirty-six years, dear God!' murmured Flambard.

'Yes, he had God. All that time, he had only God. The condition of his imprisonment varied in response to the news from England. Sometimes it was even lenient. But when William heard that Harold was bidding for the throne, Wulfnoth found himself in harsh confinement, chains even. Later, things were easier. There were periods when he was given permission to ride or hunt. But he never saw any of his family again. His life was wrecked when Harold's ship was driven ashore at Ponthieu, and all his plans unravelled. There was never a second chance. Time stopped for him. Hastings never happened. He lives in an everlasting present. The old-young man who lives without a life. His mind could not hold the horror of that truth. The only truth in his world is his faith. Christ is merciful.'

Ranulf Flambard sat silent for some time, thinking over what he had just heard.

'But are you saying that he has never been released? That, in fact, as he sits here tonight, here in the same room as the king, he is still a prisoner, still a hostage against that long-ago event?'

'Technically, yes. As I said, when the present king, acceded to the throne it was thought that Wulfnoth might be amnestied. But what was the point? Where would he go? He was beyond independent life. So he came to us at Winchester, to the Abbey. We care for him. The brothers love him as one does a child. He lacks for nothing. He has found, at the end of a long and wearisome life, a refuge in Christ.'

Flambard looked across and saw Wulfnoth's face lifted towards the small doorway where one of the brothers would enter to signal that it was time for evening prayers. His expression was ardent, his face alight, transfigured with expectancy, as if his life did have meaning, a meaning that was concentrated into one instant of waiting. His whole life had been waiting. But now, for this moment only, he knew what he was waiting for. Then Flambard realised what Prior Godfrey had meant when he said, 'Christ is merciful.'

'His life has been an ordeal,' said Godfrey 'He was caught up in human bonds, the bonds of kinship and the bonds of imprisonment, they entangled him in an incomprehensible fate, but, as you see, ultimately bound him to God.'

'I am not a man given to sentiment,' said Flambard after a time, 'but this story has moved me. I came for a very different sort of feast.' He was snatching at his own errant thought earlier in the evening; how the king, Bishop Walkelin and himself comprised in their persons a representation of the Norman hierarchy, the vast machinery of government which had been put in place by the Conqueror. And here, unexpectedly, in the piteous form of old/young Wulfnoth, was the last representative of the defeated Godwins, the old order, and Harold, the last English king. For a few brief evening hours their impossibly divergent paths had crossed. This thought flared in Flambard's mind for an instant then departed like a ghost, leaving him with an unaccustomed shiver in the spine. Then he turned towards Wulfnoth, feeling that something momentous ought to be said, some sort of apology made, forgiveness asked for, regret expressed. As if, somehow, it was possible to make amends for the vagaries of life and the cruelties of history. All Flambard could think of to do was to give him back the dignity of his title.

'God give you peace, Earl Wulfnoth,' he said.

But Wulfnoth had already turned his eyes towards the doorway where the expected brother monk appeared, signalling that it was time to go up to the Minster for evening prayers.

Prior Godfrey rose. 'The king will not notice my absence,' he said. 'We must go to compline. Goodnight to you, Flambard. I think you have heard a story tonight that you will not soon forget.' Then he led Wulfnoth away by the hand. Flambard watched until they had gone from sight, imagining them making their way up through the town from Wolvesey Palace to the choir of the Abbey. And there they would sing compline. And Wulfnoth would be happy.

***

Chapter Three
The Tragic Love of Gunhild and Count Alan

Occasionally great romances escape out of history, slip away into private lives, and never quite get caught by the fame they deserve. They disappear into archives, lie scattered in the remains of written material, sometimes in diaries, journals or private letters. Perhaps in this case it was the letters that ensured the story would come down to us. Remarkable letters, letters written by a man desperate to obliterate the story. They exist and their existence testifies to the great importance of this unique love story. The letter-writer was Anselm, Archbishop of Canterbury.

As Literature and History often observe, great passions have the power to disturb the spirit and overthrow the virtues of discipline, denial and the spiritual life. Although they might bring moments of intense joy, great passions can have terrible consequences for individual souls, thus they arouse the antipathy of churchmen to whom the only great love and central passion of the soul is Christ Eternal. Archbishop Anselm was one of those who believed this. And in the two letters he wrote in the summer of 1093 and early in 1094, he expressed it in unequivocal terms. These letters are not in the usual run of episcopal correspondence. Far from it. They are full of panic-stricken, urgent pleading, wracked by fear, and they amount to a desperate attempt to save a soul. Yet, ironically, Anselm's letters remain an enduring confirmation of a scandal he wished to obliterate. In one of those ironic twists of history, the letters bear witness to a sequence of events that Anselm, and the church he represented, wanted, above all, to keep secret or suppress altogether.

Anselm has already become the third party in this love story, but he must not be allowed to intrude at this point. His intervention comes later, and we must begin with the two lovers. Their stories are genuinely unique, and their romance belongs among the greatest legends of love: Tristam and Iseult, Romeo and Juliet, Helen and Paris, Dante and Beatrice, Eurydice and Orpheus. In the great cast list of fabled lovers, there really ought to be room for Gunhild and Count Alan. This is their story as far as it is known.

***

The extremely distinguished Norman lord, Count Alan Rufus, was descended from the Breton Counts of Penthièvre. Many superlatives can be used about this old companion of the Conqueror: the most powerful nobleman in England, the greatest magnate of the north, the strongest defender of the border country. In 1070 he was granted a huge swathe of northern England, centred on Richmond where he built a fortress. Around it, great stone walls strengthened with turreted bastions, curved away from a massive keep along two sides of a triangular hilltop. The third side was protected by a sheer drop down to the River Swale. From these heights a complete survey of the surrounding country could be taken, the road winding up the valley, the Swale looping through pastures and bosquets, the dales and hills rolling away to distant crests. Up against the southwest corner of the site, close to the sheer drop down to the water, he built for his personal use a great hall.

In contrast to the huge militaristic keep, the great hall was a place of comfort where the habitual fierce hardihood of a warrior overlord could be seen giving way to embryonic luxury. A two-storey, well heated, well decorated set of rooms, which a Roman Praetor on leave from the Wall might not have scorned, formed the focal point of domestic living for the count's private household. It was accessed via an undercroft where all the menial services were housed, but once up the wide flight of steps and through a magnificent doorway with columns and a moulded inner arch, brightly painted with scenes of the Penthièvre ancestors, an impressive effect of wealth, power and opulence met the eye. A rectangular hall with flued fireplaces and wide recessed windows was the setting for formal occasions, feasts and ritual entertainments. Beyond this large hall, and divided by a stone wall at one end, was a smaller, intimate chamber or solar, where Count Alan would receive his closest friends, or those he wanted to impress. Even today the mere ruins and remnants of this building complex has the power to impress. Such were the surroundings of an impressive man. By all accounts, and in spite of the tag of Rufus, or *le roux*, he was neither florid nor red-haired, nor given to flaming tempers. It is said that his brother, also called Alan, was given the nickname 'black' or *Niger* for reasons we do not know. One suspects that, in this period, such tags were ascribed a little too frivolously by bored monks and have been misleading historians ever since. The brothers maintained close relations, perhaps because the younger Alan was a loyal liegeman and dependable companion. There were said to be seven legitimate brothers, several called Alan, and innumerable illegitimate half-brothers, as well as milk-brothers who had shared the same nurse's breast in infancy, so that it was often joked that the lord of Richmond could muster an army from his relatives alone.

At the time our story begins, in the summer of 1093, Count Alan Rufus was a grizzle-headed warrior of fifty-three. He still enjoyed excellent health and was able to spend all day in the hunting field and was limber enough to ride half the length of England on horseback which he did for the last time in the summer of 1093. The count's extraordinary vigour and natural good health is part of the tragedy of his story.

Count Alan Rufus had no heir save his brother. However, in the north that was not necessarily a disadvantage. Here an ancient code of property transference called *tanistry* was still in existence. Based on a Celtic tradition, it involved the selection of an heir by the senior members of a clan. This was often practised in Scotland and the border country where there was every likelihood that a minor would be struck down by his own relatives before he could enter on his inheritance. So his brother, Alan Niger, was heir designate to the entirety of the Northumbrian and Cumbrian possessions. One day this situation would involve both brothers in the unfolding of a strange tale of passion and tragedy, so unlikely and bizarre that, had it not been for the subsequent interventions of Archbishop Anselm, it might never have come to light.

Whether in the comfortable security of his solar at Richmond, or at King William Rufus's southern court, Count Alan's attention was a prize for which men and women competed. He was widely admired for his personal qualities as well as for the extent of his power. He had winning, not to say gallant qualities. But why had he never married? Count Alan Rufus was said to be distinguished both in looks and manner. When he spoke, he commanded attention. His accent was distinctive, Norman French laced with Breton and a sprinkling of Border gutturals. Many would say that a kind of bluff amiability enveloped this hard man without the least trace of counterfeit. But his reputation of old, when he had fought in the Conqueror's campaigns after 1071, was of a different order. No-one could be harder, more implacable, more resolute than Count Alan Rufus in those days. And yet something about him fascinated men and women alike. In his own house, many thought he was more kingly than the king himself.

King William's attitude to Count Alan Rufus was based on the respect of long and faithful service in defence of the northern borders, mixed with admiration of his personal qualities. Here was the type of man that women admired, men aspired to be, and kings schemed to get in their inmost circles.

In the summer of 1093 King William Rufus was in search of a bride. On the advice of his chief minister his interest had been aroused in Edith, the thirteen-year-old daughter of King Malcolm of Scotland. She was then residing at the famous Abbey of Wilton, a nunnery specialising in the education of high-born ladies. Famous for its learning, Wilton was also the sheltering home of many dispossessed women whose husbands and fathers had been killed in the violent repressions that followed the Conquest. But, having made an abortive visit to Wilton to view the intended bride, spying on her from behind some rose bushes in the garth,

King William suddenly dropped the idea of marriage to Edith, scuttled away and remained unmarried for the rest of his life. He returned to Gloucester where he was due to meet with King Malcolm. Travelling in the suite of the Scottish king, Count Alan Rufus was to witness the embarrassing scene at Gloucester that summer when King William suddenly refused to negotiate with Malcolm or even to acknowledge him. At this, Malcolm, whose temper was legendary, feeling doubly insulted on being snubbed by the very man who had just spurned his daughter, took off in a fit of resentful outrage and went straight to Wilton. With him went Count Alan Rufus who, according to some accounts, was also interested in Edith as a marriage prospect.

A few days later, the gentle Abbess of Wilton, in her quiet Wiltshire nunnery, found herself suddenly confronted by the angry power of the north. Malcolm raged and stormed, Edith wept, the nuns scattered in alarm and the upshot was that Malcolm dragged his daughter from her schooling and took her off to Scotland exclaiming that she was not a nun and was not going to be turned into one. Count Alan Rufus, however, remained in the vicinity of Wilton. He had discovered that Edith was not the only royal princess of high marriageable worth to be living at the nunnery. There was another. Her name was Gunhild.

***

Gunhild was the daughter and last known descendant of the English King Harold. Like many of the women at Wilton, she was an heiress seeking refuge from the Norman land-grab. This made Wilton something of a unique institution. Noble and royal women were educated there. Heiresses, secular women, wards of the king, were given protection. It was a place where refugee stories of violence and suffering were swirling about with stories of privilege. It was both a Benedictine nunnery with a high reputation for scholarship and learning, and a sanctuary for women who made no pretension to the conventual life but were simply seeking the shelter of the church in lawless and violent times. Those heiresses who still possessed legal entitlement to pre-Conquest estates were often in danger of being forcibly married, kidnapped or even murdered by ruthless warlords. In the violent and lawless years of the 1070s, many crimes were committed against the women who had already suffered the loss of their menfolk. As it happened, Gunhild still had entitlement to lands bequeathed by her mother, Edith Swan-neck. She was an heiress with a considerable inheritance which she fully expected, in due course, to bring to the abbey. It was widely understood, so she believed, that on the day of her appointment as abbess she would convey her landholdings to Wilton. But in 1093, Gunhild was not even technically a nun. She had taken no vows before a bishop and although she wore the habit and sometimes the veil, she did not regard herself as consecrated to the religious life although she was deeply committed to the Benedictine order. Well- educated in holy texts and scripture, she had no thought of changing her life but rather had in view, as a serious but not imminent prospect, one day achieving the office of abbess. Yet, like many then and now, there was in her nature a latent eagerness to embrace a different way of living, to try new experiences and even to take risks. Under the self-possession and poise of her daily life there stormed the secret ardour of unrenounced passion, a longing for something as yet unknown. Like her father, she would be ready gamble everything on a single turn of fortune's wheel. And, like her father, she might lose.

Remarkably, for a figure little-known in our times, Gunhild was well-known in her own. Far from being an obscure nonentity, a faceless semi-nun in a provincial house, she was known in her own times by people who mattered. Although never part of the legendary or popular fable of Norman history, in her quiet way she was a person of renown. One of the most striking facts of her story is that she personally knew the man who had just been appointed Archbishop of Canterbury, Anselm, formerly Abbot of Bec. How or when they met is not known, but they did meet, and the meeting was never forgotten by either of them. This was why, when Gunhild faced her darkest moments, she appealed to Anselm for help, and why, when he knew her to be in danger, Anselm wrote two powerful letters of love which can still be read.

'Dearest and most longed-for daughter', he called her, or sometimes 'beloved sister and daughter…' or 'sister of mine truly beloved in God…' 'You once spoke to me and said that you wished to be ever with me ….and afterwards wrote me a letter full of sweetness….'

They had met, they were correspondents, they were devoted to the Benedictine order, they shared a spiritual bond. This much is known and this much is extraordinary. It may be that ecclesiastical scholarship has not yet fully grasped the extent of Anselm's emotional attachment to Gunhild. But now Anselm is beginning to intrude again. His proper place in the story comes much later and then it will the time to solicit the motives for his vigorous intervention.

In the summer of 1093 Gunhild was present at the infamous visit of King Malcolm of Scotland. She may have witnessed the unfolding drama as Malcolm vented his anger on those, he held responsible, most particularly, Christina, Edith's aunt, who was a nun at the convent. Malcolm was not known for self-control. Even though the abbess and the nuns may have been embarrassed they may have also sympathised strongly with Edith's plight.

Yet however much Edith wept and pleaded, there was no way to change her father's resolve. She would be removed from the convent immediately and return to Scotland with her father. Scotland was far off and unknown, filled with relatives she barely knew, including her mother, Margaret. Before leaving the convent, it would have been customary for Edith to have an interview with the Abbess before leaving in order to establish her grounds for doing so. King Malcolm would have formally explained his reasons for withdrawing his daughter from Wilton. As was also customary, the abbess would have given her consent. Then father and daughter would have ridden away from the place that had been Edith's home for the last seven or eight years, into an uncertain future.

If she had been an observer of these dramatic scenes, Gunhild might have reflected on the speed with which the lives of women and girls could be changed, overturned or redirected. Sometimes for the better, sometimes for the worse, but very often suddenly. And most often these great changes resulted from the agency of others, rarely themselves. Men of power waging war, making agreements, brothers or fathers settling debts, arranging marriages, or just getting angry, could change the lives of women with stunning swiftness by a single decision. The life of a little girl was subject to events and occasions made by others, by men arranging their affairs through war or treaties or marriage bargains. She had observed it innumerable times. Chance circumstances caused swift changes in the lives of women without ever inviting their own agency. This was the natural order of things disposed by God who had subjected women to the rule of Adam at the dawn of time in the garden of mankind. This was what the church taught, what she believed. But she had longed for something quite different. Perhaps it was then that Gunhild began to wonder whether, given free agency in a decision, given the freedom of choice to decide her own future, she would choose to stay at Wilton, or choose some other path in life?

We do not know exactly when and in what circumstances Gunhild and Count Alan met. Perhaps they were introduced by the abbess. By tradition, the abbesses of Wilton held an entire barony from the king, which gave them considerable power and made them substantial local figures with a right of attendance at court and a duty to supply soldiers to the king. Only three other nunneries in England enjoyed such a privilege: Shaftesbury, Barking and St Mary's Abbey Winchester. Often nobly born, or the daughters of prominent families, these women enjoyed prestige and were acquainted with prominent people. It is possible that Count Alan was known to her.

Perhaps Count Alan, hearing that an heiress of the old English royal house was present, asked for an introduction. Perhaps they met by chance in the cloister garden. However, it happened, they were able to recognise that they were both mature people who occupied serious positions in life. They may have spoken of recent events: Malcolm's anger, perhaps, and the departure of Edith. Count Alan might have talked about his journey from the north or reported news from the king's court at Gloucester. Whatever was said, we must deduce that it was pleasing to both parties and very soon some sort of courtship was in progress.

It is probable that Gunhild, being a convent-bred lady, had no wiles, no subtleties of any kind in the armoury of love. What was she to do? Being mindful of the limits of her order, of her rank in the abbey and the lustre of her ancestry, she would not suddenly act unwisely. She knew that Benedictine rule made obedience and conformity high priorities. Anselm had often instructed her in these matters. Her most likely course of action, if Count Alan had advanced his suit, would surely have been to seek out the abbess.

And that wise and experienced lady might have said something along the lines of: 'It is sometimes no bad thing to test your commitment to the religious life before you take the final step. Your spiritual life is dear to us all at Wilton, Gunhild, but we do not wish you to renounce worldly happiness, if it should happen to be offered.'

Perhaps. But however, it happened, there at Wilton in the late summer of 1093 with all the nuns as witnesses, Gunhild and Count Alan Rufus began to fall in love. The story goes that one day as they were admiring the deep red roses in the cloister garth, Count Alan took out a little knife he kept in a leather pouch at his belt and cut off a rose. In doing so he pricked his finger on one of the sharp curved thorns that grew thickly on the stem. It pierced deeply and drew blood when he pulled it out. He sucked away the blood, laughing that he had taken many wounds in his life, but never before in the service of love. Had Gunhild known then what was to be the true result of this incident, would she have acted differently? We cannot know. In all likelihood she was committed. There was only one course of action open to her. The chance had come for Gunhild to make her own choice about her future life. No longer at the command of others she was free to choose to act. It was entirely characteristic that she would have acted with decision and agency. She was free to make a choice. She chose love.

***

Time, it is often said, means less to lovers than to other mortals. Having known each other for only a few days, spread over a period of little less than a month, Gunhild was ready to gamble everything on the thrill of an adventure. She would leave the convent immediately with Count Alan.

Before she left, mindful of her duty to the abbess and all the nuns of the convent, Gunhild would almost certainly have written a letter. Letter writing was something she was skilled at as her many correspondents among the prelates of England and Normandy would agree. Prominent people admired her letters as models of the epistolary art, often written in Latin, sometimes in Norman French, rarely in English. This one was addressed to the community of Wilton, thanking them for their many benefactions over the years, begging forgiveness for any disrepute her actions were about to bring on the nunnery and promising that the settling of her legal affairs in the new marriage would result in a large donation to embellish St Edith's shrine at Wilton. There may have been a part of Gunhild that was shocked by her own behaviour, or rather the emotions that were guiding it. Such a state of mind is hinted at in her letters. Was she throwing over the decades of Benedictine obedience, the strong spiritual commitment and loyalty to the convent that had sheltered her, on the strength of emotions alone? Had she become indistinguishable from all those secular women whose common experience it is to fall in love?

We do not know the date on which she departed from Wilton, leaving behind the many friends among the nuns with whom she had shared her life for more than twenty years. But at some point, she must have ridden through the great arched gateway beside Count Alan. It was probably not exactly the thrilling, headlong gallop into a new life that she had envisaged. She knew little of the outside world and would have relied on Count Alan to plan and organise the journey. Perhaps he was touched by the great unquestioning trust she was placing in him. They would have ridden together ahead of the entourage of followers, servants and tenants which went everywhere with him. Powerful noblemen would never travel anywhere, even on a private elopement, without the accompaniment necessary for prestige and protection. Count Alan's retinue was made up of servants and relations, some brought up as wards of his father, some stepbrothers. One of them, whose name was Bodin, was actually Count Alan's illegitimate brother, now a tenant on one of the count's vast holdings in East Anglia. Stretching through Cambridgeshire, Herefordshire and Essex, these estates had been acquired over the years as a result of innumerable transferences since the time of the Conquest. In accordance with the practice of the more civilised magnates, the count endowed many holy houses, foundations and abbeys. The great Abbey at St Edmundsbury was a favoured depository of largesse but, unlike St Mary's Abbey at York, which he was instrumental in founding, St Edmundsbury Abbey had origins prior to the conquest.

Count Alan had holdings in the Fleamdyke Hundred, about thirty miles from the great Abbey of St Edmunds. Details are lacking but there are accounts which put Count Alan and Gunhild at the home of four named people living in this area, probably because they held property from him, a manor or some estate in tenure.

One of them was the Bodin already mentioned. The others were Bardulph and Rebald. Most likely, these men, were milk brothers of Count Alan, having been reared at the breast of one, Orwen, a peasant woman who is the fourth named person. These figures from Count Alan's childhood, his baby days and rawest youth were still in his service, still loyal and living as his tenants under his protection. It is sometimes overlooked that, in the medieval period and long afterwards, people of the highest rank enjoyed close friendships with people of lesser rank because of the way household living was arranged. It was difficult to keep the levels of society strictly separated, there was more mixing in the great halls and sleeping places of medieval England than probably at any time since. The habit of employing wetnurses from a different social class also meant that the offspring of noble families had their first sustained and intimate contact with a woman of the people and with her other sucklings and the babies she cared for, even long after they were weaned, so that mixed social groups of children might be seen playing in the courtyards of many a manor and castle.

Gunhild may have been surprised by the situation, for she had no knowledge of growing up in a Norman household, but she might have observed that the three tenant brothers and their wetnurse were utterly devoted to Count Alan. It would have been a happy observation that a man who can inspire such loving service in others is the most worthy of love.

From now on we can only muse and conjecture on the course of events, shaping them to what we know of the aftermath. In all likelihood a feast would have taken place in the great raftered hall. This would have been the practice to welcome a returning lord to his demesne. But the celebration of the bridal couple may well have added to the evening's bustle. All this would have contrasted sharply with Gunhild's quiet, reflectful convent meals. If the count's tenants had wives and children there would have been a boisterous evening of festivity. Did Gunhild find herself at ease in a homely atmosphere, so far from the muted and reflectful surroundings she had known? Did she ever have any doubts that she had done the right thing? She was far from Wilton now, entirely dependent on the Count's good will and honour. Had she made the right decision or had her choice been the most reckless sort of gamble? Did Count Alan give her cause to believe she had made the wrong choice? Or was she was convinced that he would keep his word, that they would live and prosper together and one day, God willing, she would bear his child? She was still young enough, only thirty-three. Perhaps she dreamed the everlasting age-old dream of a happy marriage and a family. But what, really, did she know of

Count Alan? How mercenary were his motives? Was this a deceptive scheme to get hold of her inheritance? By turning to the correspondence between Gunhild and Anselm, we can be fairly sure that Gunhild was at this time sincerely engaged in the great romance of her life. But we don't know how far Count Alan believed himself in love or whether he was capable of knowing that in the rose garden at Wilton, he had found and won a worthy lady. What had he promised her? What vows had they exchanged? Had he promised in good faith to do right by her? He was a man who understood the keeping of oaths. Surely, if he had made such a promise, he would keep it to the end of his life.

***

It is probable that Gunhild was never certain when it started. And it would have been in Count Alan's nature to make light of it. Typically, he dismissed all indispositions as scarcely worth noticing. He was fit and strong, he had hardly had an illness in his life. So when, over the next few days he began to feel ill, he may have rallied himself and carried on as usual. It had started as a swelling in his right hand, the hand with which he had plucked the rose at Wilton, pricking the index finger and drawing blood. That event was over a week ago. In the world of medieval medicine, there could be no possible connection between that act and his present illness. Today, from the few clues we have, we can track the likely progress of Count Alan's disease. During the next few days, he suffered little pain in his hand, which remained swollen, but he became weak and feverish. He was able to attend to business, receiving churchmen and important tenants from the surrounding estates, or those seeking a favour or a signature on a writ. But even this fatigued him.

Then he began to complain of feeling unwell; the swelling spread to the arm which became bloated and puffy from hand to shoulder, and he began to suffer painful contractions of the muscles. Some sort of powerful poison seemed to be spreading through his body, weakening him hour by hour. Next, he became short of breath and complained he was suffocating. At this point he was forced to his bed, something he had resisted until then, being convinced that, if he once lay down with the disease, he would never rise from it. We can assume that Orwen prescribed homemade infusions or herbal treatments from her country medicine chest, using various mints, honey and marshmallow, distilled extract of meadowsweet. If she did, nothing worked.

What was this mysterious affliction that had arisen so swiftly in a healthy man? At this moment, for the first time since leaving Wilton, it is most probable that Gunhild's thoughts turned to God. Was this a visitation of heaven's anger at her renunciation of convent life? The thought may have been momentary, dismissed quickly as unworthy of anyone who believed in the forgiving love of Christ. It would later come back redoubled in the letters from Anselm, for this illness seemed to have no earthly or rational cause.

What Gunhild must have suffered as she watched the progress of the disease through the body of her lover can only be guessed at. At what point Count Alan knew he was dying, having been brought down on a bed of sickness just days before his wedding day, we don't know. Death and a broken heart had not figured in the plans they had been making in the last few weeks. What had come upon them was as grievous as it was unexpected and cruel. Details are lacking but we have fairly reliable estimations that, within a period of ten days from the onset of the illness, Count Alan was dead.

***

It was perhaps inevitable that in this medieval age a connection would be made between the renunciation of convent life and subsequent suffering. Today we might easily identify the cause of Count Alan's death as tetanus due to the *bacterium Clostridium tetani* which is commonly found in soil, saliva, dust or manure, and enters the body through a cut or puncture wound. That Count Alan's death occurred suddenly, without prior illness, ten days to two weeks after leaving Wilton, on or about August 4th, 1093, is attested in many sources. That he plucked a rose to give to Gunhild is at the very least possible. It is known that roses grew in the cloister garth there, as attested in the story of King William's visitation earlier in the year. Even in the days before *amour courtois* and the invention of romantic or knightly codes of behaviour, it is possible that someone with Count Alan's remarkable character may have come up with this civilised practice *avant la lettre*. But the great corroborating proof of an important and controversial love story between these two distinctive figures of the Anglo-Norman world, are the letters of Archbishop Anselm. It is now time for the archbishop, who was personally involved in the aftershock of these events, to enter the story.

When he heard that Gunhild had eloped with Count Alan of Richmond from the nunnery at Wilton, Anselm was deeply disturbed. She was his spiritual daughter, his sister in Christ; they had a shared love of the Benedictine order and a close and personal correspondence. Determined to intervene to save the soul of his beloved daughter, he took up his pen.

'Anselm, by the ordination of God, Archbishop of Canterbury, to his beloved sister and daughter, Gunhild,' he began.

There was only one course of action he could advise and that was a speedy return to the convent. In his view, Gunhild had a spouse in Christ whom she had spurned by running away, exchanging the purity of spiritual vocation for the impurity of carnal pleasure. Setting out to write in a consolatory and encouraging tone, he found it impossible to prevent a shrill note of panic, for he was convinced that Gunhild had risked eternal damnation by what she had done.

'It is impossible for you to be saved in any way unless you return to the habit and the life of a nun,' he wrote. Her choice was stark, her position precarious, her soul at risk. To put off the habit and renounce the conventual life was a great sin. Almost beside himself with anxiety about the state of Gunhild's soul, Anselm did not mince words. 'Strive and shatter your heart, grieve deeply about your fall. Throw off and trample the secular dress you have put on and assume the habit of the spouse of Christ which you have cast off. If you refuse to do this,' he ended darkly, 'everybody will be against you and I and the Church of God will do what we know is to be done in such a case.'

Although sprinkled with kindly phrases to his 'dearest daughter' and 'my daughter', the letter was full of affrighted admonitions to return to the convent and throw herself on Christ's mercy.

What was Gunhild's reaction on receiving this letter? Was she stung? Had she expected more gentleness, more understanding from her spiritual counsellor and, as she had always thought, friend? It seems that, although in a state of grief, she roused herself to argue in her reply. She wrote that she had not taken the veil or made vows before a bishop, she was not consecrated to a religious life and therefore, in accepting the love of Count Alan she had broken no vows. Moreover, 'I was never offered the abbacy at Wilton that had long been promised to me. At which time I should have made over my inheritance and accepted the high honour to lead that venerable foundation. But promises made to me have not been kept, whereas I, in making none, am now accused of breaking them.'

In the meanwhile, it is probable that the Abbot of St Edmundsbury oversaw the burial of Count Alan with all due rites, for it is known that Count Alan was buried in the abbey, possibly in the nave, for some time until his remains were removed and transferred to St Mary's Abbey, York, a monastery which he and his brother Count Alan Niger had jointly founded. This same Count Alan now comes to the fore as a protector of Gunhild. It would fall to him to arrange his brother's affairs and try, if he might, to secure Gunhild's future.

It would be understandable if Gunhild was desperate for consolation when she took up her pen and wrote to Anselm once more, appealing for pity and trying to justify her actions. It appears that she wrote that Count Alan Niger had taken her under his protection and had even offered marriage in order to secure her lands and reputation.

Whatever was contained in this letter it appears to have alarmed Anselm so much that he wrote with a frantic new urgency, bordering on the cruel. He could see no sign that Gunhild was minded to return to the convent. Was she now adding the sin of disobedience to the long list of her transgressions? Anselm's disturbed reply is still painful to read. It betrays a state of mind bordering on the frantic as he sees Gunhild in peril of losing her soul. Was he too harsh? Had he become more entrenched and dogmatic in his views since becoming Archbishop? Gunhild, who was probably hoping for high-minded but warm consolation, must have been disappointed. In her fragile state, such a reply was a great blow.

'I still greet you and call you most beloved daughter,' he wrote, 'because I do not yet despair of what I desire for you, namely that you may yet regain your senses through the visitation of divine grace and return to Christ.' He reminded her that he was her 'true friend' and was admonishing his 'sister and daughter' out of concern for her immortal soul. He decided to spare nothing in order to save her, even the harshest words. 'Your loved one who loved you, Count Alan Rufus, where is he now? He delighted you while alive, now he is rotting flesh and putrefaction.' What if God had taken him away from this life as a punishment? he asked. Or as a prevention from further wickedness? In his panic, he did not scruple to bring out the weapon of moral blackmail, targeting her tender feelings towards Count Alan Niger, even stooping to making puns on his name.

'Why are you not afraid that, because of you, God may kill Count Alan Niger by a similar death, or - what is worse – if you are united with him, God may condemn him with you to eternal damnation? Oh, would that he be black to you and you black to him.' The blackness of sin and the name 'Niger' led Anselm to obvious and needless, if not obtuse, puns which he regretted later, but as he thought about these events, solicitude turned to panic and then to desperate and rather cruel admonitions. 'You know that I advise, beg, beseech and command you by the authority which permits and obliges me to do so, to resume the habit of monastic life and return to the grace of God.' Anselm would leave Gunhild in no doubt about the peril of her position. All dreams of a worldly life, of passion and love for a man of flesh and blood, were shattered. She must now think only about her divine spouse and a soul which was perilously close to damnation. In this way, dashing off equal amounts of love and consternation in tortured panic-stricken phrases, he laid out in the starkest terms what she must do. She must return to Wilton.

***

Various interpretations have been made of the thin evidence about the ultimate fate of Gunhild but it is likely that she did return as also did the other 'nun' who left the convent only a few weeks before her in that same summer of 1093, Edith, the daughter of the King of Scotland.

In late November of that year 1093, Edith's father died. King William Rufus did not welcome the news although it was, from his point of view, rather favourable than otherwise. King Malcolm of Scotland, the troublous neighbour, was dead. The fiery king who had spent more than thirty unfriendly years prowling up and down the borders, and occasionally raiding into England, had been killed. It was not so much the death but the manner of it that caused William's anger. King Malcolm and his eldest son, Edward, with a small party of riders in attendance, had been ambushed near the River Arne. Malcolm and his son were said to have been unarmed at the time. The thing smacked of the sort of vile, low, treachery which William could not countenance. The affair was dishonourable. It coupled the king's name with an act of downright villainy. William did not fear open fight, in fact he rather relished it. He believed he could have taken Malcolm in open battle whenever he thought fit. This murderous attack, thought to have been carried out by Robert Mowbray and his henchmen, bordered on *lese-majesté*, the basest form of treachery. It disturbed William for many days, for the killing of a king was a source of great disquiet among kings.

At first no clear connection was made with the events earlier in the year when Malcolm had swooped down on Wilton and taken away his daughter, Edith. Although by no means a nun, being only thirteen years old, Edith was under the protection of the cloister. Malcolm's act was deemed to be an outrage, an attack on the sanctity of the holy house, at the very least a needless confrontation that left bad feeling it its wake. An act that ought to be punished. An act most fitting to be punished by God. And when this event was placed into the unfolding sequence of the events of that summer, observers were forced to an ominous deduction. Both men had been punished by God. In the light of the news of Malcolm's death, King William himself began to reflect on Count Alan's death in what now appeared to be an instructive series of events.

The truth was that the king did sincerely grieve for Count Alan, a man he deemed fit for admiration and respect. A loyal and brave vassal. What had possessed him to snatch a nun from her convent, to carry her off and promise to marry her? Had the man lost his senses? The king had been shocked when the news of the abduction first came, but when, less than two weeks later, news came of Count Alan's sudden and inexplicable death, the king began to give ear to the stories that began to circulate that Count Alan had been struck down by God for violating a nun. Intrigued by the tragic story which ran counter to everything he knew about Count Alan, the king began to make inquiries about Gunhild, wishing to know what had happened to her. But no news was forthcoming. She seemed, for the moment, to have disappeared. King William would not be fully informed of these events until he heard from Count Alan Niger who, being aware that his brother had intended to marry without royal permission, delayed his appearance at court.

Count Alan Rufus in August, King Malcolm in November. Dead by unforeseen and sudden smitings, a short while after abducting from Wilton women who enjoyed the protection of the holy house. Within a few weeks of leaving Wilton, both men had encountered terrible fates. Two such sudden and inexplicable fatalities could have only one interpretation in that unscientific age. Certainly, this is the view that Anselm took. And, after a time of remorse and introspection, Gunhild, too, for it seems that she may have returned to the religious life. Her gamble on worldly happiness had failed, just as her father's gamble on a crown had failed.

Although evidence is thin, there is enough to suggest a fact lurking behind most of these claims and, at the very least, a possibility behind every speculation. For example, the view of the medieval scholar R.W. Southern seems to be soundly based and persuasive. His opinion is that Gunhild did indeed return to Wilton because "she was later remembered there with honour." Wilton remembered *her*, not her scandal, which implies an afterlife of redemptive presence at the convent. Even more notable is the fact that she appears in a chronicle by William of Malmesbury where she figures in a holy story, which is unlikely if scandal sullied her memory. Another indication that she returned to Wilton is that the scandal died very quickly and, indeed, might have passed out of recollection altogether, had it not been for the survival of Anselm's letters. Short-lived scandals are ones that are effectively smothered, and this would have happened if Gunhild had returned. Wilton's powerful patrons, the ecclesiastical hierarchy, the Archbishop of Canterbury, even the king himself, whose goal would be the protection of Count Alan's reputation rather than Gunhild's, all would have endeavoured to stifle the scandal or quash it entirely.

However, due to Anselm's ardent letters, written in panic to a soul at risk, this tender, romantic tale did not quite escape out of history. Its high drama, great passion and sorrowful outcome have left readable traces. The tragic love story of Gunhild and Count Alan, which belongs with the great romances of literature, can still be told. It is still worth telling.

Chapter Four
William Rufus – Accident or Murder?

The Anglo-Saxon Chronicle is a collection of annals chronicling the early history of England. It was created late in the ninth century, probably in Wessex, and continued into the twelfth century. Written at various monasteries, by a number of unknown monks, its purpose was to record for the memory of mankind significant names, dates, acts and events as they unfolded according to God's divine plan.

Had the Anglo-Saxon Chronicle embraced the use of headlines it is very likely that, on August 2nd, 1100, they would have been bold and exclamatory. Here indeed was a story command attention: Royal Death Horror! King Slain in Hunting Accident! New Forest Tragedy, King Dead!

However, the Anglo-Saxon Chronicle did not appeal to the world in headlines, nor was it concerned to form opinions. Its business was the discreet and meditative recording of the vicissitudes of the world. It was read by very few people, reaching only a limited number of readers in monastic libraries and scriptoria. We know something of its many writers. They were nearly all monks who would almost certainly be following the institutional line taken by the monastery in which they worked. These monasteries were not concerned to mould or manufacture current opinion or form the view of the common man - so necessary today in winning votes for politicians - but rather to record the events of the passing years and to comment on them insofar as didactic moral lessons might be drawn from them. As it has turned out, these chronicle histories have come to play an important part in forming the opinions, not of contemporaries, but of later generations of historians.

On August 2nd, 1100, the monk at the Benedictine monastery of Peterborough Abbey charged with writing an entry for that day, might have undertaken the task with relish. He might even have indulged in some unseemly gloating. For there were many monastics who would have found the news of that day a cause of relief, or even, dare it be said, secret rejoicing. Even the most fair-minded of them, the ones who in their daily lives would forgive the poor man who stole the loaf, the soft-eyed monks who stood at the serving hatch of the *cella* to hand out food to strangers, the ones who pitied the poor widow and gave her employment, even the most Christian souls among the Christian monks might, on that day, have experienced deeply unChristian feelings.

But although the events of August 2nd, 1100, deserved the fullest attention of the monks, some of them at Peterborough had other things on their minds. There was a significant cause for distraction because, at that time and for some time afterwards, the abbey administration was under investigation for corrupt practices. There had even been several convictions. Indeed, the abbot, Godric, fell under suspicion of simony and after investigation was eventually deposed. Also, around this undisciplined and unpropitious time there was a serious theft at the abbey. Robbers broke through the window above the altar of Saints Phillip and James and stole a great golden cross studded with gems, two chalices with patens, and two gold candlesticks. Morale was low and the monks prayed for some turn in their fortunes, some good news that might indicate that God had not abandoned them. It came on August 2nd, 1100.

It was a memorable day, for days on which kings are killed are memorable. And yet a terrible warning against the vanity of greatness lies in the speed of this king's oblivion. Certainly, the Peterborough scribe seems happy to help the king into oblivion with a few choice accusations and condemnatory remarks: "He humiliated God's church; and in his days, when abbots and bishops fell, he either granted them all in return for money or held in his own hand and put out at rent." Here William is condemned for his blatant practice of simony. And further specific charges are laid: "on the day that he fell he had in his own hand the Archbishopric in Canterbury and the bishopric in Winchester and that in Salisbury and eleven abbacies, all put out at rent." This represents a vast fortune siphoned off from the church and diverted into the king's coffers. Monastic opinion viewed this as tantamount to theft. Then the writer draws the moral lesson: "he is hated by well-nigh all his nation, and abhorrent to God, just as his end showed...." There was never any possibility of a balanced assessment of the reign from this point of view. To the monks and clergy, judgement was clear. God had struck down the sinner in the midst of his sins.

***

What were the events of that day? Who stood to gain? Who had a grievance? What might have made sense to a jury of the time? To address these questions, it is first necessary to know something about the victim: his character, his friends and familiars, his advisers and ministers, what kind of man he was, what kind of company he kept and what kind of enemies he made. We need to know something about the milieu of the court, to look into the character and background of the key actors in the drama, the preceding events, and the scene of the action.

The immediate scene of action was the hunting field. In an age of frenetic devotion to the sport, hunting accidents were not uncommon, even among William's own family. Indeed, in May of the same year Richard, William's nephew, the illegitimate son of his brother Duke Robert, was killed while hunting in the New Forest. Years before, another Richard, the king's own brother, had suffered a similar death when his horse galloped too near an overhanging branch which caught him in the throat and killed him. These and many other precedents suggest that the king's death may have been an accident. But it could equally have been deliberate; a murder, a plot, a conspiracy. If so, by whom? The basic questions of an inquiry were never asked at the time nor was there ever any investigation into these events. No-one was held to account and, although there was a chief suspect, no-one confessed.

***

It is with the events of spring 1093 that our inquiry might best begin because two events, crucial to the next thirteen years of William Rufus's reign, happened almost at the same time. First, he was struck by a serious disease which was expected to kill him. Second, during the time of his illness when his judgement was impaired and he was unable to resist the pressure of churchmen en masse, he made one of the worst appointments of his reign. It was a forced error, one might say, over-riding his judgement at a moment of weakness, one that would involve him in endless disputes and controversy with the church, ensuring that in later years monastic chroniclers might not sincerely deplore the fact of his sudden death. But let's step back and take a longer view of his thirteen-year reign.

William Rufus, third son of the Conqueror, born into the middle ranks of the aristocracy, was still a landless knight bachelor when his father died in 1087. He was never designated as successor to the kingdom his father had conquered. Neither he, nor the eldest brother, Robert, nor the second brother, Richard, nor the youngest brother, Henry, had cause to feel they had been favoured by fortune or the regard of their father. As already noted, Richard had been killed in a hunting accident many years before; Henry had been set to study and at one time seemed likely to be destined for the church, while Robert, being short and inclined to overweight, had suffered from his father's mockery for years. 'Shortlegs,' 'Fat Legs,' 'Gambaron,' these contemptuous names had perpetually dogged him through his youth, finally settling down into the insulting nickname 'Curthose' by which he was widely known. Contempt and mockery, compounded with unfair treatment and preference for his brothers, eventually drove him to rebellion. Although later reconciled, father and eldest son were never again on mutually trustful terms. So William had inherited the throne of England while Robert Curthose got only the duchy of Normandy, for which he had to do fealty to the French king. And the two realms which the Conqueror had unified, were split apart.

Among the Norman aristocracy there was great discontent about this division. Most preferred to see England and Normandy governed as a single administration, as it had been in the Conqueror's time. Noblemen and castellans enjoying vast estates in both realms, did not want to be beholden to two overlords, or to have their loyalties split by owing allegiance to two contending rulers. So when William had taken up arms against his brother, he found many supporters who wanted to see the two realms under a single ruler. Thus, his early years on the throne had been marked by aggressive policies against Robert Curthose as he sought to bring Normandy within his control. With the exception of a few periods of truce, they were to go on battling all their lives. However, in the spring of 1093 it seemed that one of those lives might be on the point of ending.

King William had always operated an obstructive policy towards the church. Many churchmen were nursing grudges about the high-handed way he had treated them in the past, imposing requisitions, keeping bishoprics vacant in order to siphon off revenues, or selling clerical offices and benefices, thereby raking in tidy sums for his own coffers. This was the hated practice known as simony. Infuriated churchmen felt constantly embattled by a king who scorned the rights of the church, refused to fill vacancies and failed to recognise a pope. In England, thanks to William's obstructions, neither of the two papal claimants then in contention had been recognised. Would it be Pope Urban or Pope Clement? William refused to say. This was a deliberate policy designed to keep papal authority at a minimum and prevent interference from the papal court or *curia* in any of the disputes between church and king. This left the higher clergy free to pursue their own interests without having to undertake long consultations with the Holy See. This, in turn, annoyed the lesser clergy who felt their collective voice was being undercut. With clerical power split, the king was left in control of the English church. Such was the divisive and unreformed state of affairs which had persisted for many years and which William had no desire to change. He riled churchmen by not taking holy things altogether seriously. He purposely annoyed them with ironic and inappropriate jokes. His old provocation about how he was thinking of converting to Judaism, so often trotted out to ruffle clerics in the act of reprimanding him, infuriated them. Although many of his jests were disarming, bluff or hearty, they went unappreciated, and he antagonised more than he amused. He could be biting or sardonic, whimsical or impious. But he was rarely coarse or cruel.

However, in the spring of 1093 he needed the prayers of holy men as never before. God forgave sinners, they assured him, but only if penitence was ardent and sincere. Unfortunately, the king had a problem with religious ardour and sincerity. These were not virtues he possessed. Humour and energy were his prominent traits. He had spent the six years of his reign in rancorous relations with the church. Even at his lowest, on his sickbed surrounded by clergy, he was not easily contrite. But in the end, he proved so ill that he became, for a brief period, amenable to the will of the church. That will, embodied in the prominent churchmen who had gathered about his sickbed in the palace of Kingsholm in Gloucester, unanimously held that one of their number, Anselm, Abbot of Bec, should be appointed forthwith to the office of Archbishop of Canterbury and so bring an end to the scandal of its four-year vacancy.

For the past four years, since the death of the previous incumbent, Lanfranc, there had been a great gap at the heart of the church in England. There was no Archbishop of Canterbury. Canterbury was therefore a vacant see, a body without a head. And all the while the rents and monies of the archbishopric, having no archbishop to claim them, flowed steadily into the king's coffers. The longer the see remained vacant, the more money accrued to the royal treasury. That situation might have continued indefinitely had not William's illness changed everything. Finally, he was too weak to resist. The clergy urged him to make his peace with God and appoint Anselm as archbishop. Only then might he be saved. If he did not appoint a man so obviously fitted by God for the office, he would bear the sin of it and take it to his grave. Hard-pressed on all sides, William at length conceded. The appointment was made. But then it became clear that Anselm did not want it. Anselm was a monk, a spiritual unworldly man, a theologian, and writer of theses and religious works, he did not want to scrum around dodging the factions at court, and he hated administration.

Inevitably and most reluctantly, however, Anselm was forced to accept the appointment and take up the burden of the archbishopric. This ill-fated moment was the beginning of their tortured story. There were many grounds of disagreement. Even though there were moods of goodwill on both sides and advisers trying to keep them talking, it was almost impossible for them to work together for the good of the church in England. From the outset it was a doomed partnership of state that would embroil not only England but

Normandy and the Papal Curia, blighting relations between church and state for years.

They split apart in 1097, unable to establish any kind of working relationship. With Anselm pushing for church reforms and William with his hands in ecclesiastical treasuries; with the king's mercurial temper and scathing humour and Anselm's increasing age and frailty, the inevitable happened. After an embarrassing falling-out at the Rockingham Conference, Anselm withdrew to his manor of Mortlake. Thereafter there was a great deal of tit-for-tat, push and push back, bad feeling and misunderstanding, exchanges of letters, superficially polite, but seething with rage in the margins. What pushed things to a head, inevitably, was a series of events that created for William a sudden and urgent need for money.

In the wake of the memorable address by Pope Urban at Clemont in 1097 when the pontiff appealed for an army of Christians to defend the Holy Places of the east, there had been a massive response. Men of every degree, including the highest, kissed the cross and volunteered to go at great personal risk and cost. One of them was Robert, Duke of Normandy. Cost meant money. It was a very expensive undertaking. A duke must take a suitable entourage, a full household, servants and retainers, an army of men and animals. Then it would be necessary to hire ships or wagons, pay for guides and supplies, buy protection, and finally maintain an army in hostile country for the indefinite duration of the campaign. Money was required. Where would Robert, at best a penurious duke, ever get such sums? The answer came in a formal settlement between Robert of Normandy and his brother of England. Basically, Robert would lease the duchy to William for ten thousand marks. William would pay over that sum and in return he would have control of Normandy for three years. At the end of that period Robert would either come back and pay off the debt, or he would fail and forfeit the duchy. For once, the brothers had agreed a plan that satisfied them both. This was the situation that produced in William a sudden need for money and would eventually lead to a crisis in the relations between himself and Anselm.

When invited to set an example to the clergy by donating generously to the royal appeal, Anselm offered 500 pounds. At first William agreed, thinking it was a substantial amount and would set an example. But some of his barons, wishing to stir up trouble between them, convinced William that this was a paltry sum and that he should demand more. When he did so, an outraged Anselm withdrew his donation and gave 100 pounds to the poor instead. From there, relations steadily declined so that by the time they met at Windsor later that year there was almost no common ground left. Their final meeting was at the Winchester court in the autumn of 1097. By now Anselm's conscientious stance on political matters was perilously close to treason. Certainly, that is how many of the most prominent barons characterised it. They turned the last meeting between Anselm and the king into a quasi-treason trial. The upshot was that the archbishop was given eleven days to quit the kingdom and go into exile. Perhaps there had never been any other possible ending to this relationship.

There now occurred a third significant happening that may have been the most critical of all. Into the vacuum left by a departing Anselm, seeped a new political force, so subtle, at first, that it was hardly noticeable. It had been operating in the margins of William's reign for many years, but now, with Anselm exiled, William in control of Normandy and Duke Robert miles away from the scene, there was scope for Henry, the youngest brother, to swell into the empty space. Henry had dodged between his brothers for years, sometimes supporting one then the other, always trying to keep below any parapet that might shield him from making a strong allegiance or committing himself to one side or the other. But with the removal of Robert from the scene, he finally felt able to declare for William. His first move was to help William raise the money to buy Robert out of Normandy. He made compacts with the Jews of London and urged tributes from priories, abbeys and other foundations under his protection. Henry began to manoeuvre himself into a more prominent position. He offered his loyalty to William, attended court, volunteered advice and accompanied him on his frequent hunting trips. Although sceptical and never fully won over by this new-found loyalty, William liked to keep Henry close. Everyone was aware of the vacuum that Duke Robert's absence made in Anglo-Norman affairs and the possibilities it afforded. None more so than Henry. Three years was a long time. There was every likelihood that Robert would never return from holy war. His martial reputation was not, on the whole, impressive. Even if he did return, would William ever voluntarily restore the duchy to him? Henry had his doubts. He viewed the transaction as conferring on William the control of Normandy without his having to fight a war for it, a situation he would never wish to reverse. William was effectively, though not in name, the single ruler of the realm their father had held years before. All that being the case, what if William were suddenly to die?

***

In 1098 William had never been more robust, at thirty-eight years old he was at the top of his game and the height of his fortunes. For the first time, feeling he had escaped the dominating shadow of his father, having matched him by welding together England and Normandy, he felt easy in his kingship and inspired by a new impregnable confidence. It was now that he had the full sense that he had 'come into Normandy'; that he was, if not Duke, at least the ruler of the duchy with legitimate title to govern. These feelings had been bolstered by an amazing stroke of fortune. While at Caen at Christmas 1096, finalising the departure of Robert and handing over the 10,000 marks, William had been approached by Abbot Gilbert, the abbot of Caen's great Benedictine foundation l'Abbaye aux Hommes, where William's father was buried. The abbot wanted to present him with a number of precious objects belonging to the previous reign which had been gathering dust in the abbey vaults since 1087. Abbot Gilbert may have wanted to benefit from the transaction by acquiring grants of land or additional tithes or exemptions for the abbey in the usual way. But as it happened, he had to be content with William's thanks and his own good deed. William was at first bemused by the gift of a large wooden chest with iron locks, having no idea what it contained. When the locksmiths opened it he realised that this was an important moment in his reign. Inside the silk-lined chest lay the royal regalia of his father: the crown, the sceptre and rod, a cup of rock crystal, a golden candelabra. These items had not been bequeathed to William and, since

Robert was not a king and had no right to them, they had lain in the abbey crypt since the conqueror's death and been forgotten. They had not been seen in public since 1087 and now it was William who would bring them back to the world. At the Christmas court he wore his father's crown, feasted by the light of his father's candelabra and drank from his rock crystal cup. The parade of the royal regalia marked the apogee of William's reign. It was a public statement that all aspects of the paternal regality were now incorporated in him. That Christmas at Caen he swelled to fill the lineaments of kingship; he had matched his father; he had laid the overbearing ghost to rest.

However, there were many Norman barons who took advantage of Robert's absence to foment disaffection and so William had spent much of the previous year, 1097, putting down rebellions in Normandy. Henry ensured that his own Norman comté of Contentin remained loyal and, although it could not provide much in the way of an army, it provided a secure base for operations in Normandy. Henry accompanied his brother on campaign in Normandy which further enhanced his reputation. William faced more bad news in October when the pope threatened him with excommunication because of Anselm's exile. William shrugged it off, not believing the pope would ever dare excommunicate a king as renowned as himself. Christmas came and went. William returned from Normandy and at Pentecost held court for the first time in his newly refurbished palace of Westminster. The following year, a crown-wearing ceremony took place on May 29th which William used as an occasion to impress a distinguished visitor, Edgar, the Scottish king. Having come south to swear fealty and render public thanks to William for helping him to the crown, Edgar was appointed to carry the sword before William at the great feast to celebrate the inauguration of Westminster Hall. It was meant as an honour, but the touchy Scots lords took exception to their king playing the role of sword-bearer and saw it as a deliberate insult. On the whole, though, the presence of Edgar went unnoticed, whereas the crown and regalia were both noticed and admired.

In July 1098, the king went to one of his favourite lodges, Brockenhurst, in the New Forest, a vast hunting domain carved out by the Conqueror, lying south and west of the ancient capital at Winchester. Here he could relax among his trusted inner circle, feasting in the evenings and spending days in the hunting field. Not that all business was suspended. There were still times when he needed to consult his ministers who were ordered to accompany him. Among them went Henry, still basking in the glow of his brother's favour. The king's hunting companions, Walter Tirel, Robert FitzHaimo, William of Breteuil, Robert of Meulan, Urse d'Abetôt, seemed to be drawn into Henry's orbit, spending as much time with him as with the king. It was noticed how they cut their hair short in the style of the 'old Normans' as if distancing themselves from William's long-haired entourage in order to establish an intimate circle around Henry. They could be seen from time to time, closeted together or standing around in suspicious huddles.

At Brockenhurst, everyone was familiar with the king's habits and the pattern of his days. What time he rose, what time the handlers departed, the order of going into the field, the course to the butts, the individual stands. All these things were well-known, and it was unusual for the king to deviate from his customary arrangements. William showed continuing indulgence to his brother and they spent good-humoured days in the hunting field during the 'fat season' of red deer stags which ran from the Feast of St Peter in Chains (August 1st) to the Exaltation of the Holy Cross (September 14th). But late in August, their sport was prematurely interrupted by news from afar, unexpected news, news that went ringing around Europe.

Jerusalem had fallen to the Christian armies. Against all likelihood, the holy warriors had triumphed. But it was not until September that the first rumours came of the Battle of Ascalon. Suddenly, William and Henry were confronted by the worst possible turn of events. At Ascalon, Robert, Duke of Normandy, had covered himself in glory. He had not only survived, he had achieved military fame, he had earned vast treasure from the Emperor of Constantinople under whose banner he had been fighting, he was rich. In the next few months, news about him dribbled lazily up from the Mediterranean: he had left Constantinople, he was in Apulia, he was prospecting for a bride. Alarm bells rang. It looked as though Robert was thinking in dynastic terms.

In England the year 1098 was wild with rumours of wars and death, prophecies of plague and tempest, forebodings of poor harvests, warnings about catastrophe in the far-off armies of holy warriors. The Anglo-Saxon Chronicle recorded that a strange star appeared in the south-west and the ray that stood from it, shining towards the south-east, seemed to be very long. Men said that such a light had been seen in the days of the Conqueror, a sign of calamities, disturbances and unnatural happenings. Hermits sprang from their cells, claiming to have seen disasters in their visions. One or two even made their way to court to proclaim that the king's days were numbered. William quipped: 'Do they take me for an Englishman?' mocking the English propensity for superstition. It was typical of William and did nothing to endear him to English chroniclers.

The following year, 1099, began in unusual calm at the English court which seemed to have adjusted itself to a different balance. Anselm was gone and the weight of his considerable moral authority was lifted. Henry was becoming more present, more weighty, more significant as an adherent of his brother. One way Henry could win his brother's favour was to share his passion for the hunt. Henry was ready to spend the whole of the 'fat season' beside William in the field pursuing his favourite sport. No-one who wanted to earn the king's favour could be absent from the hunting field. In the summer they went again to Brockenhurst. Even in sport, William always used to be vying with his father's ghost, driving himself fast and hard in order to excel. But that summer his companions noticed a change, as if the acquisition of Normandy and his father's regalia had assuaged his thirst for excellence, as if he was no longer striving to match himself against his father's reputation, as if he felt, for the first time in his life, an energy and mastery that put a stride in his kingship. When he rode out with Henry at his side in the hot August days of the fat season, he appeared gratified, confident and in excellent spirits.

The hunting field drew on a vast body of servants for its functioning. Huntsmen, foresters, verderers, fewterers and lymerers, beaters, and the marksmen appointed to kill off any animal wounded by a poor shot. The king was attended everywhere by noblemen, some of them shamelessly on the make such as the members of the powerful Clare family, Gilbert FitzRichard and his brother Roger; some powerful old stalwarts like Robert of Meulan and his brother Henry Beaumont; others who pushed themselves into the field out of a desire to please, such as the cupbearer William D'Aubigny. And then there were the close companions, men he thought he could trust. Among these, Robert FitzHaimo, Walter Tirel and William of Breteuil. The hunting field was the king's court outdoors where favour was sought, and places were contested in the unceasing competition for royal attention.

In England, William celebrated Christmas 1099 still unaware of Robert's plans. He was certain that, even if Robert was to return against all the odds, he would have no money to redeem his dukedom. Even if the Emperor had heaped him with treasures there was plenty of opportunity on the road between Apulia and Normandy to dissipate a fortune. And if he came by sea, the lawless ports of the Mediterranean or the loose pirate prowlers who were always on the lookout for rich victims could strip a traveller in moments. He was more likely to arrive penniless. In the improbable circumstance of Robert being able to repay the loan on the nail, William would find ways to prevaricate. He felt secure enough. Even so, much of 1099 was spent in Normandy putting down the last remnants of rebellion at Le Mans, making treaties, pushing back the French, marching through Maine, Touques, Bonneville, Lillebonne, impressing his authority through successful military actions and diplomacy. Pope Urban obliged him by dying in July, which left him free to deal firmly with the recalcitrant Norman bishops.

By the end of that year, he felt more secure than at any point in his reign. He was king of one of the richest realms in Europe, he had a grip on Normandy. After nine disorderly years, orderly administration had been achieved. William's secretariat was producing crisp instruments of government. Jurisprudence was being strengthened and could be left in the control of the most reliable bishops and justices. He had gained a reputation for military success and command in the field that made some observers compare him not only with the Conqueror, but with Caesar. William held his Christmas court that year in Gloucester at the palace of Kingsholm where, six years before, he had been dying. Like a king, he had taken the place of his father, and, like a ghost, he had risen from death. But death was closer than he could have imagined. As winter turned into spring 1100, King William II entered his last year.

Holy Sunday in the year 1100 fell on April 1st. The Easter court was held in Winchester, the former seat of Bishop Walkelin who had been dead for two years. William had not appointed a successor to the vacancy, exploiting it as another source of revenue. He was also keeping an eye on the royal treasury there. Henry kept close to the king. With a resurgent Robert on the horizon, the brothers seemed to be united in a mutual protection of interests. Throughout the spring, the news of Robert Curthose grew more and more alarming. Robert was about to marry, Robert had married, Robert was coming home with a shining reputation and a pregnant bride. The news affected Henry even more than William. While William felt at his most secure, the youngest brother, the boldest, the shrewdest and politically astute of the three, stood to lose. As early as Easter, Henry was ready for anything, keeping all options open and prepared to act opportunistically, instinctively, to his own best advantage.

But in July, when word came that Robert was likely to reach Normandy at the end of August, he knew that time was running out.

Henry had known, all his life, that if he wanted to succeed to his father's throne, he would have to fight for it. One way or another, in battle, honourably, man to man, or underhandedly, by means of a stratagem, a plot or a conspiracy. He had no love for William, the brothers had never shared any kind of fraternal bond, rather they were used to the rivalry and contention that their father had always fostered. But he was not entirely unscrupulous, not without conscience, not without some religious feeling. During his years eating crumbs from the tables of his brothers he had observed much misgovernment. He had seen blunders, wasted resources of men and money, mishandling of negotiations, failure to engage with allies, high-handed treatment of the temporarily disadvantaged. At William's court he had witnessed abuses of the church and had often sympathised with churchmen who were concerned by the persistent failure to fill vacancies. Starved of money, some foundations were struggling, the poor could not be fed, young monks could not be trained, discipline could not be maintained let alone upkeep of buildings, some of which were falling into disrepair. During the time of Anselm's absence, the decline of the churches had increased. It was a scandal to all England and a matter of interest to the Papal court. Henry did not forget that the new pope, Paschal, had already threatened William with excommunication.

In the summer of 1100, as the days passed in hunting and the nights in feasting, William was in broad good humour, he glowed with strength and showed himself hearty to his companions. With Anselm out of the picture he bounced the pope's threat harmlessly away, accompanied by a suitable jibe. What did he have to fear? He was surrounded by courtiers in a land at peace. Towards Henry his natural suspicions began to relax. He would slap him on the back in morning greeting and offer some comment on yesterday's hunt and how it could be surpassed that day. His favourite oath 'Holy Face of Lucca!' which had once given offence when he spluttered it out in anger, now joyfully indicated high spirits. He saw no danger anywhere. Nothing, it seemed, could dent the king's good humour. Meanwhile during those hot, fervid July days of the hunt, Henry grew more unsettled and restless. He had received a princely education, he had been schooled to search out wisdom, to read books, to study Latin. Was all that to go to waste? Could he not achieve the greatness in kingship which had eluded both his brothers? Why was he wasting his talent and energy in hunting when a whole kingdom needed reform? Reflecting on these things, he felt the bile of resentment rising in his throat. Yet his head was turning no plan even while his brain kept endlessly repeating: 'Now, what if William were to die?

***

And so we come to August 2nd 1100. As far as can be established, this is what is known about the events of that day:

On that Thursday William was at his hunting lodge looking forward to a day of sport. It was his habit to rise early but that day he was unusually late in rising and decided to delay going out until after his dinner, a meal eaten usually at around 11 o'clock. The dog-handlers, who had gone out at dawn and got tired of waiting, came back to ask what was the cause of the delay. They were told that the king was at dinner but was determined that the day should not be lost. 'Go back and wait with the beaters,' they were told, 'the king will come soon.'

William dined rather well in the company of his brother, Henry, and his closest companions, among them Walter Tirel, Robert FitzHaimo, the two Beaumont brothers, Robert of Meulan and Henry, Gilbert FitzRichard and his brother Roger, and William of Breteuil. Afterwards, just as he was pulling on his boots to go forth, laughing and joking in his customary way, a local smith arrived with six arrows, saying he wished to offer them as a gift to the king. Taking them in both hands, William looked them over, tested them for weight and balance and, praising their craftsmanship, took four for himself and gave two to Walter Tirel who was standing beside him. Just as the king was finally on the point of departing, a monk came from Gloucester with letters from the Abbot which he took and put aside. Some sources suggest that these letters may have contained a warning.

The king, followed by his hunting party then went outside to where the horses were waiting to carry them into the forest as far as the butts. When they entered the woodland, they sent beaters off in different directions to drive the game towards the waiting archers, as was usual. Marksmen were detailed to stand behind the individual members of the royal hunting party in order to fire at the deer at the same time as they did. This was to enable the aristocratic hunters to claim the kill, even when they had missed, but mainly to ensure that no wounded animal escaped into the undergrowth. Meulan, FitzHaimo, Breteuil and Henry went off to their separate stations with their huntsmen. The king and Tirel took up position at their butt. By the time the deer were heard racing into range they were alone, save for two marksmen standing behind Tirel and the king. Attendants with the horses were some way off and concealed from one another by the foliage. At this point, any words spoken would be in a whisper.

It was by now late afternoon. Out of the dazzling light of a low sun a deer passed within bowshot of the king. He fired and wounded it. Shading his eyes against the blinding glare, William looked round for the marksman who should have shot and finished it off. There was no-one there. He and Tirel were quite alone. He turned his head, following the injured stag, trying to assess the prospect of a second shot. While his attention was still on this stag, another came within range. It was now, while the second deer passed before the king, whose eyes were turned away, that Walter Tirel drew his bow, aimed one of the arrows William had given him, and fired.

The king made no sound. As he fell forward on the arrow, he broke off the shaft, pushing the head deep into the wound in his chest, fatally cutting an artery. Running up, Walter Tirel found him unconscious. At that moment there was no-one else in sight, the forest was deathly quiet, no sound, not even from the horses, though they were tethered not far away. Tirel looked once more at the fallen body, lying motionless in a spreading pool of blood. Then he ran to find his horse, leapt on it and got quickly away. There was no pursuit.

***

Above is the account on which, more or less, most sources agree. A degree of consensus presents these as the facts of the case, and they form the basis of the most reliable version of the story. Even so, speculation is inevitable. Were these events the result of murderous intent, or a tragic accident? Did Walter Tirel fire the arrow? Had he mistimed his shot, as sometimes happened? The sun was low since the king had departed late in the day. Did that affect the aim? Walter Tirel is one of those characters who pops into history at a crucial moment and then sinks below the horizon, as if all his life was destined for shadow save for one brief moment. In one sudden ephemeral ray of light, he is seen, caught centre stage with incriminating evidence in his hand, then swiftly he is gone again, gone not only out of the story, but out of England altogether. A few mentions of him appear subsequently in scattered documents in relation to land ownership in Normandy, and there is a report that, on his death bed, he denied firing the fatal arrow.

What can be said about him? We know he was the son of the Norman, Walter Tirel, whose domain was Picardie de Poix. He was born in Tonbridge, Kent and later held the manor of Langham in Essex, which in 1086 was worth 1,000 pigs, 22 cattle, 40 acres of meadow, 2 mills, 200 sheep and eighty goats; a substantial holding for a small man of few abilities, and enough to supply him with the horse and weaponry of an aspiring nobleman. Through his Norman connections already established at the English court, he was able to advance into the inner circle where his prowess with the bow and his stamina in the hunting field got him noticed. He was a regular at the 'fat season' and the after-hunt feasts where William liked to drink and revel his huntsmen, high and low together. The lubricated bonhommie of these parties led many ambitious men to overstep the limit of William's forbearance. It seems very unlikely that such a one as Walter Tirel was 'his most intimate friend' as some have written. He may have been a mate of the hunting field, but hardly on the level of 'friendship' especially the kind of heightened male love-bond friendship that the medieval world readily embraced. It seems from the accounts of that day, that Walter Tirel stood in William's estimation as 'a good shot', hence the onward gift of the arrows. Who the generous 'smith' was who sent the arrows can only be surmised. Was it even a smith who sent them? Might it have been someone richer, who could afford bespoke arrows such as might delight a king? And who might that be?

Where was Henry and what was he doing on the day in question? Again, our knowledge is limited. But we can and do know, with some degree of certainty and in considerable detail, what he did afterwards. Can his motives be deduced from his subsequent behaviour?

***

When news broke of the discovery in the forest, Henry galloped straight to Winchester, aware that what he did next would have infinite consequences for himself and the kingdom. The death of a king without heirs or a clear line of succession opened up a dangerous void of power. To prevent the whole kingdom expiring in lawlessness and anarchy,

Henry must act. If his brother was dead, he must assert his right to the throne, get the backing of the barons and clergy, and get moving. Swift action was vital because another brother stood in the way: Robert Curthose, Duke of Normandy.

In Winchester, he met up with those who had been in the forest and had scattered when the news broke: William of Breteuil, Robert Fitzhaimo, Robert of Meulan and his brother, Henry Beaumont, Gilbert and Roger FitzRichard, members of the powerful Clare family. Gathered in council with these courtiers, Henry demanded their support. William of Breteuil, thinking to sound a reasonable note of caution, misjudged the force of Henry's resolve. Breteuil reminded them that, in former times, they had all sworn fealty oaths to Robert Curthose. The greatest challenge to Henry's seizure of the throne was the imminent return of Robert Curthose from the pilgrims' war to liberate Jerusalem. Once back in Normandy, he would set about asserting his dominance in the duchy so that he could challenge Henry's right of succession. In the long term he would probably, by one means or another, have to be put out of the way. From this moment Henry's oath to Robert was null.

In these first hectic moments after the death, speed was the first essential, the second was discretion. Let there be no official announcements, no letters sent out to sheriffs for promulgation to the people, not yet, not until the thing was done. Henry's plan was to present a *fait accompli*, leaving no room for dissent. The first thing was to obtain control of the royal treasury, located in the Conqueror's castle at Winchester. Having secured the strongroom and mint, Henry took control of the whole castle, winning over the constable and seizing the arsenal. He summoned scribes to write letters to the Bishop of London, the clergy of Westminster and Bishop Gerard of Hereford, urging their support for what would come next. He assembled all the barons, those who had come with him to Winchester and those who could be called from the surrounding area, including Henry de Port, the principal lay magnate of the county, and got them by dawn the following day to acclaim him king. Leading the acclamations was Robert of Meulan, along with Henry of Beaumont, Earl of Warwick, Robert Fitzhaimo and William of Breteuil. This show of support was then touted among the English as an 'election' according to their old rights of accession and, being familiar to them, did not meet with open disfavour. These things done; Henry turned his thoughts to his coronation. Only a coronation could give legitimacy to all his foregoing actions and establish the legality of his reign.

It had to be in Westminster, and soon.

About noon on Friday, before the funeral of his brother had taken place, Henry left Winchester with his closest supporters and raced to London, reaching it, as planned, late on the Saturday night. He was crowned the next day, Sunday 5th August, a mere three days after his brother's death. Sunday coronations had been the practice of English kings for as long as anyone could remember, and Henry was keen to uphold the tradition. With this in mind, he had helped himself to the royal regalia that William had kept in the treasury at Winchester. No-one could say he was not prepared for a coronation.

The ceremony was conducted in the nave of St Peter's Abbey, Westminster and although arranged in frantic haste, Henry thought that it achieved a surprising measure of polish. Magnificent, spectacular, a ceremony charged with great solemnity. Yet something jarred, some indefinable thing. There was an undercurrent of menace, some nebulous threat. Henry felt it in the hush of the nave and saw it in the faces around him. He had gone too fast. Rebounding from this frenetic speed of action, in the lull of the ritual, many began to feel that the repercussions from this overhasty crowning, inaugurating the reign of a man long kept from power, had every likelihood of turning bad and plunging the country into war.

Bishop Maurice of London, called upon to perform the coronation at two days' notice, was wholly unacquainted with the ritual and had to improvise as best he could from the first *ordo* that came to hand. But even if Anselm, Archbishop of Canterbury, had been present to perform it, and not in exile where he had been for the last three years, he could barely have improved on the ceremony since he had no better understanding of these things than Maurice. Anyway, as Henry knew only too well, the only part that really mattered was the anointing. Even more than the crowning itself, it was the anointing that would transform him from a mere mortal into a consecrated deputy of Christ on earth. The holy chrism, dabbed in little crosses about his body and on his brow, would keep him safer than whole armies.

Another notable absentee from the proceedings was Thomas, Archbishop of York, the very same who had consecrated Anselm seven years earlier. Being infirm and elderly he could not undertake the journey, even had there been time. Thus the two great pillars of the English church were absent and Henry had to make do with Bishop Maurice of London and Gerard Chancellor, Bishop of Hereford who, between them, devised a ceremony that did not disgrace the church and satisfied Henry.

Coronation had developed into a sanctification of the cooperation between churchmen and kings. Through this elaborate and potent ritual any man who had inherited a throne or made his way to it by whatever means of political intrigue or bloodshed, could be transformed into a holy person. In exchange for some public pledges to keep the peace and maintain justice and mercy, churchmen had the power to legalise kingship. Above all, Henry was hungry for legitimacy. Kept out of power, forced to rove between his brothers, begging crumbs from their tables, witnessing all their mistakes and what he viewed as their shameless neglect of good government, spending his entire adult life up to the age of thirty-one as an observer of misrule, Henry at last felt liberated, justified and ready to make his mark.

He began at once. Standing before the altar, he publicly declared a threefold promise: to keep the peace, to prohibit iniquities and to maintain just laws. On this platform he would base his reign, as kings had done before him. But Henry went one better. These pledges, making known the terms on which he had received the support of barons and clergy, were to be written into a charter and issued that very day. It was his way of expunging the abuses of his brother's reign. Of course, he was aware that William Rufus had issued written promises in 1093 at the time of his recovery from illness. They had been placed by Anselm on the altar of Gloucester Cathedral where they remained, ignored. William had never made any effort to keep, renew, or promulgate them. Henry demonstrated the difference of his proceedings by having the fourteen clauses of this charter widely disseminated and soon copied into compilations of law. There would be a record of them, whereas William's promises were written on wind and running water. This was a charter designed to satisfy the church, the baronage and common laity, both English and Norman, and, as he put it himself, 'all people of good will.'

But Henry, whether innocent or guilty of the killing, was aware that events had happened with such astonishing speed that they might now run out of control. Even with the coronation under his belt, he knew himself very far from secure.

At this crucial moment, two things headed Henry's list of things to do. Anselm, the exiled Archbishop of Canterbury must be recalled urgently, placated and won over. In this way Henry would demonstrate his credentials as a good Christian monarch. It was imperative, too, that all the new bishops and abbots he had already appointed should be confirmed in their titles by consecration. Lastly, and closest of all to his personal satisfaction, he wanted Anselm to officiate at his marriage.

That was the second point on his agenda. He must marry and put to shame the long bachelorhood of his brother. He must secure heirs to his line, unlike William who had carelessly left the way open for him. Marriage at the first opportunity, marriage to a suitable lady of high birth and undoubted virtue would bring about popular acceptance of his accession. But it needed the approval of the church. Anselm, as primate of the church in England, was necessary to bestow it.

Soon after the coronation, Henry sent a letter politely recalling Anselm to England. By November he was was back home and officiating at Henry's marriage. The bride was that same Edith from Wilton, daughter of King Malcolm of Scotland, whom William had refused years before. She was now nineteen and called herself Matilda. She was educated, resourceful, ambitious; a spirited partner for a king wishing to make his mark.

Is there anything in this series of speedily executed actions and events to suggest a plot? Were the pledges and promises that Henry made at his coronation meant to assuage a conscience darkened with the sin of Cain? Does the succession of events: the swift take-over of Winchester, the seizure of the regalia, the hurried journey to London, suggest a conspiracy hammered out by Henry perhaps with the collaboration of Tirel, Fitz Haimo and others of his circle? Or are Henry's actions those of a man who, given an unexpected slice of good fortune, seizes it with supreme mastery and turns it to his own advantage?

Chapter Five
Eadmer's Dilemma

(*Dilemma n. (Gr) a position where each of two alternative courses is eminently undesirable.*)

The Romans, who built a fort by an alder carr and called it Cantiacorum, had long been gone when a Christian church was founded there by St Augustine in 597 AD. During the following centuries of expansion, feeding on the Roman rubble, the church grew into an important seat of learning. Buildings were added. In the 10th century it became a Benedictine Abbey and expanded to fill the needs of the monks with a library and scriptorium. By the middle of the eleventh century, it had a dormitory, a refectory, an archive, a chapel, a chapter house. In shrines and tombs lay the relics of English saints whose feast days and legends were a source of pride among the monks who kept alive the memory of St Augustine, St Dunstan and other illustrious precursors. By the time of the Conquest the monastery was known as Christ Church and occupied a building resembling a Roman basilica with an eastern apse. It is here at Christ Church, Canterbury that we can find Brother Eadmer in about 1067.

Eadmer never set out to be famous. Fame was never his goal, and he would have been repulsed by anything as shallow as celebrity. On the other hand, he might be pleased with the limited renown among historians and scholars that he has achieved over the centuries. Although he believed that in his writings he was leaving something for posterity, he could not have imagined that his name would be known hundreds of years after his death. At least, not in the early days, when he was a boy at Christ Church, an oblate child raised by the monks who became mother and father to him, for he had no other that we know of. Perhaps his parents were dead or had farmed him out to relations or a patron as was the custom of the times. If his parents were alive there is no record of them handing him over, a tender lad of six or seven. But if someone else gave him to the monastery there is no trace of them in the records. Yet, the records do not suggest that he was a foundling.

In whatever way Eadmer came to be there, it was in Canterbury he felt safe, snugly attached to an ancient source of nourishment, his roots deep in the Kentish countryside and his heart in Christchurch. He never felt at home anywhere but in the monastery that had bred him. These feelings were bound up with his own English identity which, however many times he travelled abroad, was never diminished.

We do not know if Eadmer thought of himself as God's instrument in telling the world about the history of his times and the powerful political figures who enacted their dramas on the stage of the world. Unfortunately, no-one left a biography of Eadmer, and other sources are few, so our knowledge of Eadmer himself is limited. But a writer is always present in his work, mysteriously woven into the text, in his style, observations, the weight he gives to particular ideas or descriptions. Eadmer's work is distinguished in its time for acute observation and vividness of expression. His descriptions have the immediacy of reportage. What Eadmer wants to convey more than anything is the greatness of his primary subject, Anselm. A man personally known to him, with whom he lived closely for many years, with whom he shared many journeys, frequent disappointments and periods of exile, a man who was the force and focus of his life for over a decade. Eadmer's biography of Anselm, covering the ten years he spent in England and the six years of his exile, remains a major source of knowledge about that period for scholars to the present day. He wanted Anselm's unique and saintly character to be known to posterity and this he achieved. But with the focus on Anselm, where do we look for Eadmer? It is true that he occasionally writes in the first person giving us glimpses of his preferences and patterns of thought; we can hear a tone. Now and again, he dangles a tantalising fact about himself and from these meagre sources we have to construct our answer to the question – who was Eadmer?

We don't know his date of birth but can reconstruct a fairly reliable date at around 1060. We don't know who his parents were but might estimate that they were either horribly poor or terribly devout for it is likely he was given as an oblate child to the monastery at Christ Church when he was about seven years old. He records that he could remember the arrangement of the old church before the devastating fire of 1067, so he was probably not much younger than seven. Other indications suggest that he may have come from a family of English gentry down on their luck after the conquest. For example, it seems that he had a nephew, his sister's son, with the Norman name Haimo, who was a monk at Christ Church in 1115; and that in about 1130 another relative, a man of some substance called Henry, was a tenant of the monastery. In one way or another, almost from the beginning, Christ Church is the hub and centre of Eadmer's life. It was where he was schooled in Latin and learned to read, where he was taught to memorise the litany, the saints' days, the chants and prayers, to become acquainted with the sonorous round of Benedictine hours. It was also where he learned the art of writing, by which he was to leave a name to posterity and where he learned to love the Old English church and its practices by listening to the stories of ancient monks whose tales went back at first hand to the days of King Cnut and at second hand as far back as the reign of King Edgar. Eadmer tells us, in one of those brief asides that is so charged with feeling that one almost breathes the musty odour of ink and parchment and sees the motes in the sunlight that fell across his arm in the scriptorium on the day he wrote, he tells us that he was a sensitive child upon whom the beauty of the ancient church impressed itself unforgettably, remaining into old age undimmed. Christ Church shaped him, and its history made him proud.

Christ Church, Canterbury had grown steadily since its founding but, not long after young Eadmer had thoroughly acquainted himself with the layout of the buildings and memorised their arrangement, they were burned down. About three years after the fire, sometime between 1070 and 1077, the monastery was remodelled and rebuilt. This was something of a trauma to the young boy. England had been undergoing such radical changes since 1066 that barely a custom or landholding remained from the old time. A few English monks, mainly working out of Worcester still held their posts, probably thanks to Bishop Wulfstan who was the only English-born bishop to remain in post after the change of government. But in the meantime, there had been a wholesale replacement of monks and bishops with Norman appointees. Eadmer tells us in his writings about his affection for the old English church, its rites and saints. Proud of the distinctively unique English rites and practices, he was touchy about any threatened interference from Normandy or Rome. Of the old English saints of Canterbury, St Elphege, St Mildrith, St Oda and many others were turfed out of their resting places and their bones deposited in unused chapels, in second-hand urns and musty corners. While their names might have remained in the cartularies, their saints' days were gradually forgotten; an oblivion which caused Eadmer considerable pain. In spite of these feelings, he tried to show, as the monks had taught him, the yielding grace of a Benedictine novice, accepting everything as God's will. At least Eadmer knew that Saint Augustine was safe from any disturbance. Saint Augustine, as the founding saint of Canterbury whose inaugural mission had begun the conversion of the British leaders in 597 AD, also established Canterbury as the first bishopric in England. Later on, successive archbishops of Canterbury, Anselm among them, would fight to defend this historic primacy.

But before we come to contemplate the gigantic figure of Anselm and all that he meant to Eadmer, we have to consider his immediate predecessor, Lanfranc. Appointed by the Conqueror as Archbishop of Canterbury, Lanfranc had been a man of considerable ability and great presence, the sort of man who goes on being a force in the organisation he has led even after his demise. He won respect, from kings, from other prelates, from the pope, and certainly from the Conqueror who felt himself to have played a masterstroke in appointing him in 1070. Eadmer, then about ten years old, would have felt the change. Suddenly the Normans put in place a foreigner, for Lanfranc was originally from Pavia, although he had been leading the famous monastery at Bec in Normandy for many years. It is quite probable that Eadmer now experienced his first feelings of indignation. Why should an Abbot from Bec be promoted over many worthy English candidates? Over time, these feelings were to grow into grievance and resentment at the treatment of his nation which later found their way into his writings. "Their nationality was their downfall," he wrote of Englishmen who had been passed over for promotion. "If they were English no virtue was enough for them… if they were foreigners, the mere appearance of virtue was enough for them to be considered worthy of the highest office."

But grudges and bad feeling sat ill with him. He desired an open heart, he longed to be a brother to the monks, he wanted to extend charity to all mankind. These feelings were to commit him to many inner struggles in his life, for he himself was no saint. In 1089 Lanfranc died and, since no successor was appointed, the see was left vacant for four years. Vacancies were regarded as scandals by the clergy, an outrage upon the church. It was a way for the king to help himself to all the monies from the estates and manors that the churches held. We don't know what effect the vacancy had on the organisation of the monastery, or on Eadmer other than that he complained. We do not know what he was doing at this time other than he was living the life of a monk in the community and, somehow, preparing himself to be a witness to history during the long writing career that was to come. At no time do we know what he looked like. Brought up on a monastic diet he might have been lean, even wiry; but he might not. We don't know the colour of his eyes, we only know that they were observant, looking on the world with an alertness to detail which he was eager to record. We don't know the colour of his hair, but it is probable that he wore a tonsure, a small, shaved circle on the top of his head, as a mark of dedication.

At some point during this period Eadmer would have become acquainted with another Christ Church monk, Osbern, who was about ten years his senior and had already written a few hagiographies. 'Lives of the Saints' and such like instructive stories were important reading material at mealtimes, where they were read aloud in the refectory, and Eadmer would have been familiar with them. Osbern was precentor at Christ Church, officially in charge of liturgy and music, and he was already an author. One of his main interests was establishing a study of local history and recording the lives of the saints associated with Canterbury. Whether it was from this early acquaintance that Eadmer adopted the idea of one day himself writing a saint's life we don't know, but he does mention Osbern in his writings with the affection a young lad can have for a sympathetic older man of great talent. They shared a kind of outrage when, not long after his arrival at Canterbury, Lanfranc caused the bones of St Dunstan to be dug up from the old church and more or less dumped in a side chapel. It is interesting to note that when Eadmer came to write his "History of Recent Events in England" (*Historia Novorum in Anglia*) one of the first stories he told was about Dunstan and how he had 'sternly denounced King Ethelred." Later in the same narrative, Dunstan's death is marked in Eadmer's mind by a moment of history when 'England is lain open to foreign foes' and there is a 'grinding down of the whole Kingdom with crushing exactions.'

Whether Eadmer was seeing parallels with his own times, and feeling the resentment of conquest and oppression, is difficult to assess. One might say that in Christ Church, in the shelter of an institution that was protected by the prominence of the Archbishop, Eadmer had less cause than most to storm and complain about the injustice of the world. In fact, his career serves to show how a monk, whatever his origins, might attain a degree of success in his chosen field. But it does seem probable that the incumbency of Lanfranc taught him the discipline of subjecting his feelings to proper scrutiny. As he grew up during the nearly nineteen years of Lanfranc's dispensation, he would have been living daily according to the Benedictine Rule which placed a great emphasis on submission of the will to a superior, on the subjection of self-will and on the principle of a shared life. By the time Lanfranc died in 1089, Eadmer would have been about thirty years old, and probably assumed that his life would pretty much carry on in the same tenor: the canonical hours, silent prayer, litany, chapter house meetings, almsgiving, work and sleep. And so it did until something happened in 1093 that would shake Eadmer and the whole Christ Church monastery out of its slumbrous Old English dream and send it hurtling into a new phase of existence. Canterbury was to have a new Archbishop. His name was Anselm.

***

Anselm's appointment was controversial from the beginning, but Eadmer was not present when it took place at Gloucester in the Palace of Kingsholm on May 6th, 1093.

Anselm, who was then Abbot of Bec, happened to be on a visit to Earl Hugh of Chester who was desirous of founding a monastery. Learning that the king, William Rufus, the son of the Conqueror, was lying desperately ill nearby in Gloucester, Anselm went to offer consolation and prayers. Or perhaps he was summoned by ministers and courtiers who were afraid the king might die leaving the scandal of an unfilled vacancy at Canterbury to pursue him into the grave. Arrived at Kingsholm, Anselm found himself pressured to accept the post at Canterbury although he protested that he had no desire for such an office. In his writings Eadmer gives an account of the scene. It is dramatic and vivid, with action and dialogue bringing all the bizarrerie of the occasion before our eyes. But it was not something Eadmer actually witnessed because it took place in Gloucester and he, as far as we know was still at Christ Church, Canterbury. The narrative of this momentous scene appears in Eadmer's *History of Recent Events in England* and was written at a later date after he had had occasion to talk to Anselm himself and some of the other participants. What he doesn't say about this event is that it would have an overwhelming impact on his life. From the moment of Anselm's appointment Eadmer's future hung in the balance; it was a seismic event which would redirect the quiet flow of his days into powerful streams of controversy and disputation. For Eadmer, for Christ Church and its monks, for Canterbury and all its religious foundations, the appointment of the new Archbishop was an event of mammoth proportions.

It may be surprising to know that Eadmer and Anselm may have met many years previously on the occasion when Anselm came to Canterbury in 1079. Or rather, they may not have met for Anselm would then have been the prominent Abbot of Bec and Eadmer no more than a novice monk of eighteen or so. But it is quite possible that Eadmer had been present when Anselm spoke informally to the monks after the evening meal. He often did this, he liked to gather the monks about him and discourse in conversational style, preferring parables and stories to more formal sermons. His relaxed mode of discourse made a strong impression on his hearers. His voice, his manner, his learning mingled with simplicity, his sharp intellectual poise with humour and warmth, stayed long in the mind. Anselm's talk was the main thing Eadmer remembered about that earlier visit to Canterbury. And it was this man who was about to return as Archbishop.

How Eadmer heard about it, is not certain. Possibly not until travelling monks brought the news, or some official of the king brought word to the Prior. How Eadmer felt about it also remains uncertain. No doubt he would have been pleased that the scandalous vacancy was at an end and that the monastery could now look forward to a time of order, discipline and direction. For during the four-year vacancy between Lanfranc's death and the appointment of Anselm, the wealth and income of the archbishopric had been exploited by the royal treasury. Buildings fell into disrepair for lack of funds. Services and prayers were still carried out but by increasingly wretched and cash-strapped monks. Eadmer complains that the king siphoned off the monies from rents and tenantries, leaving only 'the bare subsistence of the monks' and reducing the house of God to poverty. 'You might see daily,' he writes, 'the most odious of men, without any respect for the religion of God's servants, engaged in exacting the king's moneys, making their way through the precincts of the monastery with grim and threatening looks, giving orders on all sides, uttering threats, displaying to the utmost their dominance and power.' This description is typical of Eadmer's vivid style when he is reporting from his own observations. Eadmer, the eyewitness to history, is here writing of what he has seen and can hardly keep his personal feelings out of the story.

It is likely, then, that he greeted the news of Anselm's appointment with relief and expectation, perhaps even hopes for a brighter future for his beloved Christ Church. Anselm had a great reputation, he was a scholar of prestige and fame who had written treatises, dialogues and theological works. He was famed as Abbot of Bec, having led that prestigious monastery in succession to Lanfranc since 1078. During those twenty-five years he had demonstrated some skill at leadership even though he hated administration and preferred the work of theology. He fostered the careers of talented young monks. He had maintained a spirited defence of the abbey's independence from lay interference. He developed his signature discourse, known as *conversatio*, in which he sat with the monks and told little parables and allegorical stories in such a way that they hardly knew they were doing theology. All this reputational glory must have intrigued the monks at Christ Church while they spent the months awaiting Anselm's arrival. For he was in no hurry. Still constitutionally averse to accepting the post, he was delaying the act of homage and complaining loudly every time he met the king.

Making homage to the king was customary among high appointees, such as bishops and archbishops, even abbots, at this time. It was a matter of extreme controversy in the church and a jealousy-guarded right among kings and princes. The church must bow the knee to secular authority, not least because secular authority was armed. The custom had been established in a more savage past when monks and monasteries really required the protection of warlike men to keep them safe. But now many questioned it. As the moral authority of the church grew so did its powers of self-protection. As men became more devout and the Pope's authority more binding, the need for protection diminished. Besides, the church could exchange pardons and absolutions for a certain amount of controlled violence towards its enemies, when necessary. That being the case, the church was beginning to ask: is there any need to pay homage, to bend the knee and bow in gratitude for something that the church itself is quite capable of conferring and preserving? This question came to be asked more and more in the ensuing years, and it would eventually become a critical matter for Anselm and his successors. But in that year 1093 the issue had not yet developed the status of the full-blown controversy which was about to entrammel him in years of dispute.

It took Anselm until September to make up his mind to conform to custom and pay homage. Six months of soul-wrestling and agonising. Besides, he still felt he was Abbot of Bec and was conscience-stricken at leaving the monks when he had given his promise that he never would. Nevertheless, at great personal cost, he did the deed. In a formal ceremony at Winchester, he bent the knee and spoke the words of the oath like a vassal of the king. King William, seeming genuinely impressed with the dignity of the old man, raised him up and embraced him.

It still took until December for Anselm to make his way to Canterbury and get himself consecrated. This ceremony was, beyond all others, sacred in the extreme. By the ritual enactments of consecration, a person was taken from the profane world and sanctified; made sacred, set aside. It was a powerful and solemn ceremony which must have impressed itself on all who saw it.

Did Eadmer witness the occasion? It is most probable that he did although he leaves us no description of it. This may have been intentional because he felt that the holy rites were private. They were not to be the subject of brazen scrutiny in the common light of history. Consecrations did not belong to everybody; they were private occasions where priests or monks were transmuted into a specially blessed state. Eadmer may well have refrained from writing about the intimate details out of scruples, either personal or institutional. But he does tell us about the controversial part of the ceremony when there was a dispute over the formulation of Anselm's title. It is not out of keeping with Anselm's character that, at the very instant of his becoming Archbishop, he is at the centre of a disputation over the form of words to be used. In after years Eadmer might have seen this as the moment his own life changed. Anselm and controversy, Anselm and dispute; they were to be an inextricable part of Eadmer's life for the next sixteen years and would one day pitch him into a profound dilemma. But Eadmer's dilemma grew slowly out of the investment he made in the man who would become his pastor, master, teacher and the subject of his writings.

At Christmas 1093, in the household of the Archbishop, the next chapter of Eadmer's life began.

***

The household of an archbishop required a large staff. It was a centre of an administration which presided over lands, rents, manors, lay tenants as well as monks, priests and canons. It needed secretaries and copyists as well as clerks to maintain the archives or manage legal affairs and receive payments from tenants. On one level the archbishopric was a business with a large annual income and the archbishop needed a loyal team of trained and talented men to help him run it. Two men had accompanied him from Bec. One was Eustace, a monk who very soon disappears from the chronicles, probably being replaced by Eadmer. The other was Baldwin of Tournai, an adviser with a talent for politics who had once been the chief agent of the Bishop of Tournai whose title he adopted.

To understand how Eadmer's life took the direction it did, it is necessary to know a little about Baldwin and get a picture of the role he would come to play as head of the Archbishop's household. We don't know what Baldwin looked like but he was about fifty at this time and had had a distinguished career as a layman before he became a monk. So he was trained in the ways of the world and, we can assume, was nobody's fool when it came to the legal and political skills that he had honed at important courts and councils all over Europe. One imagines a cool gaze not unfamiliar with the iniquities of the world, a diplomatic manner, a confident bearing. Eadmer gives us plenty of information about his ability to think on his feet, to come up with solutions to sticky situations, to cajole or persuade his master into wise decisions. Many times he saved Anselm from going astray when he was at risk of alienating the king's favour or failing to read the prevailing winds blowing from Rome. It may have been Baldwin who encouraged Anselm to take Eadmer onto his household staff and give him a position which would enable him to observe and get to know the man who would become his subject of study. Exactly when and how Eadmer formed the idea of writing a 'life' of his master and identifying that life as 'saintly' we don't know, but it seems that he was making notes and writing down what he observed from the beginning of their association and may have been encouraged in this by Baldwin.

The work that grew from these notes, the *Vita Sancti Anselmi*, represents hours of laborious devotion and remains a testament to Eadmer's dedication to recording the life of Anselm as well as a history that reflects his own life. This is medieval chronicling at its most bountiful and dramatic. Eadmer cannot keep himself out of the work, his enthusiasm, his diligence, and also, very occasionally, the moments when he is tested to the highest pitch in his beliefs as a man and his capacity as a monk.

***

The destabilisation of Eadmer's quiet life began almost as soon as Anselm was consecrated and set out on his episcopal reign in earnest. From now on he would spend as much time on the road as at Christchurch, travelling to the court or to important meetings, or from manor to manor around the numerous domains of the archiepiscopal estates in half a dozen counties in England. In early December, Anselm was summoned to the court at Gloucester where he found out that the king wanted one thousand pounds as a thank-offering. In other words, a pay-off, or in Anselm's word, simony. The king wanted a big thank-you for having made Anselm Archbishop of Canterbury and thus a very rich man. But Anselm had no idea that he was rich, nor would he much care since wealth would not change his ideas or his way of life. He carried on living the life of a monk, as far as possible, leaving Baldwin and his private office to do most of the paperwork. The king found, to his dismay, that Anselm not only would not pay up but was so insulted by the king's insolent demand that he abruptly left the court. He went south, roaming round his scattered manors, until some weeks later he received the royal summons to go to Hastings. On the point of leaving for Normandy, King William was delayed in crossing by contrary winds and thought he might profitably use the time by reconciling with his archbishop. Tempers having cooled, they met in goodwill and, thinking himself forgiven by the king, Anselm began to preach to him about the need for the relief of the churches and reform of morals at court. Naturally, this met with a royal scowl. When Anselm failed to read the signs of the king's displeasure the king told him to leave Hastings as soon as possible. Perhaps this was the moment when Eadmer realised that constant bickering was to be the pattern of Anselm's relationship with the king.

Certainly, things had got off to a bad start. It even seems that Anselm became a little depressed and regretted the decision he had made to accept the post. He "began to think of all the peace he had lost and all the labour he had found," writes Eadmer, "he saw his days and nights taken up with secular business...unable to devote his attention either to God or to his neighbour in God's name." Eadmer alleges that "the king's mind was worked up into a fury against him." In fact, Baldwin was handling most of the secular business and the king was simply trying to address the problem of how to deal with a man of principle who could not be bought.

It was not long before Eadmer had to confront his own beliefs in relation to a factor central to writing the life of a saint – how to deal with the miraculous. In any saintly life there must be miracles. All saints trailed these glorious stories in their wake. Wherever saints went miracles would occur, from the healing of the blind man to the putting out of a fire with a single prayer. In all his life Eadmer had never witnessed such a thing, nor did he know of anybody who had seen any deviation from the natural course of things which might be labelled a miracle. Yet a touch of the divine must dwell with the saintly man as it had dwelt with Augustine, Elphege, Dunstan and all the other saints of Christ Church.

Eadmer must have known that if Anselm was to reach posterity through his writings, it must be as a saint; a saint to follow all the previous saints of Canterbury, the first and most holy of all the dioceses of England. A saint must perform miracles. But Eadmer had never seen any and, worse, doubted his own ability to do so. This uncertainty tested Eadmer for a long time. Sensitive to the values he represented, in the spiritual realm as well as in the integrity of writing, having respect for honest labour, and resolved to attest to what he had seen, Eadmer began to lose faith in having been chosen for the task. But then with felicitous timing, the problem was solved for him.

Baldwin, who from the first encouraged Eadmer in his writings and praised his abilities, was a man of such conflicting qualities that he remained something of an enigma. Eadmer soon realised he was a monk without great piety who preferred legal wrangles and business affairs to praying or reflection. Yet Baldwin was devoted to his master whose intellect he measured as far beyond his own and never missed an opportunity to present him as a person of exceptional holiness. Devoted, pragmatic, Baldwin could advise and guide the older man who, in turn, trusted him implicitly and looked to him to take from his shoulders the burden of daily affairs. Although a monk for many years, Baldwin's attitude to most things seemed completely secular. In only one particular did he suspend all doubt. He believed Anselm to be a saint because he had witnessed a miracle performed by him.

But it wasn't Baldwin, it was Eustace who told the story to Eadmer, who reports it to us. 'Once,' said Eustace, 'when we were all on a boat at sea crossing to the port of Wissant, rough weather threatened to sink us. Anselm started to pray for a safe harbour and not long after the storm died, and we came safely to port. As we disembarked, Baldwin swore that he saw a hole in the keel. Swore it. Swore that Anselm, by prayer alone, had kept the boat afloat despite a great hole where the sea had poured in.'

'Did you see the hole?' asked Eadmer.

'No.'

As soon as he found the opportunity, Eadmer asked Baldwin whether the story was true; 'for,' he writes, 'I was unwilling to describe anything about which I had the slightest doubt.'

Without hesitation, Baldwin swore it was all true. At a later date Eadmer would come to write up this story and other numerous miraculous stories in the *Vita Sancti Anselmi*. As he asserts, he would not willingly write as true something of which he was in doubt. He is willing to rely on third person reports of miracles, but he never so much as hints that he has seen one.

A similar incident occurs later in the text.

Eadmer tells us that Anselm has just celebrated mass and is alone in the church. A man guiding his steps with the aid of a stick comes in, approaches the chapel and tries to burst in. A monk called Alexander, who happens to be waiting outside the door for Anselm to come out, stops the man and demands to know what he wants. 'I am blind!' the man shouts, 'I beg Anselm to heal me! In the name of God let him lay his hands on me!'

Anselm, hearing the commotion, tells Alexander to come and explain what is happening. When Alexander has done so, Anselm says: 'Let him come.'

Then Anselm, with his thumb, makes the sign of the cross over the blind man's eyes and speaks restorative words. Then he sprinkles them with holy water and tells the man to go. Alexander leads him away, telling him to come back tomorrow if there is no improvement. At that, the man leaps about madly, saying 'I can see! I can see!'

Again, it is worth noting that at the end of this story Eadmer places a little disclaimer. "I have written this as I heard it from the mouth of Alexander," he says, "for I happened to be busy and was attending to other things." Later in the work, Eadmer is even more assertive about the rectitude of his writing: 'And I affirm', he writes, 'that it is a shocking thing for anyone knowingly to write what is false in sacred histories.'

This is Eadmer's method. He presents the miracle stories as told or observed or reported by someone else, never by him. It is tempting to think that this indicates Eadmer's sense of integrity as a writer. He feels himself called to the vocation of writing which, though not holy, is a task of high calling. He won't put his name to 'anything about which I could have the slightest doubt.' This is a serious assertion, the *non plus ultra* of his morality. I believe it suggests how seriously Eadmer took his task of recording the life of Anselm, a task made doubly difficult because, although he believed in the sainthood of Anselm, he never witnessed a single proof.

***

Eadmer's life entered yet another phase when, in 1097, after four years of wrangling, Anselm was exiled by the king. Finally, having inadvertently stumbled into a position which was close enough to treason for alarm bells to ring, Anselm was commanded to proceed to Dover, having been given eleven days to get out of the kingdom. Eadmer writes movingly of the leave-taking of the community at Canterbury in a passage entitled: "How he spoke to the monks of Canterbury on setting out for Rome; and how, after receiving the pilgrim's purse and staff, he went to Dover." A long passage records Anselm's words to the monks, reminding them of the nature of their service and urging them to 'bear everything with steadfast minds.' Eadmer may be recording at least some of this verbatim, from notes or from memory. Parting in tears and with a kiss for each monk, Anselm and his entourage 'set forth with much weeping and lamentation.' He would not return for three years.

Before they left England a final humiliation occurred which Eadmer describes in great detail and with obvious feeling. So deeply does the scene seem to be imprinted on his memory that he records the exact date: 8th November 1097.

Anselm's party had arrived in Dover and spent fifteen days waiting for the wind to change so that they could set sail. That morning they were told to ready themselves and go on board as the wind was favourable. It is likely that small boats were used to get out to the larger vessels and Anselm was on the beach, waiting for his luggage to be put aboard a transit vessel when he was accosted by one of the king's most efficient court servants. This was William Warelwast, who appears in Eadmer's book frequently and almost always as a precursor to misfortune. Warelwast had come with a last-minute message from the king, to say that Anselm must take nothing except personal effects out of the kingdom. By that he meant that the king forbad the carrying of letters to the pope, or money, gold or any church treasures. Such an act would be regarded as illicit. An enraged Eadmer invites us to imagine the scene: 'the Father of his country, the Primate of all Britain, was detained on the seashore like a fugitive or common criminal. This same William, (Warelwast) on behalf of his lord, forbade him to cross the sea until he had shown him, piece by piece, everything that he was taking with him.' And so, with a vivid picture of Anselm desolate on the shore with a state official turfing out his baggage all around him, Eadmer takes the archbishop out of England.

The next few years were spent wandering about Europe. After a trip to Rome to visit the Pope and register his complaints against the king, Anselm, Baldwin and Eadmer, along with a few monks and servants who had come with him into exile, spent time at Bec, travelling between various courts in France and in Apulia. Hugh, Bishop of Lyon, was a particular friend with whom he spent many months. At one time, Eadmer tells us, 'we took up our abode on a mountain top, as far removed from the thronging crowd as it were in a desert.' There Anselm finished writing a book: *Cur Deus Homo* which had been in composition almost since his appointment as Archbishop. Exile turned out to be not so irksome after all: he could travel, visit friends, speak to the pope, write his works, study. Actually, there was a lot to be said for it and Eadmer certainly gives an upbeat view of Anselm during these years.

All this time Eadmer, too, was writing, taking notes, observing, recording and collecting accounts of miracles. We don't know exactly how the work was written and over what period but at some point, when the book was at an advanced stage, something happened that stopped Eadmer in his tracks. It was such a shock, such a serious knock to his self-esteem, to the course of his writing and his unfailing faith in Anselm that you can almost feel him reeling from the blow as he recounts the incident in a paragraph attached to the end of the work.

One day, Eadmer tells us, when the work was far advanced and he was copying his notes taken in wax onto the parchment sheets, 'Father Anselm himself called me to him privately and asked what I was drafting and copying.' At this moment we realise that Eadmer's great writing project has been undertaken below Anselm's radar, that until now he had been unaware that Eadmer was writing about him. When asked, Eadmer preferred to remain silent rather than answer falsely: 'when I had shown my desire to conceal the subject by silence rather than disclose it…' Obviously Eadmer does not want to declare what he is doing, probably because he feels Anselm might disapprove. At this moment Eadmer's life's work hangs in the balance, all his labour, all his love, all his writerly integrity is on the line. What will Anselm say? Anselm then gave him a choice; 'either to desist from what I had done and begin to turn my mind to other things, or to show him what I was writing.' This seemed hopeful. In the past Eadmer had shown Anselm other things he had written, and Anselm had been helpful with corrections and advice. Perhaps he would be again. So Eadmer "willingly obeyed, hoping that out of his natural kindness of heart he would correct whatever needed to be corrected and rearrange in its proper order anything which had taken place otherwise than I had described." In other words, Eadmer was hoping for some revision and editorial input from Anselm. At first, the prospect seems promising: "Nor were my hopes deceived in this belief for he did, in fact, correct some things and suppress others, change the order of things and approve others…" Eadmer at this point is bursting with pride "my heart was not a little rejoiced' he says, downplaying a moment of high delirious relief and exaltation. Anselm has conferred his blessing on the work, it can proceed, Eadmer has not written in vain.

For a few days Eadmer trod on air, in a state of blessed cheer, feeling he had received the highest accolade from the best of judges, for no-one in his view was so consummate a writer as Anselm. His life's work had been vindicated by the highest authority. He felt more proud and more justified in his pride than any monk should ever be. But then, just as he was bounding on clouds of joy with his head clipping the stars, his whole universe came crashing down.

***

Eadmer tells us how it happened, how the world changed for him.

"But a few days after the work had been corrected," he writes, "the archbishop called me to see him." One can only imagine what Eadmer was feeling as he answered this summons. What does Anselm want? Is it good news or bad? Is Anselm going to congratulate me on my inspired work and the quality of my prose?

What happened next was a devastation so profound that he never really recovered from it.

Imagine Anselm sitting in his private office, the parchment sheets before him. On five quires of parchment, finely written, was Eadmer's work; the representative labour of the last eight or nine years, the work by which he measured his worth, the work which was his life. Imagine Anselm turning towards Eadmer as he comes in and saying very cordially and without the least intention to hurt: "I am far too unworthy of such a tribute, Eadmer, my brother. Future ages will not place the least value on a literary monument to me.

You must destroy this work, destroy the quires of paper which you have shown me and devote yourself to worthier objects. My life will be of interest to no-one."

In the *Vita Anselmi*, the pain of the next few lines is understated as Eadmer tries to master himself.

"This was certainly a severe blow to me," he says. "I dared not entirely disobey his command, and yet I was not willing to lose altogether a work which I had put together with much labour." This barely registers on the scale of his personal devastation. As if to evade the memory, Eadmer withholds from telling us what happened next or what else was said at this time. It is likely that he withdrew at the soonest possible moment, taking his quires of parchment with him. It is also likely that he sought out some person who could comfort him, someone who could give him advice, reassurance, someone who might think of an answer to the impossible dilemma in which he had been placed. It was a dilemma in the true sense. Anselm had presented him with a position where each of two alternative courses is eminently undesirable. Either he must destroy the work or else he must disobey a superior. It was an impossible choice. As a Benedictine monk, in a religious order which placed great emphasis on obedience to the Rule, to disobey, or even contest, a command from a superior was a great sin, a demonstration of self-will and pride, not to be tolerated. Equally, to destroy his manuscripts, to destroy the quires of parchment on which he had lavished labour and care for so long, was unthinkable.

Confronted with this soul-destroying directive, Eadmer is now in a state of shock, his heart races, his hands grow clammy as he clutches the parchments to his chest like something beloved that he will never let go. Imagining this scene, conjuring it up in the imagination, even so many centuries after the event, is to experience immense sympathy for this disconsolate monk who aspired to nothing more than to record the life of his spiritual father. In the last few moments his world had fallen apart, ripping away his spiritual certainties and the secure faith he had in the Benedictine life. For now, as he gazes inward, he knows that he wants to disobey his superior. Not only that. Although outwardly struck dumb, he is raging with inner fury. To be spurned, to have his life's work set at nought, to be ordered to destroy what he had created over eight long years of labour by the very man who had inspired it, was to be cut to the soul.

At such a moment would it not be likely that he would take his trouble to Baldwin? Baldwin knew Anselm, knew his moods and his quirks, knew how to handle him; Baldwin was politic and sharp-witted. Surely Baldwin could advise him what to do.

Although Eadmer does not state this was the case, it seems at least possible that it happened; that Eadmer sought him out and told him about the terrible dilemma into which he had so innocently fallen. The scene might have played out something like this:

BALDWIN: Destroy it? Are you saying he told you to destroy it?

EADMER: Yes, and I can't do it! God help me, I can't do it! At the risk of disobedience to a superior, I can't do it! Yet, if I don't, I can't continue in obedience to him! What should I do, Baldwin? What should I do?'

Seeing Eadmer's excruciated state of mind and having some sympathy for his unhappy situation, as well as a vested interest in the work, Baldwin might have given the matter some thought. Perhaps he went out and walked up and down the cloister for a while, thinking of an angle, some way of saving both the work and Eadmer's career as a monk. Surely, after a proper amount of reflection, he would have come back with a solution.

BALDWIN: There is a way to resolve this. Just as Our Lord made the distinction between flesh and spirit, where one was strong and one was weak, we can make the distinction between letter and spirit.

EADMER: What do you mean?

BALDWIN: Well, obey the master in the letter of the command, but not its spirit.

EADMER: How might I do that?

BALDWIN: What you have to do is destroy the quires of parchment you showed him. That fulfils his command to the letter. But, before you do so, copy out the work onto other quires, thus you retain the spirit of the work in another form. Since Anselm has not forbidden the copying of the work you are not committing the sin of disobedience.

This exact conversation may not have occurred, but something very like it is recorded by Eadmer, and this is the course of action that he took.

In the days that followed, working at every moment he could spare, he began the huge task of copying out all that he had written. Many years later, just in case anything of this tale should be lost to posterity, he included in the work itself an explanation of what had happened. "Perhaps my action was not free from the sin of disobedience," he wrote, "for I carried out his order otherwise than he intended."

By suppressing any mention of Baldwin or anyone else in the affair, Eadmer presents the story as a dramatic conflict between personal will and the obligation of obedience, a pure parable of the struggling soul. But that, surely, was not how it felt. Nothing so metaphysical or instructive. From that moment Eadmer's life changed. He felt bruised. He lost confidence in his work, in his life's purpose. Although no reproaches came from Anselm who still marked him with favours, nothing was ever quite the same. It seemed like a kind of fall, a crash to earth, a casting-out from his own private Eden. It took many years for Eadmer to recover from the shock of this incident which, as far as can be deduced, happened sometime in 1100, the very year in which Anselm was recalled from exile, the year William Rufus was killed, and his brother Henry ascended the throne. For seven years Eadmer had lived closely in Anselm's small intimate household, one of the privileged who had daily dealings with the archbishop. Many times, in those years, Eadmer had been outraged on Anselm's behalf when he was being unjustly treated, never more so than at the time of William Warelwast's bag-searching at Dover. Now he was outraged on his own behalf, by the very man to whom he was devoted.

The shock and trauma found their way into Eadmer's writing and, from this point on, there is a marked change in the quality of the work. There is a notable drying up of dialogue, as if Eadmer had ceased taking notes from speech. The tone is downbeat, the form changes, the colour fades. What had given sinew and vigour to Eadmer's writing is muted.

It was only when Anselm was dead, and Bishop Ralph had succeeded him that Eadmer added the passage about disobedience quoted above. The last eight years of Anselm's life occupy only eight pages of the *Vita* whereas the previous eight years occupy thirty-two pages. Nor do we fully understand the dating and arrangement of the text which was worked on over a long period. We don't know if Eadmer ever wholly destroyed the original work or how much of it he copied out. But we can be fairly certain that it was not finished during Anselm's lifetime. After 1100 it seems that Eadmer is less prominent as a member of Anselm's entourage and his place is taken by another monk, Alexander, who becomes the recorder and copyist. Eadmer is no longer in a position to keep a record of talk and events as he had done for so many years. Certainly, Eadmer makes no mention of any further conversation on this matter. It would have been left to him to reflect on St Benedict's Twelve Steps of Humility which defined the religious life of introspection and prayer for those committed to the Benedictine Rule. The third step, as Eadmer would have known, was simply: "Obey your superior."

Some scholars have claimed that, in this situation, Anselm had been severe without being effective, that he had spoilt the unselfish joy of Eadmer's work and seriously injured his life. And certainly, at this moment his confidence is undermined. He stopped writing, not only the *Vita Anselmi* but also his history, the *Historia Novorum*, giving up the pleasure of a work that had been the most creative part of his life for the past seven years. He made notes, but they were terse and lacking in detail. The *Life* and *History* would lie for a further nine years without a word being added. For twenty years he would carry the unspoken pain of this disturbing episode before finding release in confession to Archbishop Ralph, Anselm's successor, who would forgive his disobedience and encourage him to complete both works.

Reading Eadmer's *Vita Anselmi* and his *Historia Novorum in Anglia* which are among his finest writings, is to have a unique glimpse into his world. The beauty of writing in Latin is that a translation must be done anew for just about every generation so that, instead of sounding dated or impenetrable like Old English writings or even the writings of Chaucer and his contemporaries, Eadmer always sounds accessible. Even though describing an old world, old problems and old ways of thinking, he still speaks to us in ways that access an unchanging humanity. The dilemma he faced, though cast in terms we would not often now encounter, was a very recognisable one. On the one side was his integrity as moral being and a writer. He valued himself and his subject matter, he had a moral red line: he would not present as true anything about which he had doubts. These were his writerly virtues, on which he placed a high importance. On the other side was his integrity as a monk, a monk belonging to an order which placed the highest value on obedience. This was his dilemma. The impossible choice. It split him along the faultline of his being where the staples of his spirit: faith, duty, truth, the worldly and unworldly, the integral parts of himself, met. The pain of this dilemma went deep, perhaps today we might even call it a trauma. Like a trauma it is hidden, suppressed, Eadmer makes oblique references, but no reproaches, his work changes under pressure of the shock and its aftermath. Though it seems that he never blamed Anselm, never lost his admiration for him, yet still Eadmer was placed in the invidious position of not being able to finish his work until the old man died. This too was part of the pain. It dwelt with Eadmer until the end of his life. He never wrote again in his early vigorous prose style. He never recovered the peak of his form in the depiction of dramatic scenes whose dialogue captured the pulse and pathos of his world. Eadmer, as a writer, was defeated by a dilemma in the truest sense: a position where each of two alternative courses is equally undesirable.

Chapter Six
Ranulf Flambard: Escape from the Tower

Ranulf Flambard spent the last twenty years of his life trying to live down the previous forty. He did this so successfully that his long, flamboyant and controversial career has never entered the popular imagination in the way that similar powerful careers have done. Yet he steered two kings through turbulent reigns, he was an adviser to earls and princes, hobnobbed with bishops and archbishops, knew everything there was to know about the exchequer and taxation. He understood his epoch and knew his own worth so well that he rose fast through a series of promotions to a position of power and great riches. Hardly any part of his life is without excitement, it reads like an adventure tale, filled with incident and danger, controversy and scandal. Favoured by some of the most powerful people of his time, he was equally hated by many. Churchmen and prelates were among his bitterest enemies and the chronicling monks wrote scathing denunciations of him. Yet the success to which he had aspired all his life came in 1099 when he was made Bishop of Durham by his patron, King William Rufus. Like Thomas Cromwell, the financial minister of Henry VIII, Ranulf Flambard was called by many contemporaries 'second after the king' and like Thomas Cromwell he was a man of humble birth who succeeded on a spectacular career path by talent and graft alone. Unlike the latter, however, Flambard did not suffer the fate of execution. But there was a moment when his career tumbled dramatically and went into reverse.

Ranulf Flambard is a difficult character to reconstruct because he had the misfortune to upset the chroniclers at the time they were writing. He annoyed the church. He was antagonistic. He supported the king in his anti-papal, anti-church policies which, naturally, contemporary chroniclers were not disposed to treat favourably. Yet, reading between the lines of the chronicles and supplementing research with other documents, writs, charters, and so on, a fairly detailed life can be reconstructed and from this it is easy to see that Ranulf Flambard was one of the key non-royal players in the politics of his time. This is surprising when you remember just how lowly his birth had been.

His father, Thurstin, had been a poor village priest in the diocese of Bayeux where he had known Bishop Odo, the half-brother of Duke William of Normandy. Through Odo's patronage, Ranulf had acquired a Latin education and had entered Duke William's household in Caen as a clerk and chaplain. By hard work, energy, clever networking and an intuition for what the duke wanted, he had progressed steadily in favour and advancement. In 1086 he was appointed as keeper of the royal seal under William's new Chancellor, Maurice, who afterwards became Bishop of London. By the age of twenty-six Flambard was already moving in the highest circles.

When William Rufus succeeded his father as king in 1087, Flambard had already come to notice as a young man who could fix things by exploiting the royal rights and maximising revenue. He was generally reckoned to be physically good looking, tall, strong-jawed, energetic, able to mix with all types and degrees of men. Never wholly accepted into the highest circles because of his humble origins, he had friends and supporters in every rank and the gift of not making serious enemies. The name 'Flambard' has the ring of a description more than a patronymic. We don't know when he acquired it. 'Flamme' suggests fire, or torch, Flambard 'one who burns brightly' or perhaps 'one in the vanguard of fashion.' It can indicate a personality, a heated temperament, perhaps, or someone with red hair, or a firebrand with a reputation of burning out the opposition. Perhaps it was simply a name for someone who loved colourful clothing. However, he came by it, it was a name that stuck and a name that, in his own epoch, was widely reviled.

Ranulf Flambard was the exact contemporary of King William II, born in the same year of 1060. One of King William's underrated strengths was his ability to recognise talent and employ it to the best advantage, whatever its origin. So when he came to the throne in 1087 he spotted Flambard's talent and retained him in royal service. Having worked his way up to a trusted position in the Conqueror's household, Flambard now became one of King William Rufus's most talented and astute ministers.

Such things don't happen by chance. It was typical of him and men of his sort to force their fortunes at necessary points: chancers playing for high stakes, never forgetting the drag of their humble origins, the low birth and lack of blood links. Yet, in spite of indications to the contrary, Ranulf Flambard believed he was living in progressive times. Times when a nobody son of a minor cleric could ascend to the ranks of national fixers with a finger in every plot and a plant in every faction. Personal good looks, a ready laugh, a quick mind and a strong stomach for dark and ugly deeds could propel the right man upward in a steady progression. As long as every upward step was measured with care, the ramifications of every action carefully judged and secret ambitions hidden under bowings and scrapings, steady progress could be made. If you slipped, you could expect help only from those you had helped in the past. That was why, though you went along taking fortune's pawns, you always made sure to guard against the moves of bishops and knights.

One of Flambard's monkish chroniclers, Orderic Vitalis, devotes a great deal of space trying to explain his rise from poor and obscure stock, alleging that he was educated from boyhood with the low born hangers-on of the ducal court at Caen. Orderic implies that Flambard was well instructed in cunning and deception and had a grasp of the specious manipulation of words rather than of polished rhetoric. This smacks a little of denigration or educational snobbery. What it might boil down to is that Flambard had the native wit and energy to thrive in the world in which he found himself. In today's terms, he was gifted, talented and upwardly mobile.

Flambard served as a minister and chief adviser to William Rufus for thirteen eventful years and never fell from favour. By 1088 he was the custodian of vacant church lands, in 1089 he was given custody of the lands of Canterbury itself and kept them until Anselm was appointed archbishop in 1093. He attested royal instruments in 1091 (and frequently thereafter) he acted as a judge and appears to have been head of both the lay and clerical sides of the royal household. Yet, in spite of being called many things, he never had an official or documented title. On at least three occasions he was appointed one of the co-regents during William's absences in Normandy. In other words, William piled work onto him which he carried out effectively and was correspondingly well-rewarded. So why did he need, as this chapter heading suggests, to escape from the tower? Who put him there, and why? Medieval politics were harsh and unforgiving. Without high-powered, influential friends, life was cheap. Did he remain free or was he subsequently captured and punished? To answer all these questions is to discover a story of extraordinary daring along with the inventiveness of an agile mind, sheer luck and a dash of political bravado.

The story of Ranulf Flambard divides into two quite neat chapters. Chapter One: thirteen years as a minister of William Rufus culminating in the high office of Bishop of Durham in 1099. Chapter Two: having accepted the Bishopric of Durham, some say for the reasonable sum of one thousand pounds, and having thus achieved his greatest ambition, Flambard might have felt settled for life. But before Flambard could take up this prestigious office, the king died. King William Rufus was shot and killed by an arrow whilst hunting in the New Forest near his lodge at Brockenhurst on August 2nd, 1100. This was a serious blow to the nation as well as a disaster for Flambard, for the new king, Henry I, had no love for him at all. There now follow six years in which Flambard's ingenuity and sheer nerve along with his considerable powers of resilience are tested to the limits. But to understand the interplay of these chapters of his life, the continuities and contrasts as well as the underlying 'character' or as we would say now 'psychology' of the man, let alone to try to grasp the complexities of his political and spiritual lives, we need to start with a very significant moment in the reign of William II. A moment when everything might have changed, not only for Flambard but for the kingdom.

***

In March and April 1093 King William fell seriously ill. He had been taken sick at Alveston, near Bristol, early in March but had fought off his fever to travel to Gloucester and his Palace of Kingsholm. There he took to his bed and became weaker and sicker until his assembled courtiers began to despair of his life. Believing himself at the point of death, William began to think about his soul's salvation, which was uncharacteristic of him and a cause of alarm to Flambard who realised just how ill he must be. Among the many sins William had to expiate and Flambard had facilitated was one that priests and monks counted among the worst, simony, the selling of spiritual offices. As well as simony, which many viewed as a form of corruption, was the practice of failing to appoint bishops and archbishops when a vacancy arose so that the wealth accruing from them should flow to the king's coffers. This was extremely profitable, and, as far as William was concerned, had the added benefit of weakening the organisation of the church. For that reason, aided by Flambard, he had kept the most important post, the supreme office in the English church, unfilled for nearly four years. There was no Archbishop of Canterbury. This meant that there was no effective church leadership and no organisation of councils. The lack of a primate meant there was no spokesman to confer with Rome, no head of the church capable of solving ecclesiastical disputes, no leading voice to speak to the king. Flambard had been administering the lands, raising rents, creating lucrative fiefdoms, and generally depleting Canterbury's resources, to the scandal of the clergy and the outrage of Rome for the last three years. But now it looked like God had taken matters into his divine hands. By striking down the king, by making him think about his soul, by putting him in need of the prayers of monks and priests, God himself was now forcing William to heal the ills of the church and appoint an Archbishop. Only then could he be saved.

Naturally William was in no condition to resist. When the foremost nobles of his court and all the clergy combined to beg, insist, persuade and urge him to make the appointment, he could hardly refuse. A candidate was produced immediately. From Flambard's point of view, the worst possible candidate. Abbot Anselm of Bec. This famous monk was renowned throughout Normandy and beyond for his saintly life, his care for the monks and priests of his order, a leader of the Benedictines, a great theologian whose writings were widely recognised as important contributions to church scholarship. A second, quite different, reputation fixed him as a cantankerous and stubborn prelate who would stand up to kings, challenge authority and generally be a nuisance to ministers like Flambard who were serving their masters by fleecing the church. Matters were made even more complicated and sensitive by the fact that Anselm did not actually want the post or pretended that he didn't by loudly claiming that he was a humble monk who wanted to stay at Bec and had no ambitions beyond the simple life of the monastery.

So, after 1093 and the appointment of Anselm, Flambard's life became more difficult. Nevertheless, as a diplomat he had to negotiate the transference of the episcopal tenantries, monies and estates from the king to the archbishop and he had to keep the relationship between Anselm and

King William from breaking down completely. There was one particularly delicate moment early on in this fraught relationship. Feeling confident that Anselm was rightly grateful for his appointment, William asked the going rate for it which was one thousand pounds. Shocked and outraged by the grossly insulting assumption that he would connive at the sin of simony, Anselm broke off relations and left court. This incident revealed just how far William was from understanding Anselm's character and how difficult it was going to be for Flambard to keep them working in harness. Right from the start, the characters of these two men were in conflict. Anselm was a dedicated Benedictine monk, a spiritual, serious-minded cleric. He was unworldly, relying on his household, in particular his chief of staff, Baldwin of Tornai, for all political and administrative matters. In Flambard's view, Anselm's whole approach to the archbishopric had been provocative. He claimed he did not want it, that he hated administration, that he was a poor monk who only wanted to write theology and follow the Rule. Moreover, he kept dashing about from place to place, making it difficult to conduct business and impossible to hold him down to a date for consecration. Until that ceremony took place his acceptance was far from certain. Eventually, after many fraught and touchy exchanges, Anselm came to Canterbury in December 1093 and was consecrated. It had taken nearly nine months to get him into office. The pattern for the next four years had been set.

  Since it takes two to be contentious, William II must not go without blame. Even as a young man he had often deliberately shocked the clergy with his lack of respect for the church. His sense of humour ranged from flippant to provocative. Once, when he was being reproached by an old priest for some lapse in respect for the church, he quipped that it didn't matter as he was thinking of converting to Judaism anyway. This was typical. He made jokes about the most sensitive issues in the most inappropriate way. His favourite oath was 'Holy Face of Lucca!' which summed up his brazen manner. The Holy Face of Lucca was one of the most sacred objects in Christendom. It was a relic kept in the Church of St Martin in Lucca and visited by pilgrims from all over Europe. It was held to be an image of the face of the living Christ, carved by an angel. The sanctity of this object can hardly be overstated, yet William often used it as an oath or expletive, calculated to shock. His taste for provocative jests often caused embarrassing moments which Flambard did his best to cover up. Perhaps William was given a taste for cruel mockery by his father who had subjected all his sons to it. Wherever it came from, William's humour was a source of frequent embarrassment at court, but it also meant that his company was often lively and entertaining. Flambard could often negotiate his way out of a troublesome situation with a matching or distracting jest.

Humour was one of the many tactics Flambard used in order to maintain relations between Anselm and the king during their troubled relationship. Another was delay. Anselm was congenitally given to the practice of delay and at strategic moments Flambard encouraged it, hoping to keep them apart. Anselm would rather give his mind to his next theological work than actually get down to business. When he did turn his mind to it he usually suggested something inappropriate which would set the king in a rage. Once he suggested instituting church councils, claiming that reform was desperately needed in all areas of the church and at court.

The king took this as personal criticism of the way he ran his court and thundered that he would no more permit church councils in his realm than become a monk.

In criticising the morals of the court, Anselm was not alone. There were grounds for believing that the king encouraged lax and immoral behaviour. He tended to encourage young courtiers in their unseemly preoccupation with fashions and hairstyles; young men traipsed about court in brightly coloured clothes and grew their hair long like girls. Anselm frequently denounced such effeminacy. Flambard began to wonder whether Anselm was right. Surely reform was needed, the court was in dire need of a virtuous female presence at its centre, and he began to ponder why the king had never married. William was now in his mid-thirties, his rule was secure, even though the Scottish King Malcolm was always ready to make trouble at the borders. By keeping papal legates out of England, he was more or less free from interference from Rome. With his kingdom so settled, why did the king not marry?

Whether it was Flambard who focused the king's mind on marriage, or some other, or even William himself feeling rejuvenated after his close brush with death, in the summer of 1093 he set out to view a prospective bride. The chosen lady would make an eminently suitable wife, being both the daughter of the King of Scotland and a descendant from the old line of English kings. She was innocent and malleable. On the other hand, she was highly educated, clever, perhaps cleverer than William himself, and capable of far more tact. She was young, only thirteen, but that was not unusual in a royal bride. Two obstacles loomed against these advantages. One, she was being educated at Wilton, a nunnery near Salisbury, renowned for the education of royal and noble girls, famed throughout Europe. Two, she was under the domination of her aunt Christina who was a nun of Wilton and an inveterate hater of William. Moreover, this aunt had sworn that the girl would become a nun and not marry a profligate like William. As usual in these cases, the girl herself, the clever, astute, ambitious Edith was not consulted.

As it happened, the romantic meeting rapidly became a farce. William was not an enthusiastic suitor and Christina was determined to thwart his plan. When William got to Wilton he was not allowed to meet Edith alone, nor even to speak to her, he was merely allowed to glimpse her from behind some rose bushes as she crossed the cloister hand in hand with her fierce aunt and wearing a habit and veil. That was enough for William. He bolted from the scene and never came back. Nor did he ever marry. This incident showed Flambard that he could not win every trick and he never tried to marry off his master again.

Flambard's greatest difficulty in the next few years revolved around the king's relations with Anselm. He managed to stall a complete breakdown in relations by producing a succession of compromises and truces until November 1097. That was when, to the great relief of the many, Anselm went into exile. It had taken four years for the inevitable breakdown to occur, but Flambard must have known it was coming. Perhaps he took stock at this moment, a chance to evaluate the gains and losses of the last four years. On a personal level, Flambard's greatest success lay in increasing the king's wealth by exploiting 'vacancies.' He was also responsible for a highly ingenious administrative experiment.

Before he left to campaign in Normandy in March 1094, King William ordered Ranulf Flambard to do something that had not been done since King Harold's time. This was to summon the old English *fyrd* as a way of supplying foot soldiers for William's wars against his brother in Normandy. Englishmen, completely ignorant of the issues or causes of war were to be sent to fight with a Norman king against Normans in Normandy. This was a time when power politics cut through everything, loyalties, blood ties, national identities, and held the lives of common people cheaply. That's what made Flambard's experiment so innovative for it actually took it into calculation the way ordinary men, farmers and thegns, English peasants with local interests, actually thought and felt.

To understand Flambard's ingenuity it is necessary to know that assembling the *fyrd* was a way of raising an effective militia from the countryside. It had worked spectacularly well for King Alfred when he had to keep an army in the field against fast-moving Viking marauders, and it worked because of the way it was financed. In professional armies where men undertake a stipulated period of service for which they are paid in properly graded salaries according to their rank, when the supply lines are professionally administered so that food and weapons are never in short supply, and when the organisation is supervised by paymasters and all is under financial control from the centre, as for example, in the Roman Army, then the link between a man and his individual upkeep is relatively unimportant. But the great armies of the Roman world no longer existed in Europe and, even though one might learn a little bit about tactics and strategy from Vegetius's Roman Handbook, the military world about which he was writing had long departed. In the savage and violent times of the Danes and Vikings, when England's Roman order had been ripped apart, the *fyrd* had supplied a much-needed way of raising fighting men and sustaining them through campaigns without wrecking the agriculture of the land they were fighting to defend.

In King Alfred's day, every burgh, or settlement, sent a certain number of men to fight but held back an equal number of men to maintain the labour of the fields and police their own villages. This meant that communities would not be denuded of active men at times of harvest or in the face of bandits and thieves. A certain number of men of each social rank would remain in the villages to feed and defend the remaining population. Those men who went away to train and fight would do so in the knowledge that their homes and fields were protected. Thus, by reducing the number of individuals raised in any particular locality, one increased their effectiveness. This was exactly the kind of practical strategic planning that appealed to Ranulf Flambard.

A second ingenuity of the *fyrd* was to connect each man to a resource of keep and pay for the time of his service. Ranulf liked this clear-eyed approach as he believed it would be useless to appeal to English labourers to fight on the basis of abstract values, such as loyalty or duty. A man needed means for himself and his family, he needed sustenance and pay. So, under the *fyrd*, each man was attached to five hides of land. This land would support him, pay him and sustain his family while he was away. Each hide would pay 4 shillings, thus a man supported by five hides would be provided with a total of 20 shillings, half for keep and half for pay. This was the model for the system Ranulf applied in 1094 in order to raise troops without costing the king a penny from the royal coffers.

There was, of course, one major drawback. Men raised in this way were not professional soldiers. However well fed and well paid they were, they were not trained to the same degree as the knights and vavasors of the feudal system, whose main purpose in life was to participate in war. But Ranulf devised a plan of audacious ingenuity, a way of using an ancient system for the introduction of a novel scheme, turning it into a shrewd money-making enterprise. When the men had been mustered at Hastings, perhaps as many as 10,000 of them, each with his 10 shillings for pay and 10 shillings for keep, he offered them a deal. If they would care to deposit 10 of their 20 shillings into his keeping, they could go home with the other 10 shillings; walk away, return home and not have to fight for some unknown cause in a foreign field for a king they had never seen. Nearly every man eagerly deposited his money and skipped home rejoicing. Never was a tax raised with so much jubilation. Once the money was despatched, William had the cash to buy trained knights or suborn local Norman barons to his cause. Ready money would be more advantageous than a rag-tag army of field hands who had no training or skill in weaponry. This, more or less, was achieved. The Englishmen went home. The king had knights. And Flambard, keeping some ready cash for himself, was marginally richer. It was one of the most satisfying enterprises he had ever undertaken.

***

Daring enterprises gave Flambard the reputation of a fixer. Whatever the king wanted, Flambard could fix it for him. Until it came to Anselm. Although he established a rapprochement with Anselm's chief adviser, Baldwin, and although they developed a mutual workaday respect, Anselm remained the perpetual difficulty of Flambard's life and William's reign. William offended Anselm by continuing to keep churches vacant. When Bishop William of Durham died early in January 1096, his episcopal estates were taken into royal custody and Flambard was given the job of administering them. Durham was one of the most prestigious seats in the English church, a semi-independent fiefdom offering the greatest freedom to its incumbent to preside over a court of law, mint coinage and play an important role in the politics of the border country. The estates were vast and immensely wealthy. It was Flambard's job to ensure that most of the wealth ended in the royal coffers. It was also said that, at this time, Flambard started to amass colossal personal wealth which he kept in a chest that went everywhere with him. During these years Flambard was a powerful force in the land, some said 'second after the king' which naturally infuriated the aristocratic classes who scorned his low birth and made him as many enemies as friends.

Flambard suspected that Henry, King William's younger brother, known as the Comte de Contentin, deplored his dominance at court. Henry was not only ambitious but resented being outdone by some no-account, base-born interloper. But Henry was a latecomer who had miscalculated during most of William's reign, often choosing to support Robert Curthose when both brothers were in dispute. Over the years Curthose had earned a reputation for unreliability.

There then occurred the strangest circumstance that had ever arisen in the relations between England and Normandy, between William and Robert, which would have the result of aligning Henry firmly on the side of William.

Robert Curthose decided to go on a Holy War. He had been caught up in the fervour following Pope Urban's preaching at Clermont in late November 1095 when he called on the nobles and princes of Europe to lay aside their differences and make war on the heathen. The object was to raise an army which would fight to defend the Holy Land in the name of Christendom. It was as if a torrent had been unleashed, men in their droves, high born and low, rushed to volunteer for a task of danger, unrelenting hardship and possible death. What made them eager, what raised their eyes to heaven was that the pope promised that if they took part they would be cleansed of all their sins and assured of their place in heaven. Pope Urban's words offered them a way to gain everlasting life. "If any man set out from pure devotion, not for reputation or monetary gain, to liberate the Church of God at Jerusalem, his journey shall be reckoned in place of all penance." This promise of immortal life unleashed an extraordinary pandemic of enthusiasm, infecting all ranks and sorts of men.

To the astonishment of William and Henry, their brother Robert, Duke of Normandy, was prepared to answer the call and become a warrior of Christ. In order to make it possible an extraordinary deal was done. Treating Normandy like a private estate, Robert mortgaged it. William would pledge his brother 10,000 marks of silver to cover his expenses in exchange for temporary control over Normandy. After three years, or perhaps five years, since the sources disagree, Robert would return, claim the duchy and pay back the 10,000 silver marks. This improbable deal was negotiated by Abbot Jarento of St-Bénigne in Dijon, trusted by both Robert and William, a reforming abbot of great repute and known as a safe pair of hands. Eventually a contract was drawn up and the date of September 1096 advanced for the handing over of the money at a ceremony in Rouen, at which time Robert would set out for the Holy Land.

And the person charged with raising a large part of the 10,000 silver marks, a sum which represented a quarter of William's annual revenue, was Ranulf Flambard. Also charged with some responsibility in these arrangements was Henry, who now emerged as a supporter of his brother, having seen the possibility of advancement in the administration of the duchy. So for a time Flambard and Henry found themselves having to work to the same ends and were sometimes thrown together in unavoidable meetings. Intuitively, they were antagonistic. Neither one had specific grounds of hostility, they simply shared a deep distrust. Henry curried favour with the church and positioned himself with Anselm when it did not damage his support of William. Henry was good at getting between the king and Flambard, loosening Flambard's grip, spreading lies and rumours, generally doing down the upstart minister. Flambard was sure his position would become precarious in a court where Henry was in the ascendant. On the other hand, William, though not sentimental and not congenitally loyal to his ministers, had come to trust Flambard and to rely on his inexhaustible genius.

In September 1096 at Rouen, the property deal went ahead, Normandy was leased to William for an unspecified duration, and the 10,000 silver marks handed over. William had taken control of Normandy without a fight. Nearly ten years after his father's death, William could claim to have reunited the two realms of England and Normandy into one unified administration under one ruler. It was unlikely that he would ever willingly give it up.

***

In 1099 the still triumphant King William rewarded Flambard by appointing him as Bishop of Durham. But the reward for his years of service was tainted. Flambard's enjoyment was spoiled by the conviction that the king was giving him this prize in order to get him away from court, leaving the path clear for Henry. Instead, therefore, of rushing off to Durham to enjoy his long-awaited prize, Flambard remained around the king, becoming more and more concerned about Henry's intentions. There was no definite proof of anything, no hint of a plot, no information from the spies he had planted. Henry was growing daily in favour, playing the admiring younger brother. With studied care he followed William's interests and always made sure he joined the hunting parties. William was a fanatic of the hunt and if anybody was to win his favour, he must prove himself in the hunting field. So Henry began to spend the August stag season at Brockenhurst, the king's favourite hunting lodge in the New Forest, getting acquainted with the routine of the household and the officers of the hunt.

All this time Flambard was in two minds. Should he go to Durham, take up his post as Bishop and begin to enjoy the rewards he felt he so richly deserved, or should he hang about, trying to keep a protective eye on William in case there was any plot being hatched against him? For a year or more Flambard hesitated, constantly delaying his departure for Durham, unable to throw off a premonition of disaster. However, in June 1099, he took the precaution of formally taking up the post of bishop in a ceremony of consecration performed by the Archbishop of York at St Paul's in London. But he still did not travel to Durham. Instead, he continued to work closely with William and kept watch on Henry. He suspected everything but had proof of nothing. He was very vigilant in his own interests; to protect William was to protect himself. Then, in the summer of 1100 news came that Robert Curthose had miraculously survived the rigours of the Holy Land and was on his way home to Normandy with a pile of treasure from the Emperor of Constantinople with which he could easily buy back his duchy. This news failed to stir William who had no intention of handing back Normandy whether Robert returned or not, indeed had had no such intention since the deal was signed. But Henry was in a different position, likely to be trapped again between his two powerful and rivalrous brothers, unless he acted.

And so we come to August 2nd 1100 when an arrow was fired in Brockenhurst Forest, hitting King William in the neck, or some say the chest, and killing him almost instantly. When he heard the news, Flambard had the most powerful feeling of failed forevision. He had known it, seen it, tried to forestall it, and now it had happened. Flambard was surprised by the sudden emptiness he felt. He had been attached to William, not in a sentimental way but in his habits of life. He was accustomed to act and think according to the dictates of a particular personality; anticipate, advise, steer, cover-up.

He had lived daily to the pulse of another life. Suddenly all that was gone. At a stroke he had lost his place at court and though he had not a shred of proof that Henry was in any way connected with the death, he knew exactly what Henry would do next.

On Sunday 5th August, a mere three days after the 'accident' Henry was crowned King of England in Westminster. The coup was played so swiftly that there was almost no resistance. It was a breathtakingly rapid seizure of power. Almost as soon as Henry was crowned in Westminster Abbey, as soon as he had been proclaimed and presented to the burghers of London, as soon as he had granted amnesties and made pledges and promised promises in the mad wave of euphoria that grips the populace at such times, Henry turned to the more pleasurable task of settling scores. He issued a warrant for the arrest of Ranulf Flambard.

Flambard's successful career came to an end on August 15th, 1100. Thirteen ill-omened days since the death of the king. Thirteen years since he had first entered upon William's service, rising to become his chief man of affairs. On that day, the feast day of the Assumption of the Blessed Virgin, he was arrested and conveyed to the Tower.

***

The place we now know as the Tower of London was part of the keep designed by Gandulph, Bishop of Rochester, and begun during the reign of William the Conqueror. It was a statement of conquest and his legacy monument par excellence. But the Conqueror's palace was not, as yet a prison.

No prisoner of state had been kept there in confinement, there were no bars or chains on windows and doors. Although a fortress and arsenal, a command post and barracks, often echoing to the sound of boots and arms, it was also a centre of administration where scribes worked in embryonic archives and clerics presided over a finely decorated chapel. As a palace, it boasted well-appointed chambers, fit for lords and princes or visiting emissaries of high rank, with fireplaces and fine furnishings.

Flambard was received into the Tower by the Constable, William de Mandeville, a young man who had recently inherited his father's lands. It is possible that this inexperienced official was impressed by Flambard's fame, or he may have simply had orders to treat him civilly. Whatever the cause, Flambard was not thrown into a cell but installed in a chamber on the second floor. Spacious, with an arched window divided by a strong central mullion, an antechamber and an entrance lobby occupied by a pair of guards; this was to be his home for an unspecified time, it being by no means clear what Henry intended for him.

There was a long list of charges which Flambard characteristically denied. Bravado never deserted him. He shamelessly cultivated de Mandeville and immediately began to set up secret communication with the outside. On principle Flambard never gave in to despair. The most enormous self-belief underlay his personal precept: never concede to your own debasement. The truth was that he was gambling that Henry would prefer to use him as a living scapegoat for his brother's misdeeds rather than stain the virtue of his own accession with bloodshed. He knew Henry well enough to know that calculation and political advantage were more important to him than empty retaliation.

***

We now come to one of the most extraordinary and daring escapades in Flambard's life. Far from being a well-known story, part of the folklore of London, or of medieval England, the wider public has almost no knowledge of these events. Even though facts are few and some are unreliable, sufficient material can be gathered to suggest just how spectacular and daring this feat was. There are four key elements in this operatic tale: a wine cask that contained no wine, a complaisant or dim-witted Constable, foggy weather and the Feast of Candlemas. Some chroniclers added more features at various times, including the manifestation of a witch, said to be Flambard's mother who conjured supernatural forces at appropriate moments. Others claimed that he used his episcopal crozier rather like a magician's wand in an abracadabra of unlikely happenings. Such flourishes are redundant in a tale that needs no enhancement.

During the rest of that summer and on into the new year of 1101, Flambard was housed at the Tower in far from unbearable conditions. He had access to fresh air when walking on the walls and received supplies of candles and logs through the attentions of a compliant constable. Occasionally, visitors were entertained in his chamber with tolerable food and plenty of wine, paid for out of Henry's allowance of two shillings a day for upkeep. Far from suffering deprivation, Flambard ran a small household from his prison and often gave suppers to which he invited Mandeville and his guards. Even so, for a man as energetic and ingenious as the former minister, the days passed in suffocating monotony.

He never spoke of the new king, Henry, nor of the old king, William, never mentioned affairs of state, never revealed any plan, never spoke of Robert Curthose, or commented on any news from outside which he ensured was brought to him almost daily. Instead, his conversation lingered on his family, and he spoke often about his brother, Fulcher, his sons, Elias, William, Ralph and Thomas, about Aelfgifu, his mistress back in Huntingdon, and her genial husband, Alcuin. Steering clear of politics, so that nothing could be reported back to the king, he entertained his guests with stories of Huntingdon life, sometimes sprinkled with regrets that he had not spent more time with his family and how much he now longed to see them. Secretly, they were being summoned. Slowly, Flambard was planning his next moves.

Sometime during November 1100, Flambard was brought the news that Henry had married the girl whom William had rejected, young Edith, now calling herself Matilda, daughter of the late King of Scotland. This was a doubly astute move, involving peace with Scotland, at least for a time, and the recall of Anselm from exile to perform the marriage. In spite of everything, Flambard was impressed. Henry was setting about his reign with shrewd pragmatism, trying to make the ship of state secure before Robert Curthose roused himself to sink it. News of Duke Robert increased over the winter of 1100. He had returned to find a stolen duchy and a usurping brother on the throne of England. Would he now gather a force to invade, punish his brother and settle the score? Weeks went by, Henry grew more secure, Robert delayed, Flambard was more and more frustrated. Robert Curthose, as he knew from long experience, was only as good as his latest adviser. Being both thoughtful and pious, as well as indecisive, Robert was capable of acts of self-sabotage, undermining his own best interests by caution or disengagement.

As winter turned in the New Year of 1101, Flambard knew that the time had come, not only to decamp, but to re-ignite his career.

***

There are many versions of the story of Flambard's escape from the Tower, some completely unreliable, but a few features occur in sufficient concentration to make a plausible reconstruction. Firstly, an inefficient Constable, William de Mandeville. If not guilty of collaboration, he was surely guilty of gross incompetence. This was the view of King Henry who, immediately upon hearing the news, stripped de Mandeville of his office, confined him to his estates and inflicted a stinging fine. Young, impressed by Flambard's suavity, duped by his apparent inertia, Mandeville was most likely seduced into laxity and fraternisation. For example, did he know about, but blink at, the deliveries of wine? It is known that wine for Flambard's personal consumption came into the Tower. This is the second key element. At some time, early in the New Year of 1101 a wine cask was delivered to the Tower. It contained, not wine, but a rope. Thirdly, the date of the escape. This was crucial. In February when the Thames's icy tides washed widely into the banks and flooded the adjacent marshes, fogs were very frequent. Thick, murky, opaque fogs which covered the banks and rose over the walls right up to the second floor of the tower. This would be the perfect cover for an escape. February 2nd was also the day when the church celebrated the Holy Feast of Candelmas. It was common practice to hold a Vigil on the eve of the Feast on the evening of February 1st, preceded by the saying of Mass which Flambard may have conducted. Although his status as Bishop of Durham was technically doubtful, Flambard had been consecrated and still laid claim to the office. As was customary, there may have been a dinner after the mass for the participating clergy and the tower tenants. In that case, Flambard would have encouraged the workforce of the tower: servants, officials and guards, to drink copiously of the wine he supplied. Then, sometime that evening, perhaps towards midnight when de Mandeville and his guards were bleary-eyed and reeling, Flambard slipped away to his chamber and changed his clothes. With help from co-conspirators, most likely including a Thames riverman, the rope was retrieved from the wine cask. Having been tied around the central mullion with a strong maritime knot, the rope became the escape route into the foggy London night. One by one the escapees pulled themselves up, leaned out into the fog and, holding fast to the rope, slipped over the sill.

Who his associates were in this escape is not known but it is almost certain that others were involved. The exact route that was taken from the Tower is not known; some stories say that horses were waiting to carry Flambard to an unknown port where a ship was waiting to take him to Le Tréport in the Pays de Caux. Whatever the precise route, there is no doubt that when Flambard jumped from the Tower window that night he was aiming to land in Normandy, in the court of Duke Robert, from where he would launch his spectacular come-back.

***

Apart from his punishment of de Mandeville, we have no detailed report on Henry's reaction to the escape. Taken by surprise, angry and frustrated, he must have known even in the first moments of hearing the news that Flambard's destination would be Normandy. Flambard would make straight to his brother's court and offer his services. Henry must have been aware that he had just let fall into the hands of Robert Curthose the only man who could mastermind an invasion of England.

In the months following his escape, Ranulf Flambard was frenetically active. He reached Normandy and found his way to the court of Robert Curthose, then possibly in Caen. Details about Flambard's movements are lacking but from subsequent events we know that he was soon in a position to advise and direct the older man's war efforts. They knew each other from years back, when Flambard had been employed as a trusted aide by Robert's father, the Conqueror. If anyone could concentrate the duke's mind on organisation and planning, it was Flambard. So we must conclude that Robert Curthose welcomed him, took him into his confidence, backed his plans and gave asylum to any associates or family who might have accompanied him in the ship from England. Financed by a subsidy from Curthose, Flambard set about the task of restoring his own fortunes by restoring the fortunes of Duke Robert.

Without question Ranulf Flambard was now the most important unofficial political player in the two realms. Lacking any formal power, with serious charges against him, holding no office and without organised backing, he had seized the Anglo-Norman stage. His name alone blazoned forth energy, panache, flamboyance, while his legendary skill in organising successful enterprises raised the tension to fever-pitch. England and Normandy were poised, once again, for confrontation.

In preparation for this event, Henry did something that Flambard had done years before when William needed troops to fight in Normandy. He called out the *fyrd*. But whereas Flambard had exploited the levy as a way of raising money, Henry really needed men to fight against invasion. He needed Englishmen to augment his Norman forces against the invasion fleet which, he felt sure, would soon be on its way. Now was the time to present himself as the most English of the sons of the Conqueror. Henry had been born in England and had married a wife of English lineage. He had picked up enough English from the monks at Salisbury and Abingdon, where he had spent time as a youth, to make himself understood and so was able to address the levied men and appeal to their native affections. English foot soldiers were one thing; however, English sailors were quite another.

By June, Ranulf Flambard had been on the loose for four months and had thoroughly roused Robert Curthose from his political slumbers. Suddenly, with uncharacteristic dash and focused energy he was preparing a fleet, sequestering and victualling ships, assembling the forces for an invasion. In response to the threat, in sheer frustration, Henry struck out at the instigator of all this, Ranulf Flambard. With Anselm's backing, he formally deposed him as Bishop of Durham and seized the lands of his bishopric. All the charges against him were confirmed: malfeasance, extortion, misappropriation of church funds and other grim offences. But none of this second-hand revenge satisfied Henry. By raising the *fyrd* and securing the ports he had done what he could to defend his crown, but he knew he could never be secure until he had dealt with Duke Robert. In a curious way the certainty of an imminent struggle was a relief. He needed to consolidate his position and validate his seizure of power. He needed a battle. Ironically, it seemed that Ranulf Flambard was about to bring him one.

By mid-June the English court was at Hastings where Robert Curthose was expected to make landfall with the army Flambard had raised for him. Henry had gone to oversee the defences and shipping. For reconnaissance and close harbour work Henry recruited some English pilots. He now ordered them out to reconnoitre the enemy fleet far out in the channel beyond Hastings.

What happened next is not clear, and not recorded in any detail, but it seems that the English pilots, once having made contact with the invasion fleet, were handsomely bribed to conduct the enemy away from Hastings towards an inadequately defended port further west. On July 20th, 1101, Duke Robert's invasion force landed, unchallenged and unobstructed. English sailors, bribed by Ranulf Flambard, had by-passed Henry's waiting army and piloted the ships safely into Portsmouth harbour.

As soon as Henry heard of the landfall, he left Hastings and moved his forces at once to protect Winchester which was assumed to be the first place Curthose would seize. This old royal town, ancient capital of England, site of the mint, seat of one of the foremost bishoprics of the south, must not be allowed to fall. Meanwhile Duke Robert was taking over Portchester Castle and dining in the company of the man who he hoped would establish him on the throne and demolish the illegal usurpation of his younger brother.

For almost six months, Ranulf Flambard had guided his campaign with astute advice and brilliant organisation for which Curthose felt himself indebted. But now fissures broke out in the ranks of his supporters. Their fierce arguments and divided opinions were reducing Curthose to such utter confusion that he was prepared to negotiate with Henry. We can speculate that this was the moment Flambard had been counting on, that it had never been his project to support Curthose, nor necessarily to hurt him. All he wanted was to use him. By careful manipulation of the dilatory duke, he planned to manoeuvre himself into a position from where he could begin to relaunch his career. For the six months prior to Flambard's arrival, Curthose had proved himself incompetent to mount a cross-channel invasion. Until Flambard came he had posed no real threat to his brother's crown. Within a very short time of jumping from the tower and landing in Normandy, Flambard had begun to make Duke Robert look like a genuine threat. A threat so genuine that not only was he now in England with an army but was actually in a good position to defeat Henry. Now came the most difficult part of the plan: to get Curthose to agree to talks and guide him towards the complete collapse of his objectives.

Even if this was not Flambard's strategy, incredible as it seems, this is in fact what happened. From a position of strength, even dominance, Curthose was reduced within a few weeks to agreeing to negotiations with his brother. Could this have been what, all along, Flambard had planned, the supreme manoeuvre of an astute political mastermind? We cannot know. But the facts confirm that instead of bloodshed and battle there was discussion, agreement and the emergence of a treaty. The extraordinary Treaty of Westminster which enshrined a peace between the warring brothers can be attributed, however indirectly to Flambard's influence. And, as if to crown this supreme piece of political manipulation with irony, the date on which the Treaty was promulgated was August 2nd, 1101. One year to the day since King William had been killed, thus initiating their struggle for the throne.

Almost without pausing for breath, Flambard was straight on to his next piece of jugglery. During Henry's sustained burst of good humour after the Treaty of Winchester, Flambard swooped. He asked for, and got, the promise of a safe conduct. This was tantamount to a promise that he would not be re-arrested. Henry even addressed a few words to him about the good governance of his see, which made Flambard think he was suggesting that a future working relationship between them was not impossible. Then, later the same day, Henry bestowed another mark of favour by sending for him to attest a charter. He could ask for no clearer indication that his previous offences were, if not forgiven, at least not going to hamper their future association. Henry was astute enough to see that a man who had been so useful to both his brothers, might also be of use to him.

Just one year ago, Flambard had been a prisoner, deprived of his possessions, ejected from office, accused of a string of offences, facing, at the worst, death or long incarceration, at the best, exile or a lifetime in the furthest reaches of the political wilderness. In less than a year his fortunes had undergone a remarkable, if not yet complete, restoration. He still had not achieved full possession of Durham. Yet there would never be a point, at any time in the future, when Henry would seriously threaten to imprison him again or to exact punishment for his escape.

***

It took many years until Flambard made that long-delayed journey to Durham and was restored to all the rights of his bishopric. There are various hints in the records that, when Henry later made war on Duke Robert in order to seize control of Normandy, he employed Flambard on some covert spying missions. Frankly, although there is little definite evidence for this, in view of Flambard's record, it seems highly probable.

Consider how events unfolded. During the next few years, the situation in Normandy grew increasingly lawless. Duke Robert was unable to keep control of his barons, whose rivalries and feuds constantly threatened the peace. Sporadic raids and skirmishes could break out anywhere, roads were unsafe except to thieves and robbers who plundered in the wake of passing troops. Flambard spent the summer of 1103 in Lisieux but began to feel unsafe. So violent and uncertain had the area become, that he might well have returned to

England in spite of his interests at Lisieux, had not a more serious purpose kept him in Normandy. Possibly a covert diplomatic mission for the English court. Two years before, as part of Flambard's reward for his loyal support, his brother Fulcher had been appointed Bishop of Lisieux by Duke Robert, in spite of the objections of Bishop Ivo of Chartres. Hardly had Fulcher settled into his new office, for which he was entirely unsuited, then he was suddenly taken off by disease, leaving the affairs of the bishopric in chaos. It was while Flambard was at Lisieux, trying to restore order, that Henry may have asked him to report on the duke's plans. Flambard seems to have played a part not only in surveillance but also in persuading Duke Robert, on more than one occasion, to come to the conference table. Henry was now determined to take his brother's duchy into his own permanent control and this, after three more years of struggle, he did. At the Battle of Tinchebrai in 1106, Duke Robert's army suffered a devastating defeat, though he himself survived to face a lifetime of imprisonment in England. During these years, Flambard shadowed the king's manoeuvres. He witnessed charters and writs, he was present at some court occasions and, also in 1106, he was instrumental in the negotiations that ended in agreement between the king and Anselm, who was recalled from exile. Finally, having achieved tolerable relations with both the king and Anselm, Flambard was able to make the long-delayed trip to Durham, settle into the bishop's palace and, laying aside secular politics altogether, begin a second career as a leading churchman.

If, from the Bishop's palace overlooking the Wear, Flambard ever looked back on the past, he might have pondered the immeasurable distance he had come from his pauper days in Bayeux where, as the son of a barely literate parish priest, he had scraped his first ideas of the world from below. On his own merits, with an inborn appetite for stimulation and challenge, he had risen fast and high. King's advocate, witnesser of charters, custodian of church lands, financial agent of extraordinary ingenuity, he had counselled two kings through troubled reigns and never, by his own estimation, given the wrong advice. He had done what had to be done, often with ingenuity and panache, sometimes with severity, never with purposed cruelty. If he had not done so, if he had not achieved something worthy of recognition, how could King Henry, the upholder of law and 'saviour of the Norman churches', have confirmed him in this powerful seat of Durham? Such a post was only ever held by a man completely trusted by the king.

Having put away his mistress, he lived a restrained life which could have borne examination by any bishop's court. He increased the number of monks and canons in the dependent houses and found the funds from his own amassed wealth to support them. He reformed the financial management of the fiefs and manors and presided over the bishop's court with proper attention to justice and the law. He had become an almsgiver to the poor on a scale unknown in Durham and was completing the magnificent cathedral that his predecessor had left unfinished at his death. For the moment, and perhaps for some time to come, Flambard was the respected ecclesiastical officeholder he had long desired to be. And in the years that followed great work was done. Assisted by his chamberlain, William, and Pinceon, his steward, Bishop Ranulf scarcely put a foot wrong in his twenty years at Durham. And, until the end, every year on the vigil of August 2nd he kept the anniversary of King William's death with a prayer a candle-flame.

As he approached seventy and his customary energy deserted him, Ranulf Flambard, who had never been a spiritual man, turned to prayer. Well aware that no-one who achieves high office in the houses of the powerful arrives at his life's end unstained, he turned more and more to good works, prayer and penitence. God might forgive him, he hoped. The chronicling monks who had spent years defaming him, never would.

On September 5th, 1128, Ranulf Flambard, who had raced like a comet across the political landscape of his times, passed from view and was buried in the chapter house at Durham.

By then almost no-one remembered his escape from the Tower.

Chapter Seven
Edith and Matilda

On the whole, ordinary medieval women were invisible. Even royal or noble women, though seen, were never allowed to live full and independent lives. The lives of secular women were not thought worth recording. Only holy or sacred life-content mattered. Ironically, the most visible women were the ones that didn't exist. They were the endlessly depicted Saints and Marys, the representational seasons of the year, or angelic manifestations, or depictions of that wicked spoiler, Eve. The lives of idealised women were told in miracle-stories, in parables and fables: the lives of anchoresses, saints and holy martyrs were written down by chronicling monks who were happily oblivious to the lives of real women. Even the nuns, who might have shared a conventual building with the monks, would lead lives rigorously separated from theirs. There is, in consequence, a lack of detail about the lives of most women in the early centuries after the Conquest. Even the daughters of the Conqueror tend to disappear into a fug of obscurity, getting married off or sent to nunneries before they have had a chance to experience a whiff of flourishing youth under the aegis of a powerful father. Girls are barely valued except as property, bargaining chips in marriages and breeders. They are bartered like commodities, and not just by royalty. Wealthy families did deals to enhance their estates, even the poorest tenant might, by an advantageous marriage, obtain an extra acre. The very poorest women, we are often told, had the freest lives. But this is most doubtful. All females were the property of males in one form or another. That was how the world was structured, that was how God had made it in the beginning, they were told, when he had promised Eve sorrow under the rule of man.

But while the detail of individual lives is so slender and the facts so rare, there are occasional glimpses of fascinating personalities that reward study in depth. In an earlier chapter, we looked at one such life, that of Gunhild, daughter of King Harold, whose tragic love affair is still reconstructable in outline and still makes us want to know more. And we can know more about the subject of this chapter.

In case you might be expecting that this chapter is going to address the lives of two women, it must be stressed that *this* Edith and *this* Matilda are the same person; that she was known under both names at different times in her life and that both names were recorded in the surviving written records. In both guises, Edith the child: intelligent, sensitive, astute and curious, and Matilda the woman: assured, educated, queenly, lived through turbulent times and made the best of what destiny dealt her. By the standards of the day her life was privileged. But it was not easy. There are sufferings, even in the highest ranks of society, that belong to women alone.

Edith/Matilda's life was far from ordinary, except in one special sense that we will come to later. Both the names and the experiences divide her life into two distinct episodes which reflect the expectations of a royal child at that time. Her royalty is of great importance, bridging as it did, the two parts of her life. In fact, her lineage could scarcely be grander. She was the daughter of Malcolm Canmore, King of Scotland, and Margaret, a lady so pious that she was being called a saint even as a young woman. Astonishingly, Margaret was born in the old Kingdom of Hungary, daughter of Edward the Exile, royal scion of the old English lineage. Her family came back to England in 1057 when she was about twelve years old. Although facts are few, it is possible that she spent some time at Romsey Abbey where she may have known Edith the Fair, wife of King Harold. Sometime after 1066 she moved to Wilton Abbey, a sanctuary for many Englishwomen fleeing the violence and disorder of the aftermath of the Conquest. During her short stay there, she may have become friendly with Gunhild, daughter of King Harold and Edith the Fair. Possibly she named her first born daughter Edith in tribute. On the other hand, the name 'Edith' plays about in the namescape of Wilton nunnery reflecting different aspects of its reputation. Saint Edith was the presiding saint of the institution, and some girls were given the name for this reason. Another Edith, Queen Edith, widow of Edward the Confessor, retired to Wilton after the Conquest and died there.

At some point Margaret and her family fled north to Scotland where she married Malcolm Canmore in 1070. After producing five boys, this pious lady gave birth to the daughter she called Edith, followed by Mary two years later. After another gap of two years, Margaret gave birth to her last child, a boy, David, in 1084. These bare obstetric facts show that for fourteen years after her marriage, Margaret was almost perpetually pregnant or recovering from childbirth. She may not have been breast feeding, since royal and noble males usually discouraged the practice among their womenfolk, preferring to hire wetnurses to suckle their heirs. Margaret would have had to undergo all the contingent ills of suppressing milk flow and denying her body a natural and sometimes fulfilling process. Noblewomen were often subject to the ill-advised practice of binding their breasts, thought to staunch the production of milk but often causing painful reactions, infections, fevers and sometimes death. There was a contemporary rumour that Duchess Sybil, wife of Robert, Duke of Normandy, died of complications caused by binding her breasts too tightly after the birth of her son. Unfairness, misguided stigma and cruel enforcements visited women of every rank and degree in every corner of their lives. Even queens were not exempt, and indeed if they wanted to earn a reputation for piety, they had to conform in every particular.

As was fitting for someone of Margaret's illustrious ancestry married to a king, the most distinguished people were chosen as sponsors at the baptisms of her many babies. Thus, standing forward at the font as Edith's godfather was no less a person than the eldest son of William the Conqueror, Robert Curthose. There is no clear indication of why he was chosen but the connection may have caused Edith some regret and sorrow in later life. Right from the first, the child Edith was caught up in the intertissued weave of powerful family connections. These, for good or ill, would shape her life.

***

In keeping with the practice of the times and because there were no really strong educational nunneries in Scotland, when Edith was about five or six years old, she was sent south to be educated. It is possible she went to Romsey Abbey first and then later to Wilton Abbey about three miles from Salisbury. As is only to be expected, substantial facts are thin and unreliable, but we do know something about Edith's later years at Wilton thanks to the reporting spirit of Eadmer who writes about her in the *Historia Novorum in Anglia.*

But the early years are sketchy. It seems that at some time she came under the thumb of Aunt Christina, sister of Margaret and a nun, reputed to be an over-protective and domineering woman. Some sources say she wanted Edith to become a nun. This certainly was a possibility for a king's daughter. The Conqueror himself had given two daughters to the church. It was a way of ensuring redemption by having the constant intercession of prayers. Spare daughters were regularly given up in this way. But Edith was not spare, she was the first-born daughter. If anyone would be destined for perpetual nunhood, it would be her younger sister, Mary, who also joined her at Wilton.

We now have a small group of important women and girls living at Wilton at the same time: Edith, her sister Mary, her aunt Christina and Gunhild. One other woman who plays a significant part but whose name we do not know is the Abbess of Wilton. Although her name is not known for certain she was a figure of great prestige and some power. The Abbesses of Wilton held a barony from the king, a privilege shared by only three other nunneries in England: Shaftesbury, Barking and St Mary's, Winchester. As the equivalent in rank of a baron, the Abbess had the obligation to supply the king with knights when so summoned and she had the power to appoint officeholders in her domain which made her a source of patronage. Longstanding relations with the royal family increased her influence and brought considerable wealth to the convent. The occupiers of this powerful baronial post are not systematically known from the archives of the monastic houses, most of which have disappeared, but it is known that an Abbess of Wilton called Matilda had correspondence with Anselm around this time and was therefore likely to be presiding over Wilton during the tenure of Edith.

Such was Edith's childhood as far as it is known. For all the rest, her character and thought, her likes and dislikes, her sadnesses and losses, her friendships, moods and gaieties, we have barely any information. In later life she showed a love of music, she patronised poets and displayed taste and appreciation for literature. Perhaps these interests, especially music, were fostered at Wilton during the sung masses and choral prayers of the Benedictine day. Here she lived for many years under the rule of the powerful Abbess who no doubt corresponded with Queen Margaret away in Scotland, reporting on the progress of her daughters. This little collegiate: Edith, Mary, Gunhild and Christina, knew each other, had acquaintances in common, shared wishes and desires and, perhaps, memories of the past.

This should be a rich source of historical material, one aches to know more, but there is little detailed information. One thing we can be sure of is that the women were educated, not only in Christian doctrine and obedience to the rule, but in Latin and Norman French, in reading and writing, particularly the skill of writing letters, as we shall see.

When and how Edith became Matilda, we don't know, but the change of name was probably deliberate and made for a variety of reasons. One reason may have been a strikingly modern one - the need for self-reinvention. A revamping of image, an adjustment of identity. There are several reasons why this might have come about which will be examined later. But first, we need to go back to an incident we have encountered in an earlier chapter and examine it from another angle.

In 1093 when Edith was about thirteen years old, King William Rufus decided she might make a satisfactory bride, so he came south to Wilton to view her. Eadmer tells us that aunt Christina hated William as a profligate king who robbed the church on a grand scale and ran a libidinous court. Therefore, as a defender of Edith's spiritual purity, she was determined to thwart his plans. It may have been Christina's wish that Edith should follow her own example and become a nun at Wilton, aiming one day at the appointment of Abbess.

So she tried to ensure that William never had the chance to meet the child or to speak to her; he was only allowed to glimpse her as she walked across the cloister wearing a shapeless imitation of nun's clothes and a veil. The veil was Christina's gambit, reinforcing the fact that Edith was destined for the religious life and was not available for marriage. Eadmer explains that the plan was carried out and William went into the cloister "as if to view the roses that grew there." Screened by the rose bushes, he was permitted a passing glimpse of the child. Unsurprisingly, William's desire to marry did not withstand this encounter. He aborted his visit and never returned. Nor did he ever marry. In this instance, Edith was lucky. One day she would make a far better marriage to a shrewd and intelligent man with whom she could share real power.

Not long after William's visit to Wilton in that summer of 1093, Edith's father arrived. He had heard rumours, possibly from William, that his daughter was being forced to become a nun. We must suppose that he was volcanic with outrage. He and his entourage descended on Wilton and proceeded to put the Abbess in a very embarrassing position. Unfortunately, there is no record of what was said, although reference is made to the incident by Eadmer and other chroniclers. Nor do we know what was said to Christina in whose charge Edith was. Known for intemperate language and fierce rages, Malcolm probably batted away all argument and made short work of rousting his daughter out of Wilton and hauling her back up to Scotland.

So Edith's education at Wilton ended suddenly in a shocking scene which we can only speculate was desperately upsetting to a thirteen year old girl. Torn away from her friends, seized from the only secure home she had known, losing in a stroke all the certainties of a stable environment, dragged across the realm in the company of a man she hardly knew, Edith herself, of course, is silent.

Some years later there was to be an official inquiry, instigated by Anselm, into the events at Wilton that summer. Many interesting facts would come out but mostly facts of interest to churchmen and legalists. What the women: Christina, the Abbess, Edith, her sister Mary and the nuns involved in these events, thought and felt about them, is not recorded and cannot be known. But when Edith was wrenched from Wilton in the late summer of 1093, there can be no doubt that, however brave or frightened she was, her life had suffered a great disturbance. There would be many more.

***

Not long after Edith was forced back to Scotland by her father, she became an orphan. In November 1093 King Malcolm Canmore, who had ruled Scotland for thirty-five years, was killed in an ambush. The circumstances are fairly well documented as befits such dramatic events. King Malcolm was travelling to a rendezvous in company with his eldest son, Edward, and a small party somewhere near the river Arne which was swollen by the November rains and in full spate. While dismounted and looking for a place to cross they were suddenly attacked. Robert Mowbray, Earl of Northumberland, in league with his nephew, Morel of Bamburgh, trapped the party in an unexpected ambush and proceeded to kill as many as possible, even though they were said to be unarmed at the time. The brutality of this act had terrible repercussions for Edith's mother. When Queen Margaret learned that her husband and first-born son were dead, she went into extreme mourning, refused food, declined rapidly and pined away. Within a short time after the ambush she, too, was dead.

Edith was now an orphan. We don't know exactly where she was when she heard the news, nor what her reactions were, but when you consider she had only recently been uprooted from her familiar home and planted in Scotland and was just beginning to know her parents after several years of separation, their deaths must have been devastating. Left an orphan in an unfamiliar land, she was, however, not without relatives. The problem was she hardly knew them. Her father's sons from his first marriage were like bearded giants from some remote haunted landscape. Her younger brothers were unknown to her, her godfather spent the greater part of his time in Normandy, she knew a few old servants and people close to her parents, but she had few close kin. This is a period of her life shrouded in more than usual obscurity and she does not emerge into the records again until, a year or so later, she returns to Wilton.

Several reasons may have brought this about. First, the precariousness of life in Scotland. When a strong king dies and there are many contenders for the throne, the factions prepare for war and line up behind their candidates. As Edith's brothers chose sides and battled it out, she was probably sent south again for her own safety. Second, financial reasons. If she was living in England as a royal orphan, she would come under the protection of King William as his ward. This meant that he would be responsible for her maintenance, but it would also give him the power to dispose her in marriage. In other words, at Wilton once more her fate would be controlled and, in all likelihood, under the restored pressure of Aunt Christina, she would become a nun. Such an outcome would be agreeable to William. It is unfortunate that we have to do so much speculation about this period of her life, but it is almost impossible to uncover the continuous story. A gap of several years, between 1094 and 1101, occurs which blanks out her teenage years when she was developing from the embattled child into the strong and spirited woman she would become.

But there is one area of Edith's life which, even if all the monks in all the *scriptoria* of England had suddenly taken to writing about her, would always have remained a blank. It is the area that is most crucial to a woman's life, most especially the life of a queen upon whom falls the serious duty of producing an heir. If Queen Anne, wife of Henry VIII, had produced a boy instead of a girl, and had not miscarried of one, perhaps two, later babies, possibly male, the history of the Reformation, perhaps of England itself, would be different. Incalculable secrets are hidden behind the doors of historical bedchambers while great suffering and sorrow goes unrecorded. So Eve was promised by God at the Fall "in sorrow shalt thou bring forth children." For royal women, the stakes were inevitably higher. And before that, before marriage, before a girl had even been given away to a man's pleasure, there was the secret suffering caused by menstrual afflictions, excessive, painful monthly bleeding and the angst of sheer ignorance. On the whole, historians don't speculate on this subject. There are no facts, no details. Of course not. Who would record them? It wasn't even as if women or girls themselves would leave any such testimony when they were taught that pain was visited by God for bad deeds and sinfulness. Rather than complain they would be more likely to hide these secrets out of fear, self-chastisement and *pudeur.*

Women's bodies were not just a problem for themselves but also for physicians. No-one understood their workings which half the time seemed miraculous and half the time grotesque. Most, if not all, physicians were monks and practised their skills under the aegis of the church. With a few honourable exceptions, monastics had a peculiar or ignorant attitude to women. So one might expect to find very little in the way of either medical engagement or sympathetic treatment of women's problems in the transitional years between late 11th and early 12th centuries. From, say, 1080 to 1118, the lifetime of Edith. And yet this time period does bring us some exceptional physicians. One of them was Faricius, or Faritius, both names appear in the records. He was an Italian from Arezzo in Tuscany a place which had several prominent institutions developing an innovative approach to medical studies. These schools were beginning to produce practitioners who did not ascribe illnesses to the devil, or to God's punishment, or sorcery, but made some attempt to consider the body's organic processes and strive towards an understanding of them.

Abbot Faricius studied for years among the best teachers in the field and prided himself on having attained a high level of skill. The curriculum was still based on the teachings of Galen and the theories of Aristotle, but new thinking was pushing the old doctrines into experimental areas: trying to understand the workings of the body: the causes and progress of disease. At this period the medical texts of Hippocrates were available, and the works of Avicenna were circulating freely. Anatomy was undeveloped at this stage, except as part of the gain in knowledge that came with surgery. Some operations were still allowed by the church, but later in the century the church became anxious about 'the spilling of blood' and forbad the practice. Philosophy and religion still dominated the training of medical students. The earliest universities, such as Salerno, or Bologna founded in 1089, were attached to cathedrals and students were required to be admitted to the clergy before commencing their studies. But although advances were few, there was a slight improvement in attitudes towards the causes of illness and its treatment. Faricius benefitted from these new practices which he brought with him to England when he became a monk at the

Abbey of Malmesbury sometime before the end of the eleventh century. There we can leave him for the moment.

***

Meanwhile Edith was growing up back at Wilton, pursuing the round of canonical hours, the prayerful rhythms of the convent. As far as we know, Mary was still her companion and Aunt Christina still a dominant presence in her life. At this point her story grinds to a halt.

At this point, therefore, I must do what historians almost never do, with good reason. I am going to stand on a fairly shaky branch of the tree of history and proceed to cut it away from its support. Without evidence I am going to put forward a theory. If correct, it would explain quite a bit about Edith's later life. If incorrect, it at least opens up a neglected field of reflection. Edith is back in Wilton sometime in late 1094. She is aged about 14 and has been well-nourished all her life. It is more than likely that her periods begin around this time. What does she know about the functioning of her own body? How well has she been prepared? One must surmise that there was little discussion of these matters at a nunnery among women who had renounced any engagement with pregnancy and childbirth. On the other hand, there may have been dogmatic instruction about the fallen state of women, their naturally wicked and unchaste instincts, their need to be controlled by penitent obedience to God's rule. Who was there to describe to Edith what was happening? Who took the ignorant terror out of it? More practically, who supplied the cloths to soak up the blood? Scenes of wretched and unnecessary suffering caused by sheer ignorance and ill-preparedness would have been widespread and it is not impossible that Edith, having had a disrupted childhood, having recently been orphaned and having been apparently abandoned by her own family, may have suffered a severe reaction to her first painful period. My theory is that not only the first, but all her periods were painful and sometimes debilitating, even into adulthood. I suggest that it was only when she was pregnant or enjoying post-partem relief from menstruation, that she was fully free of monthly pain. This, I am arguing, is why she had difficulty with all her pregnancies and why, after only a few years of marriage and two healthy babies, she failed to have more even though still young, being only twenty-three years old. Although it does not amount to evidence, there is information enough to suggest the private, hidden, untold heartache of female anguish. And if this theory does not precisely apply to Edith, her case might be deemed at least representational of a large part of the female population of the time.

  In the remaining years at Wilton, Edith continued her education: undertook religious studies, read the lives of the saints, learned the psalter by heart, became learned in French and Latin, reading whatever she could borrow in the way of manuscripts or codices from the library, and learned to compose superbly diplomatic letters, some of which survive. She may also have been involved in some of the other activities of the convent: the cultivation of the herbarium and the kitchen gardens, collecting hips from the roses to make healing syrups, the distillation of plants for the infirmary, the raising of livestock, especially sheep on the Abbey farms, and all the other activities of a self-sufficient rural Abbey which might have contributed to fill the long hours of growing up. All the while young Edith may have been nurturing dreams of real-world power; not the prayerful power of a nun, but a role of distinction in the realm of politics, the dream of one day becoming the true daughter of her royal parents.

***

One day in August 1101 the news must have reached Wilton that the king was dead. Shot and killed while out hunting in Brockenhurst Forest. Such news, at any time, would be sensational. For Edith it meant that her official guardian was dead; she was now unsupported financially and without a protector. While Aunt Christina might have rejoiced at the news, having long hated William, Edith's position had become precarious. Everything now depended on what Henry would do. As we have seen, Henry seized power in a swift coup and within three days had himself crowned in Westminster. This news, too, would have come to Edith. She would have realised, being politically astute and having had the experience of William's blunt wooing a few years back, that she was a desirable candidate for marriage with the Norman royals. Her ancestry gave her status, placed her squarely in the royal succession. She had lived all her life with such expectations, now suddenly came the opportunity.

We don't know when they first met or how the marriage negotiations were conducted, but we do know that things were being pushed forward at a tremendous pace by Henry. He quickly recalled Archbishop Anselm from his three-year-long exile, not only because he needed to regulate relations with the church but because he needed Anselm to officiate at his marriage. These things were being put into effect within days of his rise to power. How soon they affected Edith we don't know, but sometime the following month, September 1101, Edith left Wilton and went to Abingdon on the Thames near London. She may have stayed at a royal house there, or as a guest of Faricius who, as we have seen, was the newly appointed Abbot of Abingdon, whose consecration was not due to take place until November 1st which made him, strictly speaking, still a Prior.

When Anselm returned from exile to be welcomed by Henry who yet again found himself having to apologise for the actions of his brother, he would have learned of the marriage plan and been asked to officiate. Anselm, as Archbishop of Canterbury and supreme representative of the church in England, was indispensible to the ceremony. His consenting presence would confer legitimacy on Henry's recent actions and inaugurate his reign with the symbolic union of the English ancestral line with the Norman dynasty. At first, Anselm seemed inclined to agree to the marriage which would signal his support of Henry's swift and bloodless coup. Although Anselm was not without sympathies for Duke Robert's position, it seemed to him more vital to preserve the peace than to open the way for the older brother to contest the throne through violence. So, when Henry announced his intention to marry, and named his prospective bride, Anselm agreed. But the name that Henry gave was Matilda, which Anselm at that time did not recognise. Later Henry explained that it was the will of both himself and his bride that she be married under the name Matilda. Why did

Edith want to change her name? This was troubling to Anselm.

Did he perhaps remember some scandal around the young Edith at Wilton, years ago? Wasn't she seized by her father and taken away to Scotland? Wasn't there some controversy around that event which had to do with the wearing of the veil? It was his view that when the veil had been worn, a commitment had been made. Had Edith therefore broken her vows?

Once Anselm's mind misgave on any matter he had to proceed carefully. So, without refusing to conduct the marriage he equally failed to give total consent. Instead, he came up with his habitual gambit, a compromise. Let there be an inquiry into those events at Wilton, let the case be examined, formally and with due deliberation, so that he might give a judgement pleasing to the whole church. After all, Anselm did not want to compromise his return from exile with an action that would annoy or offend his fellow churchmen. Henry had no alternative but to agree to this suggestion for he needed to establish Edith/Matilda's credentials for a marriage that would make her Queen. The archbishop's reputation was crucial to Henry at this delicate point in his affairs. If Anselm would agree to sanction his marriage and crown his bride, it would be the strongest statement that he had thrown in his lot with Henry against Robert Curthose. If, on the other hand, he should refuse, even for religious rather than political reasons, the damage to Henry's position would be costly. Costly, too, would be any hint of scandal. All scandal must be squashed at the outset; adverse comment or resistance of any sort must be crushed, once and for all. And so, under these terms, the inquiry went ahead. Prominent prelates were summoned to Lambeth Palace, not then the seat of the Archbishops of Canterbury, but of the Bishops of Rochester.

When and how these arrangements became known to Edith, who was calling herself Matilda, is not known. From the security and stable rhythms of life at Wilton she had once more been jolted into the world which, though frightening, offered her the possibilities she had always desired. Something great was presented to her imagination through the magnified figures of her own late mother, Margaret, and her long-dead mother-in-law, Matilda. They had both been queens, both politically astute, both fecund in the extreme: Margaret giving birth to eight children and Matilda nine. Although her mother's name was as cherished as a saint's, which indeed it was since she was the subject of a Saint's Life, although not yet canonized, the name Matilda was more powerful. Widely revered, the Conqueror's wife Matilda was still present in her battling sons, of whom one had recently seized a crown. She was present, too, in the many stories told about her, in her fame as a lady of piety and good works. Matilda of Normandy, mother to nine surviving children, had travelled extensively, even during pregnancy, often on horseback; she had conducted affairs on behalf of her husband, held the regency during her husband's frequent absences, found time to give to the poor, to endow churches, to attend council meetings, to govern her squabbling sons and build the magnificent Abbaye aux Dames in Rouen. No paragon like her existed in any fable. The mere name 'Matilda' evoked the indomitable, commanding figure of the Duchess of Normandy and Queen of England, wife of the Conqueror. Perhaps in the hope of emulating this extraordinary woman, sometime during the summer and autumn of 1100, Edith began to use the name Matilda.

It was under that name that she appeared at the Inquiry at Lambeth. One can only imagine her horror at this imposition. Not only was the whole embarrassing episode at Wilton, (basically a dispute between her father and Aunt Christina in which she was the injured party) going to be aired before a collection of priests and monks, she herself was to be questioned about the whole dreadful story. That terrible time, when she had been under the thumb of Aunt Christina, then wrenched away by an irate father, was to be rehearsed in public and submitted to the scrutiny of doctrinaire prelates whose heads were full of canon law. Intolerable! Nevertheless, on the appointed day, she went to Lambeth, probably by river-barge, to appear at the specially convened council where the dramas of her female childhood were to be subjected to the judgement of old men. Naturally, in all this babble about events that had happened years ago and which were quite beyond her control, no attention was paid to Matilda as a person, either to her feelings or her physical presence. It was as if, although present at the occasion, standing there in full view of the court, she was invisible. She may even have been suffering from monthly pains at the time of the inquisition, she may have been bleeding and in pain; none of that mattered.

As might be expected, the council of churchmen, after due deliberation, in which Anselm sought to exert no influence one way or another, though everyone knew which way he was leaning, found their verdict in accordance with that drift. There was no bar to marriage. Matilda had not broken sacred vows when she left the convent, she could not be considered as having taken the veil, therefore she was free to marry. Moreover, added Anselm at the end of the proceedings, there must never at any time in the future be the slightest doubt about the ruling. If anyone sought to dredge up any scandal in the future, he would be cast out of the church.

    This painful episode behind her, having undergone a considerable transformation in a mere three months, Matilda married her king on St Martin's Day, Sunday November 11th, 1100, and was immediately crowned. She now enters history as Matilda II, Queen of England.

***

    The private life of Henry and Matilda is not a matter of record but in the few hints and references that we do have there is general agreement that they were well-matched and had a relationship of trust and companionship. They presented, at any rate, a united front and Matilda, as a young wife who had sworn to serve "her dear lord" at her coronation, took her word seriously. Not only was she prepared to vie with her own mother-in-law, the legendary Matilda, in the fecundity of her marriage, she also wanted to emulate her subtle practice of advising her husband on sound policies and keeping him on the right side of the church. In this she proved immensely useful for it was her relationship with Anselm, conducted mostly by letter, which often eased the tensions between king and archbishop when both might have made irretractable errors. In that sense she upheld the wifely virtues and the queenly code, being peacemaker, settler of disputes and soother of troubles.

Did they love each other? In some ways the question means little since we cannot know and have no idea if what they expected to feel or allowed themselves to feel would be what we today call marital love. They would both have known that by reason of their status they would be condemned to long separations. They would both have known that one of their prime duties was to get legitimate offspring. Yet, this royal couple, so enamoured of power, so clever, so strong-willed, tenacious and hard-headed, might well have more chance of making each other happy than lovers who merely love. What they probably both had in common was a desire for power and that in itself may have been a strong bond. Then they prided themselves on charitable works and religious conformity, although that was an understood part of royal obligation and aimed at creating a favourable public image. In the early days of the reign, when Henry's right to the crown could justifiably be contested and was to be contested the following year by Robert Curthose, public presentation was immensely important. Youthful, and by the very fact of youthfulness, fair, and by the finding of Anselm's inquiry, pure, and with every probability of supplying legitimate heirs in the near future, Matilda was popular. She was to retain that popularity throughout her reign.

But the couple were not without critics, even within their own court. In the early days they were subjected to satire and mockery, not openly but in the subtle way of sly name-calling and smirking. A clique of courtiers took to calling them 'Godric and Godiva,' English common names, in mockery of their pretensions to an older, native, royal line. Such ridicule may have implied criticism of the plainness, even dullness, of the court, in sharp contrast to the flamboyant and flashy style of William Rufus.

Such criticism was probably stifled sometime around April or May 1101 when Matilda fell pregnant. This was proof that God had blessed the marriage, for which prayers were offered and candles lit. It looked as though she was about to fulfil the chief duty of a royal wife and produce an heir. But this first pregnancy was not easy and there were moments of great danger.

We have seen in the last chapter how Robert Curthose invaded England in July 1101, landing at Portsmouth unopposed in order to make war for the crown. This extremely alarming news, although not entirely unexpected, was to catch Matilda while she was at Winchester where Henry had assembled his defensive army. She may have been lodged at the castle, or possibly at the Bishop's house, Wolvesey Palace. But Winchester being a small city, almost entirely surrounded by hills, she would have been able to see the gathering troops of her godfather from almost any high window. How she felt as her husband and her godfather prepared to make war on each other cannot be known. In all likelihood she was entirely supportive of Henry's cause, whilst regretting her godfather's decision. On the other hand, she knew that Robert Curthose had a valid case, and indeed had signed a treaty with the dead king William in 1091 under which terms he had every right to claim the throne. Perhaps it was the burden of this anxiety or the long journey to Winchester or perhaps some other reason that caused her, a few days after arrival, to fall ill and take to her bed. This 'illness' is mysterious. In some obscurely worded references, there is a hint that the 'illness' referred to her pregnancy. If she had fallen pregnant in May, she would by now be about two months or thereabouts. It is quite possible that these references concern a threatened miscarriage which caused her to take to her bed.

Lying in bed in a city that was about to be attacked, unable to get away, fearing for her unborn baby while armies gathered outside, a frightened Matilda might well have turned to prayer. Facts are bare but it is known that suddenly and unexpectedly, as if in answer to prayers, Robert Curthose withdrew his forces, deciding not to try to take the city but to draw Henry's troops further off towards Alton and attack them there. Did Robert Curthose withdraw in order to spare his goddaughter the trauma of unleashed violence in the midst of her own personal distress? Did someone tell him that his goddaughter might miscarry the child and die? We can't know. All we know is that he did withdraw, and the baby was not lost. The loser in this story is Robert Curthose himself who, from a position of strength, went on to fail in all his objectives.

Before the birth of her baby, we know that Matilda went to stay at Abingdon, either at a royal residence in the vicinity or at the Abbey of Abingdon, whose prior had, since his consecration on All Soul's Day the previous year, become Abbot Faricius. The mere fact that Faricius was a physician and one, moreover, who was later to be appointed by Henry to the post of Royal Physician, might indicate that Matilda was lodged at the Abbey due to fears about the state of her health. We do not know what part, if any, Faricius played in the accouchement of Matilda, but he is widely reported to have later earned a reputation for helping women in childbirth. It may have been now that he won the king's confidence by the part, he played in bringing a healthy baby into the world, sometime around the Feast of Candelmas 1102.

The first duty of queenship as Matilda knew full well, was to produce an heir. When she realised that her firstborn was a daughter, a healthy, thriving, lusty-lunged daughter, but a daughter nonetheless, did she experience any disappointment? Is it possible to be disappointed at such a moment? Surely even the demands of sacred duty and sworn oaths shrink to inconsiderable trifles at such a moment, a moment when all status is cancelled, and all women participate equally in the exhilaration of bringing forth life. Matilda, I like to think, felt like that.

Did Henry suffer disappointment? If he did, he disguised it well. He went through the ceremonial kissing of the baby, acknowledging it his, and naming it, as was customary among fathers of the time. The name, naturally enough, was Matilda, later shortened to Maud. Henry already had numerous sons. He was reputed to be a first-order philanderer, having had mistresses and illegitimate children in many different places in England and Normandy. He was known from his youth to be singularly libidinous. But in the early years of marriage to Matilda it seems very likely that he made efforts towards restraint, confining his attentions to his wife. Within a short time of being 'churched,' the ceremony of blessing after childbirth with thanksgiving for the survival of the mother, Matilda was once again pregnant.

***

Sometime during her pregnancy, between late 1102 and 1103, Matilda wrote Archbishop Anselm a letter which still survives. It is written in Medieval Latin of bravura style, festooned with images, similes and scriptural references in which she tells him off for overdoing his penitent fasting and appeals to him to take more care of his health. She addresses him as "venerable father" and signs off as his "faithful handmaid." In the many lines between opening and closing, for this is a long letter, she sprinkles innumerable learned references: to Cicero, Pythagoras, Socrates, as well as Saints John the Apostle and Martin of Tours and Books of the Old Testament. In this letter she fully demonstrates that the years of education at Wilton had not been wasted; perhaps she is trying to impress, or appeal to Anselm as someone who can engage at an intellectual level, or simply trying to please an old man.

At this time Anselm would have been about seventy-three years old and probably very thin, worn to a whip by fasting and anxiety. There was plenty to worry about. By the end of 1103 he would be in exile again, having been forced out of England by Henry because, in a case of history repeating itself, Anselm refused to recognise lay investment of bishops. It was the same dispute that had ruined his relationship with King William Rufus. But in the years since William's death the Pope had been pressing the issue. Then, in 1099, at the Council of Rome, the Pope had ruled most strictly on the matter by decreeing that "no king or prince or layman whatsoever" was to appoint a churchman to high office. Unexpressed but thick in the air was the threat of excommunication. Anselm could not disobey the pontiff; Henry could not give up his royal prerogative. Exile was inevitable. So Anselm went, though neither he nor the king relished such a breakdown in relations between them. At times like this, Matilda's aid was vital. Matilda was Henry's way of maintaining some credit with the English church, whose leader and premier luminary he had forced into exile.

Matilda's pregnancy, we must assume, advanced without incident. With many things to occupy her mind, and the consolations of prayer and piety, she was soon establishing a public persona in her own right. Religious conformity and queenship were her two strongest cards, and she was dedicated to promoting Henry's cause in whatever way she could. There were many ways. As we have seen she could act as intercessor between her husband and Anselm, and did so, often by letter; she acted as co-regent during his absences in Normandy, in partnership with Roger, Bishop of Salisbury; she interested herself in building projects; she endowed charitable causes; she was involved in plans to build a bridge and several religious houses including Waltham Abbey. Besides these activities she would have been acquainted with some of Henry's councillors and chief supporters, among whom was the loyal Robert Beaumont, Count of Meulan, who had backed the king from the first day when they had ridden to Winchester hours after King William was shot. Robert and his brother, Henry Beaumont, remained staunch through the uncertain early days when the more powerful concentration of Norman nobles was backing Robert Curthose. Boldly choosing Henry, Robert Count of Meulan became his chief aide, an adviser whose political wisdom was widely celebrated among the chroniclers. It would be fascinating to know what Matilda thought of him. It was to her advantage to remain on the best terms possible with those who had influence over her husband. She may well have been astute enough to use Meulan by sounding out his views on policies or personalities, particularly those associated with affairs in Normandy about which she had little first-hand knowledge. Others may have advised her too, but it is tempting to think that she was more than capable of forming her own wise counsels.

At Christmas 1100, while she was in the full bloom of pregnancy there was a great court held at Westminster. This formal occasion, known as a crown-wearing, was a major public statement of Henry and Matilda's right to reign. By wearing their crowns, the royal couple was reminding everybody that a coronation had taken place which conferred legitimacy and could not be undone. Anyone now contesting that legality was a traitor. What made this ceremony particularly impressive was that it was attended by the heir to the French crown, the future king Louis VI. Afterwards, at the banquet, Louis sat between Henry and Anselm with Matilda on his other side, an image of France and England cosying up. Matilda would have been the presiding grace at the table, hopefully making more than small talk. Robert of Meulan would have been somewhere close at hand for he was almost certainly the agent responsible for securing the royal visitor. Meulan also knew Anselm from his long-ago days in Bec, for the Abbey of Bec lay on Meulan's territory and they had clashed fiercely over 'traditional' rights to the abbey's direction and control. Since then, their relations had undergone various convolutions, but at that Christmas feast they were reconciled. Undercurrents of past disputes and the tensions of international politics may have given the atmosphere a taut depth but, on the surface, smiling politeness was the order of the day.

***

On August 5th, 1103, Matilda was brought to bed of a healthy boy. The rejoicings around the birth of this baby must have been truly ecstatic. Henry had an heir, Matilda had a son. She had achieved the single most important virtue of the queenly code. This put her on a par with Duchess Sybil, wife of Duke Robert, who had produced a son about the same time baby Maud was born. Both Henry and his brother now had sons and, as if to make a deliberate statement of rivalry, both sons were named William. Two sons of the same name, sons of brothers locked in bitter enmity. As if in further contention, the two Williams each bore a title which signified a special destiny. Duke Robert's son bore the title 'Clito' a Latin tag meaning 'renowned' or 'worthy', which conveyed a sense of princely entitlement. In an effort to match this, Henry and Matilda added 'Aetheling' to their son's name, the ancient title for a prince of the royal house deriving from old English custom. The name had been given to Matilda's uncle Edgar Aetheling, the brother of her mother Margaret. If it is accepted that every family has an embarrassing member, Uncle Edgar fulfilled that role. Both his sisters, Christina and Margaret went on to have rather more distinguished careers than he did, Christina becoming an Abbess and Margaret a Queen. However, this black sheep had a moment of pure white glory. Like Robert Curthose, whose cause he embraced at the moment of its doom, he had shone with the burnished glamour of the Pilgrim's War. He had fought for the liberation of Jerusalem and returned with the stains of all his sins washed away as the Pope had granted. Nevertheless, the cognomen, Aetheling, given with all the braggadocio of aspiring parents, failed to designate a kingly destiny. Undaunted, Matilda and Henry persisted in conferring it on their son. By coupling the Norman 'William' with 'Aetheling', the parents hoped to make the point that their marriage had united the old English lineage with the new Norman one and that William Aetheling was the fruit of their happy union. A fragile fruit, and so far, a single one.

It was now Matilda's dearest wish to provide another heir for Henry. Although her daughter, Matilda, known familiarly as Maud, was a strong and forceful child, she could never inherit in her own right. More sons were needed, and in her prayers of thanks, Matilda surely asked God for increase of such a blessing. It wasn't only Henry's mother who existed as the exemplar of motherhood, there was another family member whose fecundity, which she found almost indecent, was held up as an object of emulation. Henry's sister, Adela of Blois, had ten children, at least five of whom were sons. Some of the girls may have been stepdaughters, but even so the family was prolific. Matilda, who found childbirth a terrible ordeal, longed for more pregnancies, and feared them.

It was not to be. Whether more pregnancies followed and ended in miscarriages or still births we do not know, but at the age of twenty-three Matilda was to have no more living children. There must have been much private anguish around these circumstances, but nothing is mentioned in the records and her letters bear no sign of personal matters. Though women could be granted a public role in special circumstances, their functioning in nature, their bodily changes, their embodiment of implacable mysteries, so frightening to the masculine ethos, deprived them of real power. Even royal women lived half-invisibly under suffrance, in a world not shaped for them. Nevertheless, the demands on Matilda were unrelenting.

In addition to courtiers, Matilda welcomed many prelates to her reception chamber, among them Roger of Salisbury, her husband's chancellor, with whom she developed a good working relationship. Perhaps he amused her with an anecdote which gave her a glimpse of her husband's youth; the story of how he first met Henry. The story, recorded for us in various sources, concerns the time when Roger was the priest of a small chapel at Avranches. One day when Henry was travelling through the town on his way from the coast, he came into the church to hear mass. Roger confessed that at that time he was an ungainly novice, unschooled in the ways of the world. It was his duty to read parts of the service, but he was so nervous that he gabbled through them very quickly. So quickly, indeed, that the young Henry was impressed, thinking such speed could save vast amounts of time, and immediately enrolled Roger in his service. Whether true or not, such a story would surely have delighted Matilda.

Throughout 1105 she continued to witness charters, to issue writs in her own name and interest herself in the founding of a priory of Austin canons at Aldgate which she had discussed with Anselm, proposing to appoint her own confessor as first prior of the holy house. Patronage now became a source of worthwhile endeavour. She valued the arts, poetry and music and always invited musicians and entertainers to the Christmas courts. But it was in keeping up relations with Anselm that her best work was done at this period. Anselm in exile was a source of embarrassment to the court. The mere presence of the illustrious old man, thin and failing, wandering in foreign exile instead of presiding over the English church from his seat at Canterbury, was a source of foreign criticism. Especially annoyed was the *curia* in Rome from where the Pope kept threatening to excommunicate Henry.

During this time Matilda maintained her correspondence, most certainly encouraged by Henry and probably by Roger of Salisbury who was well aware that the monks at Canterbury were getting impatient at their pastor's continued absence. In late 1104 she wrote again to her "piously esteemed father and devoutly reverend lord." This letter is a masterpiece of redundant verbiage. Sometimes she is abstruse, if not nebulous, referring at one point to the "presence of your present absence" and hinting at unknown things such as that Henry "is more kindly disposed towards you than most people might think." Towards the end she attempts to heal the rift between them by urging him vaguely "not to turn away the sweetness of your love for him."

If these letters did nothing else, they kept a channel of friendly communication open between the king's court and the archbishop. Matilda might have been gratified when she heard the news that an understanding had been reached. At last, under pressure from foreign courts and the English church, Henry was brought to a compromise solution in 1105. With great reluctance, fearing that he would be universally blamed if Anselm died in exile, Henry renounced the right of investing bishops. This royal prerogative, which his father and brother had both enjoyed, had been the source of contention with Anselm since the latter's first recall from exile in 1100. Now, five years later, as a result of the agreement, he was being recalled again, this time in a stronger position. The balance of power between the church and regal authority had shifted towards the English prelacy. This meeting, which produced this staggering concession by Henry, took place in Normandy, at Anselm's former monastery at Bec, which had been harbouring him in exile. As soon as the deal was done, the old archbishop, tired and frail and recently recovered from illness, set out on his final journey to England, the last voyage across the channel which in his long life he had crossed so often.

***

According to the chronicles, Anselm landed at Dover on the morning of September 3rd, 1106. By a curious coincidence, noted by some as ordained by God, the date happened to be the Feast Day of St Gregory. St Gregory was the 6th century Bishop of Rome who had sent St Augustine to found Canterbury in 597. What date could be more fitting, more symbolic, or perhaps more contrived?

Matilda played an important part in the celebrations around Anselm's return. While Henry was preparing to make war against his brother in Normandy, she went to meet Anselm at Dover in order to welcome him home after his exile. There was great rejoicing among townsfolk and all those nobles and prominent clerics who gathered to welcome the returning shepherd to his flock. After resting at Dover, Anselm set out for Canterbury escorted by monks and canons from Christchurch, headed by Prior Ernulf. All along the twenty-mile route delegations of townsfolk, knots of villagers and representatives of religious houses, came out to meet him and receive his blessing.

The journey took several days and there were overnight stops. This was to enable Anselm to be seen, to greet and receive as many well-wishers as possible. Matilda led the ceremonies and saw to Anselm's comfort. She ensured that all the proper arrangements were in place by going on ahead with her entourage to prepare the way. All the lodgings, including the religious houses, were inspected by Matilda's officials and placed under seal until the archbishop's arrival. As an eyewitness to her efficiency, Eadmer notes her part with approval in his *Historia Novorum in Anglia.*

The same year put an end to the constant warfare between Matilda's husband and godfather. After six years of contestation, threat, assault and counterassault, negotiation and treaty, the long fratricidal struggle came to a definitive end. In the damp tail-end of a wet summer, on 28th September 1106, the finale came at the Battle of Tinchebrai. Henry won outright. Duke Robert was taken captive, but it was some time before any news came to Matilda. She must have waited anxiously, aware that her family was deeply implicated. Uncle Edgar had made another of his bad decisions and chosen to back Curthose in the climactic denouement of this long tussle. It is likely that, in the anguished days awaiting news about a battle in which three close relatives were involved, not to mention the hundreds of Christian souls teetering on the edge of eternal judgement, Matilda spent her days engaged in charitable acts, in prayer, at masses or attending special vigils.

As soon as he could, Henry dispatched letters to Matilda and Anselm informing them of the great victory won by his forces under the disposition of God, adding supplementary news that the uninjured Robert Curthose, with a few of his retainers, would be dispatched to England on a royal ship. To Bishop Roger of Salisbury, he sent notification that the duke was to be held prisoner in his charge at Devizes Castle until further notice.

***

The Easter Court at Windsor in April 1107 marked the summit of the royal couple's endeavours. Henry not only ruled England and Normandy, he had re-established good terms with the papacy, had a son and heir and was still only thirty-six years old. One brother was dead, struck by an arrow in Brockenhurst forest, by what design or accident was still unknown. Another brother was imprisoned under the jurisdiction of Roger of Salisbury and could pose no further trouble. For six years he had struggled, first to secure the throne of England, then to acquire the dukedom of Normandy. In all this he had been magnificently aided by Matilda, who had established a widespread popularity among the people. The royal couple had been clever, diplomatic and lucky. They had succeeded by using the best and worst qualities of useful people, by negotiation, by astute manipulation of propaganda and, as always when war is involved, relentless taxation.

Whether Matilda ever suffered regrets about the imprisonment of her godfather is not a matter of record. But no doubt she was wise enough to know that strict necessity enforced it. A free and embittered Robert would seek revenge or find himself the figurehead of endless plots against his brother. So, he was kept prisoner, first in Devizes and then at other locations around the country, including Bristol and Cardiff. When rumours began to circulate about his cruel treatment, Henry wrote an exculpatory letter to the Pope: "I have not kept my brother in fetters like a captured enemy but have placed him as a noble pilgrim in a royal castle and have kept him well supplied…." This is more or less convincing. The reference to 'noble pilgrim' shows that Henry recognised his brother as a warrior of Christ who had taken part in the greatest Christian enterprise of the century, the Pilgrim's War that had won Jerusalem for Christianity. It is more likely that Robert was kept in conditions befitting a nobleman, with access to books, a retinue of servants, a personal chaplain and possibly, with due supervision, permission to hunt.

Meanwhile, Robert's son, William Clito, Count of Flanders, was roving around Normandy, making trouble, trying to obtain his father's release. Like his father he suffered numerous setbacks and his life, though privileged, was far from easy. At the age of four he was effectively orphaned. His mother, Sybil, had died not long after his birth and his father was a prisoner in England. It may be that the trauma of his early years never left him. William Clito's subsequent story will be followed in detail in the next chapter. A life dedicated to avenging his father's imprisonment and seizing back the duchy which he always believed his uncle had stolen from him.

Did Matilda ever see her godfather again? There is no record of any visit although it is easy to imagine that she would have wished to pay him that respect in his misfortune. Perhaps she wrote to him. No letter survives but it is at least possible that she might have sent him some religious works, extracts from Boethius's *Consolations of Philosophy*, perhaps, writings of the Stoics or Lives of the Saints. He was, and she would have known it, the most pious of the brothers, the least aggressive, the one who preferred to negotiate wherever possible. Even Henry recognised him as a 'pilgrim warrior' who had answered the Pope's appeal and won glory on the field of Ascalon. Robert had spared his goddaughter by withdrawing his troops when he knew she was ill in Winchester. He had not been a major figure in her life, but she may have felt that a debt was owed.

In 1109 Matilda would have heard of the death of her old correspondent, Archbishop Anselm in his seat of Canterbury, surrounded by the monks of Christchurch, including Eadmer. She may have been informed by letter from Anselm's head of household, his personal secretary, Baldwin of Tournai, who would have told her, in the style of the times, that Anselm went to Christ at dawn on Wednesday 21st April 1109, in the sixteenth year of his pontificate and the seventy-sixth of his life. He had been ailing for some time and in the final month was unable to go on foot to the church for mass. He had himself carried in a chair every day to be present at the consecration of the Lord's Body.

Anselm had played a great a part in her life since the inquiry of 1100 into her suitability for marriage. As a result of that ruling, she had married her king and gone on to live the life of queenly power and privilege. During all that time,

Anselm had been a correspondent, a mentor, a spiritual guide, a collaborator in building projects and charitable causes. They had met on many occasions and were intricately bound up in the tissue of interests and conflicts that always beset relations between the court and church. But they had something else together, a warmth founded on aspirations towards Christian charity, both desiring a state of blessedness, both seeking the good in events and people wherever they could. Matilda was wise enough to know that when Anselm died, a great life had ended. A life that embodied an age, the best of all ages, the age when she was young.

Another prelate who had played an important part in her life, the learned Italian Abbot Faricius of Abingdon, the royal physician, was proposed by Henry and Matilda as Archbishop of Canterbury in 1114. At Anselm's death the seat was left vacant for five years to the increasing outrage of the English church and the curia in Rome. The wishes of the royal couple were batted aside by a thin-lipped faction of magnates and prelates who preferred a Norman to a 'foreigner.' But some said it was not Faricius's 'foreignness' that they disliked, but the fact that he had tended women in childbirth in the course of his professional duties. He was tainted. Such were the prejudices of the times.

Matilda had no more babies after the birth of William Aetheling when she was twenty-three. Why? The cause might have been Henry's neglect, though it seems doubtful that he would allow his whole dynastic future to depend on the frail life of one young lad without setting about an energetic remedy. On the other hand, it is not impossible that Matilda had been damaged internally by the birth of William or that a series of subsequent, secret miscarriages had made it impossible to carry a baby to term. Any unhappiness, or pain or long-term ill-effects remain hidden and can never be known. Matilda's life is in part vividly painted in bright colours and visible to us from detailed chronicles about public acts, and in part unknown, unrecorded, invisible. The woman's life, the life of pregnancy, pain, miscarriage, the agony of long labours, the pain of internal rupture, wrecked insides and terror of death, lie beyond the ever-closed door of the private chamber, the birthing room. The woman's life was the life in which Matilda was ordinary, the life in which all women were equal.

Matilda died on May 1st, 1118, at the age of thirty-eight, having reigned as queen for eighteen years, and was buried in Westminster Abbey. Her post-mortem reputation was taken care of by the chroniclers: she was a woman of 'exceptional holiness', generous towards the church, called 'Good Queen Matilda' by her people, and committed to the pious task of commissioning from Thurgot, a monk of Durham, a Life of Saint Margaret, her mother. Mercifully, she did not live to experience the devastating death of her only son in 1120, nor the terrible strife of 1130s - 40s when her daughter, Matilda or Maud, made continual and ineffectual warfare to establish her right to the throne of England. Maud had not taken on board the lesson that her mother would have taught her. In these times a woman cannot rule in her own right.

The dreadfully bloody strife of the Anarchy lay ahead: long, wasteful years spilling so much blood for so few gains, reducing the countryside to blasted wastes and grinding down the starving people with swingeing taxes. All this was yet to come and would have broken Matilda's heart.

Chapter Eight
The Cousins' Tragedy

After the death of Matilda, Henry's life changed in many ways. He may not have indulged in outward shows of bereavement, but he led the public mourning of the court and ensured a burial worthy of his queen. Whatever private grief he suffered, whether grief-stricken or solaced by a new paramour, whether cast down, unconsoled or serene, he now entered alone upon the difficult middle years of his reign. Many felt that he was not the same king after Matilda's death. Still strong, still astute, still in full control and gifted in negotiations, his temper grew shorter, he had bouts of irascibility or moods of depression. Yet he remained, as always, in control of his court and anxious for good relations with the Pope who persisted in annoying him by threatening to send legates to England, something that Anselm had always resisted. Disputes in the church, rebellions in Normandy, a sequence of poor harvests due to bad weather and a series of wrangles with the grudging neighbour France, were among the many disappointments he was to encounter in the next few years. But one in particular was, almost beyond belief, tragic, cruel and terrible. As always, it is the personal stories we are trying to access, and they are the most difficult to discover.

Our obscurity would be even darker than it is without people like Eadmer, the writing monks who are virtually our only source of news from these times. Eadmer himself lamented the lack of sources, complaining about the paucity of documents. In his Preface to the *Historia Novorum in Anglia* he writes: "What an inestimable benefit they have conferred on posterity who, with an eye to the good fortune of future generations have committed to writing a record of the events of their own times." This may be self-praise, but it is not undeserved. He goes on to observe that, without these witnesses and reporters, "events [are] all too quickly buried in oblivion." Unfortunately, the inner life of individuals is for the most part "buried" as Eadmer suggests and the entire area of human existence so valued by us today: thoughts, feelings, emotions, psychological states, hopes, fears, desires; the whole armoury of what makes us human and suggests the ground of our actions and the basis of our nature are literally left out of the account. Thus, the figures who play out their lives so vividly in illuminated manuscripts, dressed in their colourful robes, sequestered within their decorated margins, inked with dazzling gold or lapis blue, nevertheless, for all that, remain little more than a shining surface.

In our non-supplicatory age when justice is expected rather than petitioned, we often lose sight of the inestimable solace of medieval belief in a world where God disposes all things according to a divine order beyond our understanding. In suffering and hardship, at the darkest moments in life, many people found that a mass or a confession, a holy vigil on the eve of a Feast Day, a prayer or psalm, a pilgrimage or the ministrations of a priest had power to console in ways we might not now understand. Even so, one wonders what Henry found on earth or in heaven that would offer any comfort for the shock of events of 1120, a personal and national tragedy almost past bearing.

***

In a reign as long as Henry's there are many turning points, moments when shifts happen in the surge of events. Some can be controlled or contained, others not. Some kings suffer a gradual weakening of their power almost at the same pace as their bodies weaken. But in 1118 Henry was fifty and still vigorous; his health was largely good; he was alert, well-counselled and he brought much experience to the role. It was unfortunate that he now found himself with two intractable Archbishops on his hands, who continued the old argument between York and Canterbury that had embittered his relations with the church since the days of Anselm. How much he missed Matilda's soothing diplomacy in those years is not a matter of record, but there must surely have been times when he remembered how she had sweetened Anselm at difficult moments and often made pleasing overtures to foreign emissaries. Her pacifying interventions had saved him endless trouble.

Barely had he time to bury Matilda in Westminster Abbey and make the customary dedications and donations in her name, than another blow fell. One month later, on June 5th, 1118, Robert of Meulan, his closest adviser and friend, the man who had backed him from the first, who had ridden to Winchester with him on the day he proclaimed himself king, Robert Beaumont, Count of Meulan, Earl of Leicester, died at the age of seventy-eight. His death wasn't altogether unexpected as he had been ailing for some time and had retired from court a year earlier. Still, it was another great blow to Henry, already in mourning for his wife. Count Robert of

Meulan was one of those aged warriors who, half a century before, had made up the ranks of aspiring young knights who defeated King Harold at the Battle of Hastings. The fame he earned there never left him. The veterans were a class apart and went on garnering the fruits of their success throughout their lives. William the Conqueror's success was not just a battle won on a particular day; it was conquest in its purest form. That is why the title stuck and why he is the only king of England to have held it. Conquest as total subjection of a population, complete control of the organs of administration, utter suppression of all resistance within a few years. To the winners, the spoils. From that day in October 1066 Meulan's fortune was made because William, for all his manifold faults, knew how to reward his friends. And so, through the reigns of three Norman kings to whom he gave loyal service, Meulan enriched himself, gained an earldom and advanced the name of Beaumont beyond the dreams of those Viking-Norman ancestors who had come in their boats to settle in Northern France over a hundred years before. By the time Meulan died, leaving many sons to follow him, his family was established and Norman rule so entrenched that hardly anyone remembered Harold or the Godwins.

Anselm, Matilda, Meulan, the old faces were passing, new troubles arising. Robert Curthose lived on in confinement, seeming to have taken on the appearance and manner of a monk. Reconciled to his necessary fate, Robert was apparently rising above his misfortune by the effort of daily prayer, wide reading and biblical study. Whether Henry ever came to hear the subsequent rumours that went the rounds about Robert Curthose and his adventures in the Welsh language, we do not know. But at a later date Robert was believed to have learned Welsh, learned it so well, in fact, that he composed a poem in the style of the bards. This may not be fabricated. The right character and mental attitude, together with long days free for the application to study, turned up some surprising prisoner-students in the medieval period. At a much later date, Charles d'Orleans, nephew of Charles VI King of France, who was captured at Agincourt, learned English and took up the study of poetry while a prisoner in the Tower of London. Student princes in prison towers make a curious footnote to history, but whereas definite records exist in the case of Charles d'Orleans, there is no proof that Robert Curthose ever learned Welsh although he was imprisoned for some time in Cardiff Castle.

The fated year of 1118, when Henry was still reeling from the loss of Matilda and Meulan, was also a year of trouble in Normandy, bringing war with the King of France and the Earls of Anjou and Flanders, involving desertions and betrayals and the loss of castles. As a result of these disturbances a vast burden of taxation was imposed on the people.

There must have been moments when Henry, bowed down by troubles, stood for a moment in the embrasure of a window or gazed absently through an open doorway, remembering the past. In those moments he might have caught an imaginary glimpse of Matilda, passing down a corridor, the veil of her coif flying out in the draught as she soft-stepped her way to meet an envoy, to hear a mass or witness a charter. She had always been hurrying somewhere. Remembering how much she had done in her short life he might have felt a pang at her loss. Or perhaps he thought about that other Matilda, their daughter who, as a child, had been called Maud.

To think about his daughter was to think about one of the great policy successes of his reign. As a very young child she had been sent into Germany to learn the manners and languages of the Holy Roman Empire. It was a preparation for the ultimate diplomatic gamble, marriage. At Easter 1110 the gamble had paid off. In the city of Utrecht, little Maud, only eight years old, had been betrothed to Henry V, Holy Roman Emperor. To secure this great prize Henry had to pay, or rather he had to force from his barons and people, the vast amount of between 10,000 and 15,000 pounds of silver for the dowry.

On July 25th of the same year the little girl was crowned Holy Roman Empress at a ceremony in Mainz. Four years later, when she had reached the great age of twelve, she was married off to her Germanic prince. Although early aristocratic marriage was common practice at the time, sending future brides far from their families, throwing them on the mercy of strangers, giving them away as tiny girls to men of middle age, marrying them off into families riven with all the jealousies and rivalries that power and wealth invariably produce, this common practice undoubtedly caused silent and unrecorded misery.

In the light of Maud's subsequent career it is not to overstate the case to say that her heart was crushed very early and pity never found a place in it. In addition to the hardships of her upbringing and youth it seems very likely that we can add the childbearing problems that had afflicted her mother. This is, of course, speculation, but the obstetric history of Maud seems to resemble fairly closely that of her mother. But while her mother had produced one male heir, her brother William Aetheling, Maud had no baby son to show forth to the rejoicing people of the Empire. One chronicler, Hériman of Tournai suggests that the couple had a child who died soon after birth. Was Maud still too young for pregnancy? Did she have the problems with menstruation which seem to have dogged her mother? How many still-births and miscarriages went unreported? It is more than possible that sufferings stifled behind closed doors added to the heartbreak of this young girl's life. Either she would be broken by it or she would overcome. In the style of her Norman ancestors, Maud hardened her nature, survived and fought.

***

With his daughter safely married off and living abroad, Henry's foreign worries narrowed themselves into sharp focus on one relative, his own nephew, William Clito. A young man about the same age as his own son, William Aetheling, Clito was proving himself a thorough nuisance, prowling up and down Normandy, fomenting trouble wherever he could. William Clito bore a grudge and had solid justification for it. Bitterness was his legacy. His mother, the wise and lovely Sybil of Conservano, had died when he was an infant, some chroniclers suggest by poison, others that it was a perinatal death caused by infection. Whatever the case, the child William was effectively orphaned at the age of four. He had been only four years old when his father, Robert Curthose, was taken prisoner at the Battle of Tinchebrai, leaving him trapped with the remnants of his father's henchmen in Falaise, the ducal stronghold that Henry had failed to take the year before. Falaise was the birthplace of William the Conqueror and of symbolic more than strategic importance, but Henry needed possession to seal his dominance. At this point the brothers agreed a pact. The boy William would be released if Curthose would order his men to surrender Falaise. A deal was struck and to their credit both sides kept their word. The boy was freed and from that moment became the focus of plots and rebellion against Henry that would only increase as he grew older.

Initially the child William was put into the care of Hélias de Saint-Saens, Count of Arques, or rather into the care of his female household. There, one hopes, he had something of a kindly upbringing where a four-year old child might have some cheerful smiles and games before the hardness of duty got to work on warping his nature. In 1110, when William was about eight years old, Henry sent agents to demand the boy be released into his custody. Not likely to give up such a prized possession easily, his governors spirited him away to the protection of Robert de Bellême, perhaps the most relentless of all Henry's enemies. Raised in the care of these warlords and nobles, brought up on endless helpings of resentment and loathing, William Clito was fashioned into a model of vengeful animosity and set upon the course of his life.

From then on, seeking allies wherever he could, William Clito dedicated himself to winning back the territory his father had lost at Tinchebrai and wiping out the stain of defeat. The teenage William Clito sought an ally in the French King Louis VI and was involved with the French in the Battle of Brémule in August 1119 against the forces of Uncle Henry. The French were decisively beaten; William Clito barely escaped capture and the rebellion was over. But this was the pattern for the next few years. In October 1119, King Louis tried a legalistic strategy, launching a claim through the *curia*, bringing the dispute to the attention of the Pope with the object of forcing Henry to justify his treatment of the boy. Meanwhile the boy's father was still a prisoner in England, enjoying a rather liberal regime which is probably what Henry would have done with William, if only he could get his hands on him.

In these years, 1106-1118, between Henry's victory at Tinchebrai and the deaths of Matilda and Robert of Meulan, Henry's rule remained strong. The peace of Normandy continued more or less unbroken, save for the skirmishes with King Louis and William Clito which were easily put down and were largely fought in territory beyond the Norman borders. Later the situation changed. There was a shift in the pattern of events, a pattern run through with darker threads. In the next few years Henry was so beset with internal problems and external enemies that his authority over Normandy was seriously weakened. Whether Robert Curthose in his confinement in England heard this news we do not know. Certainly, he would have expected that his son would seek redress and lay claim to the title Duke of Normandy. At first, Henry had not asserted his right over the title, having satisfied himself with seizing the duchy *tout court*. But as his son, William Aetheling, grew older and was recognised as heir to the kingdom of England, Henry also conferred the title of Duke of Normandy on him and tried to force the King of France to recognise it. Naturally, William Clito was enraged. Resentment against his uncle was almost certainly exacerbated by the misfortune of his father which had deprived him of the possibility of filial pride. His father had nothing; his uncle everything. The inequity was stark. Even more infuriating was the ease with which every good thing seemed to come to his cousin, William Aetheling: status, patrimony, titles, pride, while he was left with nothing but shame.

But fate was about to play an inhumanly cruel trick on one of these two young lads who, in better times, might have shared strong ties of cousinship or close bonds of friendship. At a stroke all the long rivalry, begun by the falling-out of their fathers in the previous generation, was ended by catastrophe.

***

It often happens that personal tragedies are preluded by a period of thrilling success, or gratifying achievement, or plain good fortune. The summer of 1120 was such a prelude. It crowned a splendid season of success for William Aetheling, who celebrated his seventeenth birthday that August. He was in Normandy, taking a leading role in the dazzling diplomatic triumph of his father. Henry had engineered something that might well have been the foundation for peace between France and England for a generation. This diplomacy functioned around the formality of making homage. Long honoured in custom, prized by those who received it, resented by those who had to give it, homage was a contentious issue among princes of church and laity alike. Sometime between May and September 1120, Louis VI granted Normandy to William Aetheling who then did homage to him. This spared Henry the embarrassment of having to make homage to a king who was no better than himself. As an equal, Henry could hardly stomach the idea of having to do homage. Palming off the duty onto his son, who by that act was formally and legally recognised as Duke of Normandy, and getting the whole thing staged, sealed, witnessed and recorded, was something of a coup. At 52, Henry still had the energy to be active about his own interests. Always canny and still prudent, he had the gift of conciliation which had so often led to beneficial diplomatic outcomes. If he was missing Robert of Meulan's counsels, he was nonetheless well advised. One chronicler was so impressed by Henry's manifold successes that he called him "the man against whom no-one could prevail except God himself."

It must have seemed to William Clito at this time that he had permanently lost out on his claim to his father's duchy. He was forced to hear the news that William Aetheling, having done homage to Louis, was now receiving homage and oaths from the Norman barony as he toured the regions in a cavalcade of acclamations. All this was merely outward show, of course, Clito was sure that the Aetheling had no real power. Nevertheless, it was a serious blow to his immediate prospects.

After a summer spent in this high-octane atmosphere of recognition, elevation and celebration, the successful duo of father and son was due to return to England that autumn. In the fables of the times, it would be said of this moment that William was riding at the top of the wheel of fortune. Life could hardly be better for a young man of his time. He was rich, healthy, heir to the throne of England and the Dukedom of Normandy; he had a wife, Matilda of Anjou, whom he had married the previous year, in the process securing

Henry a powerful ally; he had good counsellors and was generally popular among the people.

Now the wheel had to turn.

***

Early on the evening of November 25th, 1120, Henry sailed out of Barfleur harbour on his way to a triumphant return to England. A successful round of negotiations had been achieved, he had sealed a gratifying pact with the French King, and he was leaving a peaceful Normandy in his wake. It had taken four years. Four years spent in crafting this peace, four years of unremitting labour. Henry could be excused a great deal of self-satisfaction as he left the harbour lights of Harfleur and headed back to England.

The evening was fair and clear with a southerly breeze and the decision was taken to depart even though it was late in the year for a major channel crossing and there was no moon that night. Henry was confident, crossings often occurred at night; he had in the past crossed many times on moonless nights. On clear nights, pilots could use the Pole Star to navigate the journey, usually of about ten to twelve hours. Henry's ship left port in the early evening and cleared the harbour, leaving William Aetheling and his party to follow later that night.

The chronicler, Orderic Vitalis, tells us about an encounter that Henry had with a man called Thomas the day before his departure. This man, a mariner, approached the king saying that his own father, Stephen, had piloted William the Conqueror across the channel in 1066 and thus he came from a family of long service to the kings of England. Thomas suggested that Henry might like to make the journey in a newly refitted vessel, the White Ship, to be piloted by himself. Declining this offer, Henry suggested that his son, William, and his numerous party who would be departing later the following day, might benefit from a more spacious vessel. If this is true, then this harmless little exchange between the king and the sailor is charged with tragedy.

Many accounts survive of what happened that night and several of them agree, so the main points can be established with some certainty. But it is worth stating that the harbour at Barfleur was notorious as one of the most difficult of the cross-channel ports to navigate. It is tidal with a stream or race (raz) reaching five knots at spring tides, making conditions difficult for ships to enter or leave the harbour. The White Ship was a first-class vessel for its time, 35 metres in length and four metres in the beam, recently refitted to top specifications with capacity for fifty oarsmen and the latest side-rudder design. On the night of 25th November, about three hours after Henry's ship had departed, three hundred people were on board the White Ship awaiting departure. A passenger manifest of this vessel would contain the names of the glitterati of the age, a harvest of titles belonging to the rich and privileged younger generation of Anglo-Norman nobles. That night William Aetheling was travelling with his half siblings, his illegitimate brother Richard and sister Matilda, Countess of Perche, his cousin Richard d'Avranches, Earl of Chester and his wife, Matilda and Richard's half-brother Outher FitzCount, a tutor to William. These were only a few of the hundreds of family members and courtiers on board that night. Ministers and counsellors of the rising generation who had distinguished themselves in the negotiations of the summer were also embarked: Ralph the Red and the two sons of Ivo de Grandesmil were travelling home, hoping to receive rich rewards for their work in the recent successful diplomatic spree. Other important officials of the royal household made up the passenger list: William Bigod, Geoffrey Ridel, Hugh de Moulins, Robert Mauduit, Gisulf the Scribe, and many others. In addition, a number of military men were on board to protect the king's treasure which was guarded in the hold.

A source tells us that before they left the harbour somebody, perhaps a sailor, perhaps one of William's circle, asked permission to drink some of the wine from the casks on board. But it may be that no permission was ever sought, that the casks were broken open and drunk wholesale. It is likely that William took part in the drinking along with his companions. After all, they had much to celebrate; it had been a long slog all summer: negotiating, placating, arguing, occasionally skirmishing; days in the saddle, nights in uncomfortable castles, and now everything was settled. Peace, agreement, homage, oaths. His father and King Louis satisfied, himself acknowledged Duke and heir to the English throne. What more could William desire in the way of glittering prizes? Who could blame him if that night he felt his head bump against the stars as he drifted over the decks in pure exhilaration. His attention wandered, his guard fell, watch was not kept. Drinking got out of hand among the exuberant young noblemen. The rowers and sailors, even the pilot, Thomas, were reputedly drunk. Forced to remain in port until the raz slackened enough for them to put out to sea, the passengers continued to drink. At this point some of them left the ship complaining that the crowd was getting too wild and headstrong. Among them was Stephen, son of Adela of Blois, Henry's favourite nephew, who would much later play a prominent part in the civil war called the Anarchy. It could be said that his luck that night was England's misfortune. There was indeed a presage of misfortune when some monks from the nearby Abbey of Coutances who came to bless the vessel were jeered at and chased away. So, the White Ship never got its blessing.

It was about an hour off midnight when the vessel put out into the harbour heading for the north-east channel where the hazard of hidden rocks could be avoided. The details of what happened at this point are not clear. There may have been some drunken wagering to go faster which disturbed the rhythm of the rowers who, drink-fuelled and anxious to show-off, caused the ship to veer to the north-west and ended by hitting the dangerous Quilleboeuf Rock one nautical mile from Barfleur and half a mile from the shore. Two planks in the starboard bow were shattered but it was only when the sailors tried to push the ship off the rock that it suddenly capsized.

We know from recent tragic experience that an overturned ship, close to port, in shallow seas can prove a death trap to those on board. That night hundreds drowned in the dark waters of the harbour while those on shore could hear their terrified screams. A rescue boat, which was eventually launched, was quickly swamped by the number of frightened people trying to clamber aboard or jump down on to it. Of those in the water, few could swim, and many were pulled down by their thick fleeces and robes of wool which absorb water and quickly grow heavy. At that time of year, the sea temperature was very low, people would have only a short time to try to reach safety. Even if they did not drown, they would die of cold. Seventeen-year-old William and all his young companions died that night. The Bishop of Coutances, whose monks had earlier been chased from the dockside, watched the whole thing from the shore, looking on in horror as the waves closed over the ship that carried his own son, his brother and three of his nephews to their deaths. Meanwhile, Thomas the pilot was clinging to a spar in the water, listening to the cries of drowning people all around him, before he too perished.

A final count reveals a monumental tragedy. In addition to the passengers already named, eighteen noblewomen died, the daughters, sisters, wives of some of the most eminent of the king's companions-in-arms and loyal servants, the men who had travelled with him all summer and helped him reap the rewards of his painstaking diplomacy. Their bodies, carried away by a strong tide were never recovered although some accounts record that divers were sent out to search.

Late the following day, the wreck of the ship was brought ashore, still containing all its cargo including the king's treasure. But that could be of no possible comfort to Henry. There could be no consolation for a king who had lost to the rocks and tides of Barfleur the irreplaceable treasure of his only lawful heir. At a stroke the waters had swept away his work of the summer; the alliances with France and Anjou were severed. It had all come to nothing. Henry had lost his son, but England had lost an heir and, as the people knew only too well, that presaged war.

The historian C. Warren Hollister states that: "The wreck of the White Ship is the most catastrophic maritime disaster of the Middle Ages." If anything, that might be understating the case. A comparison with the Titanic is sometimes made but the White Ship passenger list constitutes a much greater proportion of the nobility, the great magnates, the heirs to powerful ruling houses, in essence the 'investment' of one generation in the next, so that the loss amounts to a fatal wound in the body politic. A wound so wide it opened the way to the horror of the Anarchy which plunged a reduced and inadequate generation into wasteful, unnecessary and prolonged war. When the White Ship foundered, the waves closed over Henry's hopes for peace. Everything changed as the backwash from that horrific wreck rippled out into Henry's policy and personal life for years to come.

***

Henry reached England in complete ignorance that he no longer had a son. By all accounts the crossing was trouble free, and he arrived in excellent spirits, still aglow from a triumphant summer of diplomacy. Observing this, those who heard the news first were the last who wanted to bring it to him. No-one dared tell him. But the news spread through the court in a miasma of grief. So many families were affected by the loss that their lamentation became impossible to keep from the king. Orderic Vitalis tells us that a certain Count Theobald, who had accompanied Henry on his return to England, staged a little scene to avoid having to tell him directly. Theobald engaged a young lad to throw himself at the king's feet and tell him of the catastrophe. Whether true or not, it adds a suitable touch of drama to a cruel and unenviable task. It is said, too, that when he heard the news, Henry threw himself on the ground and wept inconsolably. Wept for the stolen future of his promising young heir, wept for his natural son, Richard, for his natural daughter, Matilda, for all their companions, for the three hundred souls, for the collapse of his peace plans, for the future of the kingdom, for his own old age. Henry had much to lament in this cruel and capricious trick of fortune. Against him, in mockery of all his triumphs, God had prevailed.

In the midst of all this misery, there was one person who probably received the news as a sure sign of God's beneficence. At a stroke, William Clito's fortune turned from defeat to the prospect of success. Overnight he had become the most plausible heir to the Norman Dukedom, possibly also to the English throne, both of which, he felt, the Aetheling had stolen from him during the course of the summer. All that oath-swearing and homage-pledging had been reduced to little more than gratuitous bravura, swept away by the icy tides of Barfleur. Diplomacy could turn on a nailhead, and often did. Now everything had to be reshaped, adjustments made, new circumstances encountered and mastered. We do not know how William Clito heard the news, or what his reaction was, but he almost certainly experienced a kind of bitter gratification. Bitterness was the one part of his inheritance that never failed him. Revenge and resentment had been fanned to leaping fires since childhood. Unfortunately, none of this made him a good strategist or leader of men. In fact, William Clito was used by others as a figurehead for rebellion throughout his life. He may have become deluded into thinking he was followed for his qualities of leadership or the popularity of his cause, but he was almost always used by other, more powerful, more canny, magnates in gaining their own ends. Sometimes though, vested interests came together in a shrewd agreement of mutual gains, as they did when the fault lines of the Norman peace cracked apart after Barfleur.

The first shift happened at the fringes, but William Clito was ready to take advantage. Count Fulk V of Anjou, who had married off his daughter, Matilda, to William Aetheling in 1119, now had her back on his hands as a dependent. Worse, he had handed over several castles in Maine as Matilda's dowry and wanted them back. Fulk petitioned Henry to return them. Henry promptly refused. At this point, Fulk, in collaboration with the aggressive malcontent, Amaury, Count of Evreux, saw a chance to repudiate their pledges and weaken Henry. They combined to persuade William Clito to marry Fulk's other daughter, Sibylla. She would bring with her the significant dowry of Maine, a buffer county between Anjou and Normandy. Eager to fall in with any plan that might damage his uncle, Clito agreed and married Sibylla in 1123.

But an even more important marriage had taken place two years before. On the death of his son, with almost unseemly haste, as if hellbent on replacing the loss, Henry, at the age of fifty-two, in a frantic move to get another heir, remarried.

***

Adeliza of Louvain, daughter of Godfrey I, Count of Louvain, enters England at the age of eighteen to marry a man thirty-five years her senior with the sole purpose of providing him with an heir. This lady is little more than a name in the archive, a shadow on water, an unknown person traded between states for the fruit of her womb which, disappointingly, failed to produce an heir. We know little about her but, in an obscure and indirect way, she was to play a part in the establishment of one of the greatest noble houses in English history.

It seems she and Henry were compatible, they spent most of their marriage together although she played little part in politics. At court she promoted a taste for French poetry and the arts. Other than the usual attributes of beauty, piety and charity, she is little more than an attractive surface. Adeliza and her King married at Windsor on January 29th, 1121, barely three months after the White Ship went down. When, years later, Adeliza was left a widow on the death of Henry, she gifted the manor of Petworth to her brother, Jocelin of Louvain. When he later married an heiress of the Percy family and took the name Percy, he became one of the founding sires of the Earls of Northumberland, the battling Percys, the lords of the north. From their seat at Alnwick Castle, these fiercesome Catholics were to play a key role in political and religious history for centuries. So perhaps it may be said that Adeliza's legacy was a little more than just being Henry's second wife.

During the next two years, Henry remained in England, perhaps paying attention to his new wife in the thwarted hope of getting an heir. Meanwhile the situation in Normandy was deteriorating steadily as he failed to keep his royal officials in check. Their high-handed methods, malpractices and injustices were whipping up feeling, especially in the important county of Evreux where Count Amaury de Montfort was losing patience. Accustomed to a free hand in his own domains, some of which lay across the Norman border, and deeply resenting the hustle of Henry's punctilious administrators, in 1123 his frustration broke into open rebellion. One of the cruellest pieces of news that would come to Henry in the wake of this rebellion was that the son of his old friend, Robert of Meulan, had thrown in his lot with them. Waleran, Count of Meulan, elder twin son of the great count, joined the conspiracy against Henry which grew into a formidable force, gaining cohesion through the marriage links that bound so many of these top-ranking Norman families together. Another distinction about these families was that while holding no lands in England they held extensive lands across the Norman border, making them effectively not Anglo-Norman lords but Franco-Norman lords whose allegiance would sit more comfortably with Louis rather than with Henry. These were the plotters who in September 1123 united in a general conspiracy to make war on Henry from strongholds in Evreux. At the same time William Clito, supported by the Angevin forces of his father-in-law, began attacking Henry from the south. Surely, they thought, now was the time to inflict final blows on the aging Henry, a man bowed down by misfortune. His son dead, the son of his best friend a traitor, his own nephew sworn to destroy him, a young wife unable to produce an heir, and now rebellion in his homeland. How many blows could the old man take?

***

What happened in Normandy in these years was a terrible foretaste of what the Anarchy would do to England after Henry's death: depopulation, besieged castles, burned towns, people impoverished, crops trampled and fired, livestock loosed or rustled, homesteads destroyed, abbeys pillaged, slaughter, mayhem. As the princes and nobles fought, the people despaired. In the past, Henry's rule had brought them a measure of safety through laws and the settling of disputes in courts. Famines had occurred from time to time, largely through caprices of the weather, not through unbridled destruction by armed thugs, mercenaries, landless knights and, as always in their wake, bandits and thieves. Riches that the townspeople had buried for safekeeping were dug up by these scavengers: gold coins, silver cups, rich garments. Householders were murdered for a ring or a silver trinket. Once again, as their fathers had done in the days of Robert Curthose, people stashed their valuables in churches: trade tools, ploughshares, copper vessels, cooking pots, jamming them in the nave up to the altar itself, leaving scarcely room to pray for God's mercy. The winter of 1124 was particularly dreadful in England and Normandy alike. Bad weather blighted winter crops, people starved or stole. Inflation rendered food staples almost too expensive to buy; a pound's worth of coins would buy only a shilling's worth of bread. Coinage was debased. And in the midst of this miserable wretchedness, taxes remained high to pay for the wars.

As Henry's world continued to unravel in the wake of his son's death, he had two pieces of good luck. Or perhaps not so much luck as good tactics, astute and bold. The first was a successful military engagement in March 1124 when Henry defeated the forces of the combined rebellious bloc of Norman barons who were supporting William Clito. This was the Battle of Bourgthéroulde. Most effective in this success was the tactic of distracting Louis to keep him out of the action. Henry got his son-in-law, Emperor Henry V, to threaten Louis and keep him occupied. The second tactic was to strike at his nephew by undoing the marriage that had brought him Matilda of Anjou and the county of Maine. Henry appealed to canon law and, with the help of hefty bribes, got the Pope to annul the marriage on the grounds of consanguinity. The result was that the backing of Count Fulk and all his supporters melted away from Clito.

Successes for Henry were setbacks for his nephew. But, in spite of them, William Clito continued making trouble and even found a new impetus through his second marriage, engineered by Louis VI who made great efforts to further his cause, seeing him as a useful pawn he could manipulate and control, someone who did not possess power in reality but only the image of it. Clito's new bride was Jeanne de Monferrat. Monferrat was a tiny north Italian appendage of the Holy Roman Empire. The gain seemed marginal, but Jeanne was in fact a relative of Louis VI who gifted Clito with the lordship of the French Vexin. More encouragement, more nudge and shove to get Clito into the field as a useful instrument in King Louis' advancement of French interests. Sure enough, soon after this, Clito led an attack on Henry's castle at Gisors from where he issued a formal claim to Normandy. Relations between England and Normandy now descended into a remorseless round of attack and counterattack.

But it wasn't Normandy or England that did for Clito in the end. It was Flanders.

***

On 2nd March 1127, the forty-three-year-old Charles, Count of Flanders was attending mass at the church of St Donatian in Bruges. According to the chroniclers, a group of armed knights entered the church and struck him down as he knelt in prayer before the altar. A scene so evocative of the murder of Thomas Becket in Canterbury Cathedral fifty years later, invites doubt or at least interrogation. Such scenes may be from stock scenarios belonging to the Christian playbook of horror. Almost nothing could be so wicked as to slay a man at prayer in a church. Nevertheless, Charles was killed, and this was the story put about. The resulting horror and repulsion at the deed rippled out from the church into the streets where mobs began burning, looting and protesting. The shock was profound. Charles had been known as Charles the Good, he was in the prime of life, popular, generous, just. The people went wild at his loss. Rioting turned to insurrection and, in the general lawlessness of the situation, competing candidates plunged Flanders into war. Who should appear in the midst of this eruption but Louis VI who happened to enjoy the status of overlord of the murdered count. It took him only a week to arrive in Arras in the south of the county and to set about subduing the violence and selecting a new count. There was only one possible candidate as far as Louis was concerned. William Clito.

The chronicles say the lords chose Clito "on Louis's advice and command" but one may be sure that more than moral pressure was exerted to secure the prize for Clito. Once again falling in with French plans, Clito was installed as Count of Flanders in May 1127. Did Robert Curthose, in whatever prison he was then residing, hear the news and rejoice for his son? Almost at once Clito granted privileges to the leading burghers of his new territory. Arras, St-Omer, Bruges, Ypres, Ghent. These towns were industrially active. Property mattered to these people. War threatened serious disruption to their manufactories, their guilds, their trade and commerce where goods flowed and money was made. Flanders wanted strong protections and an end to war. The burghers thought that, by pulling together a renewed league of French, Flemish and Angevin interests, they would protect their trade and bring peace. William Clito's long-term aim was to secure Flanders as a wealthy base from which to launch a challenge against Henry in Normandy.

***

When Henry, at his Easter court at Woodstock, heard the news of Clito's elevation he is reported to have been "much distressed." As well he might be. Was this cursed nephew never to leave off making his life a misery? But Henry must have quickly got over his distress because he was soon acting to keep his enemies off balance. Secretly, he sent money to various disappointed claimants to the comital title, backing them and placing himself nominally at their head until he could work out which one would prove the best investment. He imposed a trade embargo on the export of English wool to Flanders, in the hope that, by damaging their highly profitable textile industry, he could incite a backlash against Clito within the cloth towns. Through the autumn of 1127 Henry fanned hostility, first in Bruges, then Lille, Saint-Omer, Ghent and Ypres, spreading discontent and impoverishment among the previously rich and satisfied burghers. Steadily Flanders was building towards a state of general rebellion and the person blamed for the catastrophe was William Clito.

Around this time, another candidate was emerging, twenty-eight-year-old Thierry of Alsace, a contemporary of William Clito but a more competent leader of men. Thierry was a campaigner who astutely promised the cloth-merchants and burghers of the wool towns whatever they wanted to hear. Touting these promises, he then embarked on a publicity tour, travelling through the towns in a procession of well-wishing: Saint-Omer in February 1128, Ghent and Bruges in March, Lille in May. Thierry was winning accolades not just from the merchant class but from the labourers and peasants. The latter were inclined to favour him because he was the first cousin of Charles the Good and grandson of Robert I of Flanders, which gave him blood-kin entitlement to the county. Moreover, he promised generous terms to the townspeople. In this way Thierry's campaign was sucking support from Clito who, in turn, begged help from Louis VI of France.

In a sudden and aggressive response, like someone stamping on an anthill, Henry made an attack against the Ile de France, forcing Louis to drop his plans to help his protégé and instead hasten back to defend the centre of his kingdom.

But Clito continued the fight, this time with uncharacteristic grit and determination. Perhaps he was not fighting for revenge anymore, perhaps now it had become a matter of survival.

William Clito always felt that he had been cheated by life. He was the son of the eldest son of the Conqueror, he came from illustrious stock, yet he had been forced to scrape and beg all his life. Since the age of four, when he had been released from the castle at Falaise and put into the care of strangers, he had fought to be noticed. Love, attention, trust were blessings rarely encountered. Apart from Hélias de Saint-Saens, who is mentioned several times in the chronicles and was present in his early and adult years, we can detect no stable figure, no close or enduring relationship in his life. Most likely, he had gone through life wrong-footed by this early disaster, full of anger, resentment, bile, never flowering into his full nature which, ironically, might have borne more resemblance to his estranged uncle than to his imprisoned father. Twice married in loveless matches to girls as ill-prepared as himself, without producing a single child, he was now twenty-five years old and felt he had achieved nothing. His father was still a prisoner, he was still fighting for his patrimony. He had thought that the White Ship disaster had opened the way for him to seize Normandy. In reality, it changed nothing. Now, five years later, he was fighting for his survival in Flanders, making war on townsfolk whose obvious preference was for his rival, Thierry of Alsace. Yet he fought on, determined to change his fate, obsessed with restoring his stolen inheritance. As though recognising a fresh impetus in Clito's actions, the chroniclers agree that, around this time, he began to show the prowess that had often been lacking in earlier campaigns.

He may have been heartened by the news that his cousin Maud was no longer Holy Roman Empress. Her husband Henry had died in May 1125. Their long and steady political partnership had been astute, but she was now cast in the role of brave and steely widow. Maud was in her thirties and had no children. Looked at from Clito's point of view, immense possibilities had just opened up. Henry had no legitimate heir and no grandsons. It was not impossible that Clito dreamed of a far bigger prize than Flanders or even Normandy. On the horizon gleamed the throne of England. Henry may have seen the same vision as a nightmare and acted quickly to forestall any possibility of Clito's succession by marrying off Maud, in June 1128, this time to the fifteen-year-old Geoffrey of Anjou, called 'le Bel', a notoriously handsome and choleric youth. It was a grotesque *mésalliance* for a woman with fifteen years' political experience at the heart of the most powerful court in Europe. The aim of this marriage was twofold: to provide Henry with grandsons and to forestall Clito's ambitions by bringing Anjou within Henry's control. Nevertheless, William Clito, bent on making Flanders the first step to future greatness, went ahead with his war plans. Towards the end of July 1128, he was at Aalst, a castle between Ghent and Brussels and a stronghold of Thierry, occupying an important strategic point at the place where the road from Bruges to Cologne crosses the River Dender. Although within the Holy Roman Empire, it was considered the capital of the county of Flanders. If Clito could seize this stronghold he might well make good his claim.

What happened next is not fully known. Chroniclers tend to take partisan views and give versions according to which side of the dispute they, or their patrons, were on. But it appears that in the afternoon of that day Clito was leading an assault on the western wall. When battle was engaged a spray of arrows was fired from the bastion to hit randomly wherever they could find a target. Looking up in response to the surprise volley, the attackers were dazzled by sunlight which bathed the top, but not the bottom, of the wall. Out of that light an arrow found its way towards Clito. That is one possibility. But however, it occurred, chroniclers agree that Clito sustained an injury and was taken from the field, leaving his loyal Hélias de Saint-Saens to carry on the fight. At first, the wound seemed light, and he was treated by a physician and told to rest. Later, however, it became apparent that the wound had become infected. The recorded symptoms lead some to believe he contracted septicaemia. During the next few days he steadily declined into fever and vomiting, becoming feverish and weak. But those few days he used wisely. Calling for a scribe, he dictated letters: to his wife, to his father, but most importantly to his uncle. He sent for a priest and took confession. A short time later he was dead. At first, news of his death was kept quiet while Hélias de Saint-Saens and his forces continued to battle for Aalst. But it was hopeless. In the end they negotiated with Thierry's castellan, informed him of the death and showed him the body. Acting generously on behalf of his master, the castellan arranged for the body to be taken under escort to the Abbey of Saint Bertin in Saint-Omer. In this Benedictine monastery William Clito was posthumously enrolled as a monk and buried in a simple ceremony.

Unlike his cousin, William Aetheling, who had died in a sudden catastrophe without time for preparation, taken off in the midst of high spirits and celebration with all his sins on him, William Clito lay in pain for several days and saw death coming. He had time to prepare, to make confession, to settle his account with God. Perhaps this is when he took the decision to request his Benedictine burial, just as he tried to settle his worldly affairs through the letters he dictated up to the end. Hours of looking back over the past as the infection steadily advanced, reflecting on his life of hatred, anger, revenge, in which the image of his imprisoned father never left him, may have brought him to a new understanding. Never, in all the battles he had fought, had he really believed he would be killed. He had not confronted death. He came from a long-lived family, his grandfather had been 63 when he died in circumstances similar to his own: battle, injury, infection. His own father was still alive, his uncle, William Rufus had died young but as the result of an accident not warfare. His uncle, Henry, well into his fifties, had hardly taken an injury in his life and was still active in battle. Long life had seemed written into his inheritance. But his inheritance had eluded him. The name 'Clito' had been a mockery, a hollow sham, for he was neither 'worthy' nor 'princely'. His life, like his father's, had been far from lucky or blessed, as this wretched ending now proved. A bitter laugh, a bitter tear and he would be gone. Having ensured that the letters were sealed and having given orders for their delivery, William, son of Robert, closed his eyes and died.

***

Who carried the news to Henry or how long it took to reach him we do not know. Eight years before, in 1120, the news of a young man's death had been brought to him with fear and lamentation. We can only assume that the news of the sudden death of another young man was brought to him with very different feelings and generated a very different response. However, royal custom forbad public rejoicing over the death of an enemy, whilst family decency and Christian teaching would condemn unseemly glee. But however he expressed it, Henry must have experienced relief at the death of his nephew, for now his diplomatic troubles were virtually at an end. The peace of his cross-channel dominions was, for a time, assured. William Clito had presented the only viable alternative to his rule and to his plans for the succession. A great obstacle that had been standing across his path for the last ten years had finally been removed. At Henry's court there was relief without exultation, decorum was preserved, prayers and masses were paid for, and the proper observances kept. But without doubt the immediate threat was gone and the future looked brighter. In the letters that had been brought to him, Henry found that his nephew had written a petition asking forgiveness for the wrongs he had committed, phrased in the proper terms of penitence. As only to be expected, Clito begged continuing mercy for his father, and asked Henry to pardon all those who had supported him in the past, if they would take new oaths to Henry. In the end even Henry had to admit that William Clito faced his death as a proper Christian warrior and knight. One can only hope that Robert Curthose, the most pious of all the Conqueror's sons, received that mitigating detail when he got the news that his only son was dead.

Robert Curthose lived on for another six years, sustained, one assumes, by his monk-like devotional habits, dying in 1134. Henry outlived all his brothers, his closest friend, his wife, his nephew and his sole legitimate son. Personal sadness dogged his later years. He was permanently troubled by the question of the succession. Illegitimate sons were out of the question because the church would not sanction them, so his beloved eldest, Robert, Earl of Gloucester, probably the most qualified of all the aspirants, was out of the running. Maud could inherit, but not rule. Henry needed legitimate grandsons, but the marriage of Maud and her debonair young husband was on the rocks and after the first few months they lived apart. In 1131 a desperate Henry brokered a peace and virtually forced them to live together. Apparently, they did their duty because, in 1133, Henry's first grandson was born, followed in 1134 by a second. Two legitimate heirs at last; but they were so young, and he was so old. As a footnote to Maud's obstetric history, these births were difficult and the second nearly killed her. She was very ill, perhaps with puerperal fever, and her strangely fortunate and miserable life seemed about to end; she even planned her tomb. But, in the tradition of her forbears, she rallied, survived and fought. From then on fate propelled her inexorably towards the years of the Anarchy. She fought for her father's throne and, in doing so, prolonged a bitter and relentless war which plunged a country habituated to peace into horrendous suffering. Perhaps the Anarchy became inevitable when Henry tried to make powerful warlords swear allegiance to a woman simply because she was his daughter. Such oaths were never likely to hold. It was a policy doomed to failure.

In November 1135, while at Lyons-la-Forêt not far from Rouen, where he had gone late in the season to hunt, Henry was taken ill. It was sudden and untreatable. He was sixty-seven years old and exhausted. When he died on the night of December 1st, Maud was not at his bedside, his only legitimate son had long been a ghost, his two grandsons were babies. Perhaps even as he lay in his final sweat he could see the Anarchy coming. A hideous vision of sustained warfare in a lawless land; bloodshed, famine, devastation. He knew, because it was known since the days of the earliest kings, that the best legacy a king can leave his kingdom is a clear line of succession. In that one particular, he failed. Years of warfare between Maud and her cousin, Stephen, the White Ship survivor, the son of Henry's sister Adela, Countess of Blois, would follow his death. This was the Anarchy, the time when the chroniclers said: 'God and his angels slept.'

But Henry is unique among medieval monarchs in maintaining peace in England for almost three decades. While Normandy was plunged into frequent warfare between competing baronial powers, in which the countryside was impoverished and the churches plundered, England enjoyed a period of peace. Ironically, it was the Norman descendants of the conquerors who brought thirty years of peace to England while their own homeland was devastated by war.

Henry was written up by many chroniclers with very favourable notices. William of Malmesbury noted his diplomatic skills: "He would rather contend by counsels than with the sword...." He was a shrewd investor in other men's characters, spotting talent, knowing how to use the best qualities of people, knowing when to forgive old offences, how to cultivate longstanding ties while promoting new ones. He knew when to maintain strict justice or inflict punishment. He was wiser than his brother William Rufus, more adroit than Robert, and certainly luckier than both. Unlike Rufus he never sought to extend his father's territories, only to safeguard frontiers already established. He had visions of a more just rule, better law, a system of justice, he valued the attainment of objectives through negotiation. For a short time, he had shared something good with Archbishop Anselm, when they had both seen a vision of church and monarch working together for the peace of the church and the betterment of the realm. Even the Anglo-Saxon Chronicle tersely acknowledged: "He was a good man and was held in great awe."

He had great tragedies in his life, supremely, the foundering of the White Ship, but he was never swamped by events. He was astute, intelligent, and if not always wise most often wisely counselled. He wanted justice for the people and limits on the power of the warlords; he wanted to preside over a peaceful and prosperous land. That he didn't wholly achieve these things is hardly a matter of reproach. Henry was, in the phrase of the chronicler Orderic Vitalis, who had written so critically of his father, "the greatest of kings."

When Henry died, he left behind him the twin glories of good government: peace and a full treasury. Within a very short time, both were gone, squandered in the war for the throne. The cousins' tragedy was perhaps not so much their early deaths and unfulfilled lives, but that the smooth succession of either one of them after Henry's death might have spared England the howling years of the Anarchy.

Chapter Nine
Unfortunate Life and Death of Robert Curthose

You might think that the eldest son of one of the most renowned figures in English history, the only man who ever held the title Conqueror, would be singularly blessed in his life. Having all the appurtenances of success, privilege, prestige; having his advancement through life smoothed by an attentive father who wished to endow him with the character and education necessary to his high duties; being nurtured from the first to discharge his duties as a strong ruler and just judge of men, you might think his life would be most fortunate. Before giving reasons why it wasn't, I need to state the obvious: these things are relative. Compared with a peasant living at these times, Robert Curthose was indeed lucky. That said, one can strongly argue that compared with his brothers, William and Henry, he was unlucky in that he never gained what he most wanted. William and Henry wanted a throne, a crown, power, the trappings through which they could emulate their father. And these they got. Robert wanted those things too, but above all he wanted the thing he could never have: the good opinion of his father.

The amount of damage that can be done very early in a child's life and have ongoing repercussions well into adulthood is now commonly understood. It was already partly understood in the 19th century when children as young as seven were routinely farmed out or sent off to boarding school where they might be ill-treated or beaten. Parents themselves might beat small children for small infringements. Even then many spoke out against such practices. The treatment of children has been debated since ancient times, became a focus of debate in the Enlightenment and remains a burning issue today. But the profound psychological damage of ill-treatment has not always been readily grasped. One assumes a common human nature in the love of offspring down through the ages but now and again it seems that nature gets out of sync with custom. Medieval custom among the nobility, was to pay minimal attention to one's children other than supplying for their upkeep and arranging a suitable education. Infants were put out to nurse; wet nurses were common among the aristocracy. Poor families might struggle to bring up children at all in the face of famine and disease. Child neglect was rampant. But what Robert Curthose suffered at his father's hands was different. If we read between the lines of some more respectful accounts, he received treatment that would, at the very least, cause a dangerous loss of self-esteem. For a young man of the warrior class, that might be disastrous.

We need to think about his name. Robert, of course, we understand. Robert was his grandfather's name, a previous Duke of Normandy to which title he, as eldest son, was expected to succeed. But Curthose? This is an insult, a wounding boorish, piece of name-calling. It is one of those cutting names that can easily crush the spirits of young people, that undermine their self-worth and go on hurting throughout their lives. The name sticks and can't be washed off. For Robert it has stuck for nine hundred years.

Who is to say that identity issues weren't important in those days? Either one's nature is made, or one has to make it. Psychologists tell us now that all the early experiences of life go to make up a character, they are the shaping and forming forces. From the experiences of life a character is forged or revealed or both. A child's concept of himself is based on what the most important people in his life think of him. From a very early age self-confidence can be encouraged or crushed. Modern studies are eager to tell us that the shape of one's personality and the direction of life are laid down in the first formative years of childhood. If this is true how long has it been true? Was it true of children in the eleventh century? Certainly, there is something in the life of Robert Curthose that suggests such may indeed be the case.

The insult of 'Curthose' is profound. The word derives from the Norman French 'courtheuse' meaning 'short-stocking'. Other insults included, 'brevis-ochrea' a Latin tag meaning short boot: 'gambaron', from the French for 'leg'. Robert suffered all his life from this cruel mockery invented by his father, taken up by his brothers, whispered around by the courtiers. Always, always, the lack of height was the centre of his suffering, the first and last essential of Robert's life. He is defined by the thing he cannot help. His observed laziness and weakness of character may have had its inception here, in the stultifying paralysis of the child who isn't allowed to flourish. His father actually encouraged his brothers, whose subsequent histories might suggest they were more naturally inclined to dominate, to insult and abuse him. One can imagine a sensitive nature shrivelling up, never fully to open. Though by all accounts a favourite of Matilda his mother, it was to his father that he looked for the image of himself. All he saw coming back at him was a sneer and a jest, and there began his earliest misfortune.

It is often the case that first-born sons are preferred by dominant fathers as the first human being that closely resembles the magnified patriarchal self. They want a first-born to reflect their own sense of themselves, a surface from which the returning image shines back to the satisfied glance. Robert's singular tragedy was that he did not shine and did not satisfy his father's self-image. Neither at the first nor later. Besides, he was soon followed by three more sons, all of whom seem to have satisfied their father's insatiable ego more than he did. In his case, being first-born was in fact a handicap; it granted him no privileges, won him no favours and put him in the situation of being constantly outdone by his brothers. The contention and ill-feeling arising in the very early days of family life laid down a pattern that was only exacerbated in later years.

Within a short time, Richard was born, followed by a number of daughters before the namesake, William, and a few years later the youngest son, Henry. As he grew up, Robert felt that all the other children were valued more than himself. This may have been a perception only, deriving from the insecurity of the family or external factors such as the constant changes in the household. The long absences of his father were not a hardship for Robert, in fact he looked forward to them. But he also looked forward to the time when he would be called on to travel abroad with his father or ride with him in battle. When he was absent, he longed for him to return; when he returned, he found his joy turned very quickly into sour feelings of humiliation and resentment. According to all the accounts, Robert was loved by his mother, Matilda, and developed a good relationship with her. We have evidence from several chroniclers that later in life she risked her husband's displeasure by supporting her son in an insurrection against his father. Thus, we have proof that Robert and his father drew so far apart that they actually entered a state of war one against the other.

**

  The breakdown in relations that led to open conflict may have begun in the destruction of Robert's self-esteem when he was very young. But surely the odd, jokey remark or name-calling cannot have caused a lifetime of damage? Unfortunately, what assailed him was something much worse, a systematic campaign of cruel and boorish insults. The mere fact that they came from his father was bad enough but, as Robert's brothers grew older, they were encouraged in this petty habit of sniding at their sibling. The chroniclers agree that there was something of a campaign of abuse going on which, on at least one recorded occasion, overran the physical boundary between name-calling and assault.

  Several chroniclers record an incident that happened in Normandy in 1077. Then aged about eleven and nine respectively, the brothers William and Henry played a prank on the adult Robert by dumping a full chamber pot over his head. At which, Robert, in a rage and urged on by his companions, started a brawl with his brothers that only ended when their father intervened. It sounds like a saloon fight from a Western, or the kind of stagey incident common in the indecorous plays of Plautus. It's a scene from a thousand dysfunctional family sagas. It is not impossible that this story, far from being the account of an actual incident is simply a graphic metaphor for the state of the family's relationships. Robert felt that his dignity had been wounded and was further outraged when his father failed to punish his brothers. The next day, we are told, Robert began an insurrection against his father by attacking the castle of Rouen. This story might be a rather weak explanation of the cause of the revolt; it might also be an insight into the kind of treatment that, perpetrated over a long period without respite, was actually driving Robert to despair; it might simply be an allegory revealing the unhealthy state of family relations.

***

In order to grasp Robert's situation, we need to look at his brothers. Richard, the second born, was only about sixteen years old when, in 1070, he was killed in a hunting accident in particularly gruesome circumstances. In hot pursuit of his game, riding at a furious pace, he caught his neck in an overhanging branch and was garrotted. It was sudden and unsurvivable. He was not the first of his family to die in a hunting accident, nor would he be the last. We know very little about him and cannot establish his relationship either to his father or to his brothers. William, the next brother steps forth into the full glare of historical chronicles, under the title 'Rufus' which has stayed with him as long as 'Curthose' stayed with Robert. But 'Rufus' was very common, a nickname so widely used that it is almost meaningless. We don't know how many bearers of this name had red hair, or flaring tempers, or burning natures or flamboyant habits. It is possible that what we have here are two different types of name-calling; a general, impersonal widespread use of a common epithet with very little personal evocation, such as Rufus, and a personal, uncommon epithet growing from attribution and affixed by constant usage. 'Curthose' belongs most clearly to the second category. As far as we know, Henry, the youngest son, had no defining nickname in his early years though in later life he was sometimes called 'Beau-Clerc', drawing attention to his recognised literacy, which may in part have been derogatory but not deliberately cruel. It is clear that neither Henry nor William suffered, from a young age, the same dismantling of self-esteem through mockery and ridicule as Robert.

In addition, Robert bore the full brunt of his father's ambitions. That is to say, during the whole period of his childhood, until the age of ten or twelve, his father was engaged in the subjugation of Normandy, fighting constant battles, often surrounded by enemies, staking his prowess against France or Maine or Anjou as they contested his right to the control of Normandy. Fierce, blunt, remorseless, absent, William was never going to be the best of fathers. It took William a decade to win the struggle and secure the dukedom of Normandy. These years coincided with the formative years of Robert's life.

Born after these fighting years, when their father was asserting his authority in more secure circumstances, both William and Henry experienced a less fraught childhood and were not regularly subjected to the cruel jests or bitter remarks of their father. As earlier chapters recount, both achieved the throne of England and, at one time or another, the control of the duchy of Normandy. Robert did neither.

But that is not to say that William and Henry had an untroubled relationship with their father. It is easier to believe that the 'Conqueror' was a gigantic figure who threatened all his sons with diminishment. He took the prize in every field: in conquest, warfare, government, virility, rule, leaving them almost no zone in which to excel. They all suffered from his dominating presence when he was alive and his colossal absence when he was dead. He left them a legacy of constant feuding because he would not be clear and precise about his wishes for the inheritance. That feuding, that habitual distrust, may have been established early in their lives. Certainly, the perpetual name-calling of young Robert did not conduce to the establishment of friendly relations or life-long brotherly affection.

Something that comes up frequently in the chronicles about William Rufus is that he had a sense of humour. He could be flippant, ironic, stinging and had a penchant for confronting serious moments with an inappropriate jest. One of the reasons he upset ecclesiastical opinion so regularly was because he would joke about sacred things. His favourite oath has a be-damned-to-you kind of ring to it: 'Holy Face of Lucca!' The Holy Face of Lucca belonged to the statue of Christ in the church of St Martin in Lucca, Italy. It was said to have been carved from the face of the living Christ by angels. It was immensely holy, an object of awe and reverence. In using this oath, it seems that William was intentionally breaking boundaries, crossing the lines of convention in a deliberately provocative way. Whether the use of this oath was a way to hit out at his father's hypocrisy, or at his tutors, or whether he wanted deliberately to offend or show what good company he was, we cannot know. But the use of the oath and many of his jests were recorded so frequently that we have to assume that satire, insult and offhand offence were part of his social armoury. Little encouragement would be needed to turn this 'humour' on his brother. Unlike Robert, William and Henry were not subjected to personal insult and ridicule and there were times when the relationship between them was almost good, though all three were sensitive to the unmatchable challenge of their father's reputation. But William and Henry were treated preferentially by their father, and this shows most clearly in the contrasting records of the important rite of passage known as the 'conferment of knighthood.'

In fact, there is some mystery over whether Robert was ever knighted. As heir he most certainly should have been, but no chronicler records it. The symbolism of the dubbing ceremony can hardly be overstated, it was a rite of passage for every young nobleman who aspired to the knightly ranks of the chivalric class. It involved oath-giving to an overlord, promises of a binding duty and it had a spiritual aspect concerning the transformation of the individual to a higher state of being. What would later become the 'knightly code' was probably already in formation.

In contrast to Robert, the knighthood ceremonies of both his brothers are recorded. William was knighted by the famous Archbishop Lanfranc, who had been his tutor, probably around 1076 just at the time when the relationship between Robert and his father was reaching breaking point.

One is inclined to ask: was this another deliberate snub for Robert?

Many chroniclers agree that Henry was knighted by his father in an even more prestigious ceremony at Westminster at Pentecost in 1086. This seems like a deliberate statement of favouritism, almost as if William is singling out Henry as his chosen heir. And although Robert did get an 'acknowledgement' as heir to Normandy before 1066, it was never confirmed. William did not bequeath either the throne of England or the duchy of Normandy in clear and unequivocal terms, almost as if he was willing his sons to fight for them. Which is what they did.

***

Historians tend to state, unequivocally, that Robert was a man of 'more than conventional piety'. Brought up in the faith, like all his siblings, and being taught by men of the church as well as a tutor, Hilger, until he was 'of age', probably about 16 or 17, he would have attended mass on Feast days and have many occasions to converse with ecclesiastics among whose higher ranks were members of noble households. His own Uncle Odo was Bishop of Bayeux, although in Odo's case we may consider his position a mercenary *quid pro quo*, rather than a sublime calling. Not all occupants of high church posts were spiritually qualified. Someone like Lanfranc, however, with whom his father had a long and close connection both in matters spiritual and lay, was a leading monk and a wise and dedicated churchman. He would have been well known to Robert and was probably his tutor at one time or another. In matters spiritual we can more or less establish what Robert had in common with his siblings and contemporaries. But how was he different, why is his piety called 'more than conventional'?

It is not impossible that there was some compensatory mechanism at work. Robert's nature, starved of parental notice, sought blessing from another kind of father. Perhaps there was consolation in prayer to a God who, he was taught, loved everybody even though he judged them harshly. God was a father who rebuked but did not scorn. When Robert became a pilgrim warrior later in life, setting off to liberate Jerusalem and win back the Holy Sepulchre, we cannot know whether his reasons for engagement were deeply grounded in religious need, or whether he was drawn by the chance for military glory. But as we look at Robert's later life there is strong evidence to suggest that he was the most conscientious Christian with a strong personal faith, the most spiritually inclined among the brothers. All through his early years there were men of considerable piety around him at court. Among the chaplains and priests of the household, plus the network of connections with abbots and bishops and other high office holders of the church, there was considerable interaction with the family. It may be here, in the religious more than knightly caste, that Robert found some compensating strengths for his father-deprived character.

And yet, it may be the case that William the Conqueror was in fact more like his son than he cared to admit. Perhaps, in Robert, he did see a reflection of himself, but not the one he wanted. In later life, as attested by many chroniclers, William grew obese and had a predisposition to portliness that, as his activity declined, grew worse. He is not described by any chronicler as being tall, so it is at least possible that William the Conqueror was physically not very imposing. Perhaps he rejected these aspects of himself that Robert embodied. The father dominated by fierce warrior skill, indomitable temperament and a loud voice. None of these things was reflected back at him in the son. As time went on, and especially after the death of Richard, the Conqueror seems to have shown increasing favour to his other two sons who had learned how to play up to their father's expectations. William Rufus thrust himself forward, 'always obedient, displaying himself in battle' as Orderic Vitalis puts it. William's later history tends to justify the assumption that he held his father's regard and was more than capable of holding his own in battle; even putting himself in physical danger in defence of his father. Henry, too, according to William of Malmesbury, received his father's notice and attention far more than Robert. But this does not mean that they were free from a troubled relationship with him. The Conqueror lived to subordinate others; he was an overreacher who threatened all his sons with diminishment. Almost to the end of his life he blazed in battle, domineered over his family, manipulated his council and took every prize. These undoubtedly prodigious achievements threw all his sons into shadow. Robert found, and his life confirmed, that it was no privilege to be this man's first born.

Perhaps it is true that all his later troubles devolve from this first one. It is certainly a contributing factor in his exile. As a result of the cruel and insulting prank played on him by his brothers while they were at Rouen, and his father's failure to exact punishment, Robert is said to have rebelled by attempting to seize the castle the following day. Although he was not without followers, the attempt failed and he was forced to take refuge with a lord called Hugh de Chateauneuf-en-Thymerais, south of Normandy and close to the territory of the King of France. Philip, King of France, might have been, in some respects, the father figure he was looking for. There are indications that he got on better with Philip than with his father. He may even have been knighted by Philip who was actually his father's overlord, Normandy being theoretically held from France, a niggling fact that the Conqueror did his best to ignore. Certainly, Philip was to prove a confederate in Robert's battles against his father, but that was likely to have stemmed from mercenary motives.

Robert married but had no legitimate children by this first union. His wife, Margaret, brought him Maine and for a time he was known as Count of Maine. When Margaret died, he went on to lay claim to Maine in his own right, as well as the title of Duke of Normandy. All such appeals went unheard. From now on there was a spiral of declining relations which achieved their most dreadful climax when Robert actually wounded his father in a skirmish. This went beyond violent quarrelling in a family dispute. The total breakdown in their relationship was now involving too many other people, landed families, the young entourage of Robert's supporters, the knights and followers of William. Why should these men die in dishonourable feuding? At this point, William of Malmesbury tells us, Robert was driven out by his father and went into exile, seeking aid from Philip of France and his mother's relatives.

This breach took three years to heal. It was probably thanks to his mother, Matilda, that some sort of reconciliation was reached in 1080. Robert travelled to his father's court to witness a charter in Rouen. A formal occasion, stiff and cold, but the beginnings of something better. At least the Pope, Gregory VII, was pleased, writing Robert a letter full of wise sayings and admonitory urgings, the sort of thing his mother was saying to him in the hopes of a family reconciliation. It seems that William was persuaded to give Robert some responsibility. After spending the summer together in Normandy, William sent him on a mission to Scotland, tasked with establishing peace between England and Scotland, a mission which was, to a degree, successful. While in Scotland, Robert was asked by King Malcolm to stand godfather to his new daughter, Edith. This formal religious sponsorship strengthened the political agreement, and it seems that Robert took very seriously this spiritual bond which was to have repercussions later in his life.

Robert's misfortune was that at the very time relations with his father might have been improving, although still subject to tempestuous outbursts, his mother, the peacemaker, the soother of inflamed egos, died. In 1083 William the Conqueror lost his most loyal supporter, his helpmeet of thirty years, and entered a time of increasing troubles. William in mourning became even more remote, so that while at court Robert was isolated. His uncle Odo, Bishop of Bayeux, was imprisoned, Archbishop Lanfranc was no longer able to help him, his mother was dead, his brothers alienated. As his father's temper worsened, he suffered constant public humiliation from sniping rebukes and name-calling. Destined never to meet his father again, he went into exile, or rather he went off to trawl around the petty states of Europe looking for support in his effort to assert his right to Normandy. At least in these years we cannot accuse him of laziness. He fathered illegitimate children, he attempted to remarry, he paced about the borders of Normandy, took part in skirmishes, meanwhile biding his time in the neighbouring county of Ponthieu until, in 1087, he heard the news that would bring him release.

***

When their father died in 1087 his sons were too busy jostling for position to grieve. In a sense, reading the chroniclers' versions of this momentous death, the Conqueror had already declined from the heroic status of warrior, a dominator in the world of cross-channel politics, the unstoppable leader and powerful personality who could subdue nations and armies. He had become morose, obese, taciturn, his bad temper had alienated some of his household and was leading him into risky battles. As we have seen in an earlier chapter, his death was painful and long-drawn-out which invited many instructive homilies from the chroniclers on the vainglories of the world. Certainly, the classical ideal of a gentle passing, crowning a life of good works surrounded by friends and family, was not the fate of William the Conqueror. Almost at once the brothers took up their stances on the dual inheritance of enormous power and wealth that their father seemed deliberately to have left unclear. William left a poisoned legacy in many ways. It was now almost certain that the three brothers whose fraught and troubled relationship had been laid down in childhood by their father was not going to improve upon his death.

In 1087 William Rufus asserted his right to the throne of England. In order to do so, to focus on the full seizure of power in a transfer that was always going to be contested, William recognised Robert's right to inherit Normandy. So, at long last, Robert secured the inheritance he had always desired. The confusing, loathed and admired figure of his father was removed; he entered upon his rightful inheritance. What would he make of it?

According to the chronicler who writes the most detailed account of Robert's rule of Normandy, he found himself, almost from the first, beset by factions. Orderic Vitalis is, however, writing about thirty years after the events he is recording, and is sometimes drawing on 'common opinion' and hearsay. But there seems little doubt that over the ensuing years Robert's reputation was mixed. On the one hand he was 'bold and daring, praiseworthy for his knightly prowess and eloquent in speech' he was also accused of exercising 'no discipline, either over himself or his men.' He was criticised for 'being too merciful to supplicants; unable to pursue any plan consistently', 'lavish in his promises' but 'thoughtless and inconstant'… 'through his wish to please all men,' Orderic tells us, 'he either gave or promised or granted whatever anyone asked.'

This is very interesting. In the terms of eleventh century statecraft, this is the portrait of a fool, a prodigal and ineffectual ruler, unable to control those around him. According to another set of terms, however, here is a generous, forgiving man, wishing to do good to as many as ask, with an ear inclined to mercy and a deep, insatiable need to please. It is easy to read these virtues as inherently Christian, fundamentally belonging not to the warrior but to the monastic class. Orderic may unconsciously be giving us an insight into the real nature of Robert. Stripped of the constant necessity to prove himself in the eyes of his father, he could become the self he had always felt himself to be. Had he been born the second or third son, he might have been allowed to go into the church, to become a monk, an abbot or bishop, situations far more fitted to his nature than that of eldest son to the Conqueror. And indeed, the weight of that burden had deranged his nature to such an extent that he was unable to hold Normandy in the long term.

***

The great exception to the unfortunate life of Robert Curthose could be said to be the four years he spent abroad in the armies of the pilgrim warriors who went to the Holy Land to liberate Jerusalem. Success finally crowned his endeavours. At last, far away from the people and scenes of his past, he was able to shine as a warrior of Christ, finding victory on the field and winning a reputation which had eluded him up till then. Here he encountered the kind of fighting suited to a totally different terrain and conditions which required deploying armies in formations that had not been seen since the days of the Roman Empire. Finally, Robert and his fellow commanders were able to put into effect some of the precepts of *De Re Militaria*, the premier military guide and the leading handbook of warfare of the period. This Roman treatise, written by Publius Flavius Vegetius Renatus, would have formed part of the education of the knightly class. A staple of theoretical military instruction, it was very well known at the time. It taught military principles and emphasised such things as the training of soldiers, strategy, maintenance of supply lines, leadership and use of tactics. But it is unlikely that the military aspect of the enterprise alone drew Robert to the Holy Land. Personal piety undoubtedly played a part in this decision, but how great a part we do not know. The enterprise was turned into a penitential pilgrimage, though its real goal was war and the winning of territory. Salvation through warfare was offered when, in 1096, Pope Urban promised the remission of all sins to anyone who took part. Perhaps it was a mixture of Christian commitment and the chance to shine in a sphere that had not been monopolised by his father, that led Robert to undertake the arduous penitential work of the fighting pilgrim. For whatever confused and multifarious reasons, Robert decided to take the oath to participate but then found he was faced with a problem. He was cash poor. He had no resources with which to fund the enormous expenses of such an undertaking. Where could he get the money?

In 1096, clearly seeing what needed to be done, and with the help of the Pope, Robert began reconciliation negotiations with his brother William Rufus. At Easter intermediaries were travelling between the English court and Rouen in an attempt to settle differences and raise funds. What emerged from these negotiations was an extraordinary piece of diplomacy that amounts to one of the greatest land deals of the medieval period. In short, Robert was to raise the money for his foreign adventure by leasing his duchy. Normandy was put out to lease and William Rufus was to pay the term. For the princely sum of 10,000 silver marks Robert pledged Normandy to his brother for a term of years. Some chroniclers say three, some say five, some say that whenever Robert repaid the loan, the duchy would be returned. Knowing a bargain when he saw one, William raised the money within six months and Robert received the cash at a ceremony in Rouen in September 1096. Since William, like most of the courtiers in England, believed that Robert would never return to claim the duchy but would perish abroad, probably of disease, he viewed his lucky bargain as another miscalculation by his brother. William and Henry sensed a misstep, an error, a wild impossible gamble, a folly beyond credence, a typical blunder by their luckless long-slighted brother.

That this folly translated into Robert's golden years of warrior success and the garnering of fame was unforeseen at the time and is rather surprising now. But this episode is unique in his life. Like the pilgrim he was, cleansed of his sins and honoured in service, he re-entered the scene four years later, utterly changed. Endowed with a reputation, a new bride, a wealthy father-in-law, and enough money to pay back the loan, Robert returned home in 1100. His misfortune was that he came too late.

***

After his success with the pilgrim armies, Robert fatally delayed his return and thereby missed the greatest opportunity of his life. Instead of immediately returning home with the treasure awarded by a grateful Emperor Alexios Komenos of Constantinople, whose call for help the pilgrims had answered, he squandered his time in Apulia, seduced by Count Geoffrey of Conservano who wanted a military hero as a son-in-law and was trying to fix up a marriage with his daughter, Sibyl. This delay meant that Robert did not arrive home in Normandy, with his shining reputation and new bride until September 1100. He had the cash to redeem Normandy from his brother William, with whom he had made the land deal four years before, and fully expected to do so within a short time of returning. He looked forward to settling into the reinvigorated rule of his duchy, aided by his reputation and his new wife, the wise and gentle Sibyl, with whom who would one day get a legitimate heir. Unfortunately, he was one month too late.

When he arrived in Normandy, he discovered that not William, but Henry was now King of England. On August 2nd, 1100, William Rufus had been shot dead in Brockenhurst Forest, whether by accident or design no one knew, or pretended not to know. With a breathtaking swiftness of reaction, Henry had raced to London and had himself crowned in Westminster within three days of the death. On August 5th, 1100, Henry became King of England and in that ceremony he deprived Robert of making a legitimate claim. The deal with William was voided, Henry would never honour the terms. Robert had missed the opportunity to make a bid for William's vacant throne; missed it by one little month. Henry had grabbed the greatest prize, leaving him nothing more than the remnants of a leased-out duchy. No self-respecting son of the Conqueror could submit to such a state of affairs. He would have to rouse himself to contest his Henry's actions. And that meant war.

As we have seen in an earlier chapter, almost as soon as Robert arrived back in Normandy his charisma left him. All the success and glory of his military endeavours in the

Holy Land, his spectacular success at Ascalon, where he led the charge into the Fatimid camp, seizing the banner and treasure, his fame as a 'soldier without fear', his chivalric reputation, all deserted him with the thoroughness of a dispersing dream. Normandy diminished him; once again he was merely Robert Curthose. In the following months, although realising that he needed to act swiftly to raise an army against his brother, Robert achieved almost nothing. As we have seen, it was not until Ranulf Flambard escaped from the Tower of London and took refuge with Robert that his fortunes turned. In July 1101 a Norman army disembarked at Portsmouth with the intention of winning a throne for Robert. But the ensuing events constitute a string of misfortunes as his proposed attack declined into delay, hesitation, poor decision-making and eventual capitulation.

After a period of hesitation in Portsmouth, waiting to see how many of the barons would support his invasion, Robert prepared for an assault on Winchester. This royal city, ancient capital and site of the royal treasury, the first city in which Henry had declared his seizure of the crown, was a great prize. Unfortunately, he had delayed so long that by the time he was ready to move into the attack Henry had already brought up his army and was ready to defend it. Worse, he discovered that his goddaughter, Edith, daughter of King Malcolm of Scotland, was stranded defenceless in the city, at risk of a premature accouchement. Edith, the baby to whom he had stood sponsor in 1080 when on a mission for his father, was now a young woman of twenty. In the interim of Robert's absence fighting the heathen, Edith had married Henry and was now not only his goddaughter but his sister-in-law. Her presence at Winchester, therefore, confronted him with something of a quandary. To attack the place where she was lying in distress and pain was unthinkable. So he withdrew his army and moved towards Alton, drawing Henry's troops in his wake, intending to give battle there. Robert's position was still strong. Some of the Anglo-Norman barons who had been wavering, came over to him. Robert de Bellême, one of the fiercest of the fence-sitters, declared for Robert, bringing his brothers, Arnulf of Montgomery and Roger the Poitevin with him. These men were representative of those powerful families who held lands in both England and Normandy. When both territories had been under the rule of the Conqueror, they served only one overlord and knew where they stood. Now the unified realm had split in two; under Henry in England and Robert in Normandy, the nobility found their allegiances divided. Did they want as overlord Robert with his lackadaisical ways, who would allow them a free hand in their own fiefdoms, or did they prefer Henry, the interfering, over-controlling legalist who would curtail their lawless proceedings? The answer was obvious, and they declared for Robert. But, so aggressive were they, so incapable of concerted action, so surly and argumentative that they very soon fell out among themselves and began advising Robert in so many conflicted directions that he was actually in danger of losing his superior position. Having wrongfooted Henry, he had now delayed so long that the momentum was lost and when the idea of negotiations was mooted, Robert agreed to talks.

Robert has never received any credit for the number of lives he spared by not fighting at Alton or anywhere else during this invasion of England. Instead of unleashing the full effects of war with all its accompanying horrors of starvation, torched villages, rape and slaughter, Robert talked. And in the course of talking, undid everything he had undertaken in the past year.

Perhaps it was crucial that these talks were private. Robert and Henry met alone in an epoch-defining confrontation that would decide the fate of England for a generation. Without advisers or counsellors, who would inevitably intimidate or try to control the proceedings, Robert was unsupported by anything but his own character. He and Henry spoke together without attendants and so, unfortunately, there is no record of this momentous conversation, only the results of it which, in the coming days, would be transcribed into a document whose terms can still be read. But during the course of that conversation Robert, for good or ill, pledged away a crown. With the Peace of Alton, or the Treaty of Winchester as it is often known, Robert's pretensions to the throne of England were rendered null. He withdrew from the fight and would never again be in a position to contest Henry's rule in England. Indeed, he was forced to spend the next six years trying to defend his control over Normandy. Again, the medieval allegory of the wheel springs to mind. The ever-turning wheel of fortune which had been at the topmost point during the four years Robert spent far away from the scenes of his previous life, spun downward within a year of his returning home. The invasion that had begun so well ended in failure and by September 1101 he was back in Normandy, surrounded by disaffected barons, lukewarm supporters, fence-sitters and potential rebels, trying to hold on to his inheritance.

A pattern seems to be repeating itself. Once again Robert finds himself having to fight for Normandy. He had been wrong to think he could just come back after four years and take up where he had left off. The delicate scales of influence in the church, the heavier weights of power among the barons, had shifted; a new king in England nullified contracts with William, and the newly concluded Peace of Alton trapped him in solemn oaths and undertakings.

By the kind of irony that was to mark Robert's misfortunes the day on which the treaty terms were promulgated was August 2nd, 1101. One year to the day since King William had been killed. It had taken Henry exactly one year to put his claim to the throne of England beyond doubt. In the Great Hall at Winchester Castle, King Henry and Queen Matilda sat under a canopy on a raised dais. Robert of Meulan, Henry Beaumont, Richard Redvers and sundry attendants stood nearby. Further back, the king's official staff, Roger Bigod, Hamo Dapifer and Urse d'Abetôt were in attendance. Duke Robert sat opposite his brother, flanked by his remaining barons. There was a hush and sense of expectancy as they waited for the terms to be announced.

In the first clause of the treaty Robert formally relinquished his claim to the throne of England. To many of those in the hall, this was barely credible. Such a renunciation meant that everything he had undertaken in the past year was, by this brief announcement, set at nought. In exchange for this capitulation, Robert was to receive a pension of 3,000 marks annually from his brother. Why was Robert agreeing to be bought off? Although Henry was extravagant with money promises, he did not always pay. It was also notable that Henry did not renounce his claim to Normandy, although he did promise to surrender all his lands there, except Domfront and Contentin. Then came a mutuality clause: the brothers agreed to help each other recover the lost domains of their father; unspecified, but doubtless referring to Maine and the Vexin. This clause was worrying for it had the potential to relocate the war in Normandy where most of the assembled magnates held estates. This is indeed what happened.

Next came the issue of amnesty. Here the treaty showed its double face, looking both ways. The clauses were contradictory and time sensitive. Amnesty for offences occurring in the present crisis of 1101 was guaranteed, but offences occurring both before and after that date were not covered. In other words, the treaty ruled out action against the barons simply for having backed one side or the other in the present crisis, but it would not protect them from other crimes, past or future.

Next came a survivor clause. If either Henry or his brother should die without a lawful male heir, the other should inherit the entire Anglo-Norman estate. When this clause was announced, everyone looked at Matilda, rumoured throughout the whole court to be pregnant, while Duchess Sibyl showed no signs of bearing an all-important lawful heir.

In the final clause of the agreement, Robert freed Henry from the homage he had performed for his lands in Normandy and then recognised him as king. At a stroke the grounds for war in England had been removed. The clauses were recorded and would later be set down but hardly anyone who heard them could believe their ears. Some even wondered about the state of Duke Robert's mind. Not only did he give up everything, he actually lost out on those clauses about mutual aid and survivorship. Where had the pilgrim-hero gone?

And yet it is difficult with hindsight to see the Treaty as just another of Robert's misfortunes. There is almost a glow of penitential surrender about it. What Robert did at Alton was to spare life, renounce war, lay down the arms of opposition and accept the status quo. Had there been some kind of spiritual revelation in the Holy Places of the East? Had he been doubly transformed, first into a holy warrior, then into a man of peace and penitence? But again, with the cruellest irony, the penitential peace of Alton laid the groundwork for the next years of constant fighting to hang on to those parts of Normandy which he still controlled. Henry's aim now would be to de-stabilise the duchy, urging on the most violent and lawless elements, subsidising treachery and undermining Robert with every tactic to be found in Vegetius' handbook and more. In the Treaty of Alton Robert may have declared his preference for peace, but Henry had not.

***

Over the next few years Henry deliberately set out to de-stabilise Normandy as a policy to weaken his brother's rule. Having waged war on the most lawless barons, Robert de Bellême and his brothers, Arnulf de Montgomery and Roger the Poitevin, he successfully booted them out of his kingdom. They went off to Normandy, where they had immense estates and a large power base and started making trouble. The fall-out from the banishment of Bellême was soon being felt in the duchy and Robert found himself confronting a situation which required decisive and vigorous response. Yet again, he failed to apply such methods and, in fact, began to make a series of dreadful mistakes. Instead of quashing Bellême as Henry had done, Robert sought to buy him off with the conferment of lands. The town of Argentan, the forest of Gouffern, with all its valuable timber reserves, even the rights over the bishopric of Sées, were handed over to Robert de Bellême. A chaos of violence and lawlessness swept through Normandy in exactly the pattern of private warfare that Henry had vowed to banish from England.

Duke Robert, utterly out of his depth, frequently short of cash and with inadequate resources, was often a hair's breadth away from total disaster. In the midst of all this turmoil another blow struck. His new young wife, Sibyl, who had recently borne him a son, died suddenly. There was some mystery around her death. Rumours that she had been killed by a plot or had bound her breasts too tightly after childbirth tried to account for the unexpected death of this lovely and popular duchess.

Grief may account for what he did next, although sudden action of an inappropriate nature often marked Duke Robert's response to events. Even so, his arrival in England, unheralded and without a safe conduct, towards the end of 1103, caused dismay at court. Such a thing was tantamount to throwing himself on Henry's mercy. Then it became known that Duke Robert had turned up in England to press a case on behalf of one of his barons. Alarming though this was in itself and suggestive of a disturbed state of mind, it was even more incredible when the baron in question was revealed to be none other than William de Warenne who had been banished by Henry in 1101.

Did the dreadful case of the bereaved duke make calls on Matilda's compassion? He was her godfather, her brother-in-law, and he had refused to assault Winchester when he knew she was in the town, pregnant and ill. For all these reasons, she may have pleaded with Henry not to treat him harshly. Certainly, Henry allowed him to come to court and put his case.

There is no clear record, but it is possible that Henry consulted the disgraced former minister, Ranulf Flambard at this time. Certainly, Flambard understood Duke Robert's mind better than anybody and Henry was astute enough to seek out information from any reliable source. In whatever way he came to the decision, Henry granted Robert's request and restored the banished Warenne's estates. In return, Henry demanded the allegiance of Warenne for all his estates in Normandy. Since he recouped the financial loss of Warenne's estates by withholding Robert's pension, Henry came out of this deal marginally stronger.

Meanwhile, in Normandy the situation was declining by the day. Barons who had previously supported Robert Curthose were drifting away. He had been forced to do a deal with Bellême in order to strengthen his power. Henry, meanwhile, in preparation for what he was going to project to the world as a necessary intervention, was busy making friends in Normandy. Norman churchmen were now appealing to Henry for help, along with the people of Domfront and the Cotentin. Fleeing to England, Gilbert of Laigle and Ralph of Tosny offered Henry their strategic castles on the Seine, at

Conches, at Portes and Acquigny. Little by little, the pieces were falling into place. Henry would soon be in a position to claim the moral high ground in the battle for Normandy and his long-cherished dream of reuniting the two domains of his father would be realised.

But it had to be by right. Given Duke Robert's status as the legitimate ruler of the duchy and the prestige of his participation in the war for the Holy Land, Henry had to justify his actions. After all, he was about to invade a Christian principality and depose a lawful ruler. Since strong justifications would be required, his position would be considerably strengthened if he could set himself up as the defender of the Norman churches. Appeals from besieged prelates and harassed monks in monasteries laid waste by the rebel barons, poured into the English court and were turned into the stuff of propaganda. Queen Matilda was drafted to write justificatory letters to the pope, to Anselm, to Hugh of Lyon and other prominent churchmen. The stage was being set for a climactic struggle for Normandy.

On Easter Sunday, 1105, a sermon was preached in the village of Carentan in Normandy. Sermons were being preached all over Christendom on that day, but this one was noteworthy and has been recorded. In a little church stacked with the precious belongings of frightened villagers, King Henry of England stood listening. Present in the church that day were Henry, his close advisers and the nobles and followers who had come from England with the object of seizing the duchy from Duke Robert. The sermon they heard amounted to a justification for what they intended. It was a piece of propaganda, possibly scripted by Henry's advisers and delivered by the ousted Bishop Serlo of Sées. It fell roughly into two parts. The first part was an impassioned justification of the invasion of Normandy which Henry was about to undertake. 'All Normandy is dominated by banditry and lacks a true ruler. Look around and see everywhere the result of savage depredations. Fear, alarm and outrage stalk the land. No man feels safe, either for himself or his chattels.'

In the second part, Bishop Serlo addressed Henry personally:

'We implore you to rise up boldly in the name of God, win the heritage of your father with the sword of justice and rescue your ancestral lands.' There now followed a personal attack on Robert. 'Your brother does not truly hold Normandy, nor does he govern the people as a duke ought, leading them along the path of righteousness. Sunk in lethargy, he is dominated by men of little worth. He squanders the wealth of a great duchy on trifles and follies.'

This was the kind of travesty to which Duke Robert was subjected in his lifetime. It is pure political propaganda. But as a piece of rhetoric designed to heighten the image of the 'saviour king', this defamatory sermon was undoubtedly effective. The speech underlines the irony and misfortune that dogged Robert all his life. A pilgrim-soldier of high reputation is reduced to a squanderer and trifler. While Robert is traduced in these scurrilous terms, Henry is sanctioned by the church to seize his brother's patrimony.

From April to June Henry's campaign swept its way across western Normandy with only sporadic and largely incompetent opposition. By summer, Henry was in control of all western Normandy: the Cotentin, the Avranchin, Bessin and two major west Norman cities: Bayeux and Caen. But this grand military endeavour turned out to be only a dry run for the real thing. No major battle was fought that year and thus the situation was unresolved. It was not until the following year, 1106, that Henry and Robert would meet in the long overdue set-piece battle that would define the future and settle their differences once and for all.

Tinchebrai is not a name that resounds through English history, or even history of the early medieval period. But it is a battle that marks the point when England and Normandy were brought under one rule for the first time since the death of the Conqueror in 1087. In terms of its consequences, it might well be described as the second greatest misfortune of Robert's life.

In the stormy autumn of 1106, with thunder, rains, miserable damp conditions, mired tracks and soggy ground, Duke Robert gathered his resources. Formidable allies such as Robert de Stuteville, Robert de Bêlleme and William Count of Mortain still held firm but were few. After a long delay, William de Warenne, whose fealty had officially transferred to Henry on the restoration of his lands, finally got around to declaring his new allegiance and left Duke Robert's camp. Soon after, Henry targeted Mortain's castle at Tinchebrai, building a siege castle and attempting to choke off supplies. The count, who was Henry's cousin, had long been an avowed enemy. A jealous schemer and long-time grudge-bearer, Mortain was reproved by the chroniclers for his 'shameless arrogance' and 'turbulence.' However, Henry's strategy of building a siege castle and investing the stronghold failed since Mortain continued to supply the fortress through the lines of the besiegers. As a result, Henry was forced to tighten his grip. At length, unable to hold out indefinitely, Mortain called on Duke Robert to bring forces to raise the siege. After some time, Robert set out, on the way issuing a pointless warning to his brother to withdraw. By now many people, including his own supporters, were baffled by Robert's reluctance to fight. How could a man of his lineage and experience, living in times when war was the touchstone of power, risk losing his whole patrimony by such inept and sluggish proceedings?

After this inexplicable delay Duke Robert headed for his vassal's castle at Tinchebrai which he reached in late September knowing that the coming battle might well be his last. Even now he seemed reluctant and was perhaps distracted by the fact that his four-year-old son might be left fatherless. The little boy, William Clito, was far away in Falaise Castle, protected by a few loyal henchmen. Falaise was the birthplace of William the Conqueror, the place where it had all begun, that long story of a family destroyed by the rivalrous pursuit of power, the oldest story in the world.

What Robert felt that day as he disposed his forces in the field we cannot know. His vanguard was led by William of Mortain, on whose estates at Tinchebrai they were about to fight. Robert de Bellême was given command of the rearguard. Edgar Aetheling, uncle of Queen Matilda, was placed at the centre, close to the duke himself.

These forces were placed in opposition to Henry's three contingents, one led by Robert of Meulan, one by Ralph of Bayeux, and one by William de Warenne. Henry kept his English and Norman forces in close proximity to himself, among them many of his illegitimate sons and high-born nobles, the scions of great families. Further off, somewhere in the rainy field, were men of lesser rank whose names have not been recorded. Count Hélias of Maine was in command of the armies of Maine and Bretagne, stationed at some distance. Because of the undulating, rain-sodden terrain, unsuitable for heavy cavalry, both armies were to fight on foot with the flanking support of light cavalry. These dispositions were put in place on the morning of 28th September 1106, forty years to the day since William the Conqueror had landed at Pevensey.

The battle lasted little more than an hour.

***

There is a letter, which can still be read, that Henry sent soon after the battle announcing his victory: "Henry, King of England, to Anselm, Archbishop of Canterbury, greetings and friendship," it began.

"We write to inform you that on a named and fixed day Robert, Duke of Normandy, with all the forces of knights and infantry which by begging or buying he was able to collect, fought with me furiously before the walls of Tinchebrai."

Few who knew Duke Robert would be inclined to agree that he ever did anything 'furiously.'

"In the end, by the mercy of God," the letter continues, "victory was ours, without great slaughter of our own men. In short, the mercy of God has delivered into our hands the Duke of Normandy, the Count of Mortain, William Crispin, William de Ferrers, the aged Robert de Stuteville and others to the number of four hundred knights and ten thousand foot and Normandy itself." While mindful that he is writing to the saintly Anselm and trying not to gloat over the victory, Henry can barely disguise his exultation. It was a tremendous victory which he makes sure to ascribe to God alone. But what has happened to the prisoners? Henry makes no mention of them. Within a month of the battle terrible rumours begin to do the rounds. Duke Robert has been blinded and kept in chains, Mortain has been butchered on the point of Henry's sword, old Stuteville has been slain, Duke Robert's son has been kidnapped by Henry and put to death. For a few months, while everyone hears of the victory, no-one knows what has happened to the vanquished.

When the truth began to emerge, later that year, it turned out that Duke Robert and the Count of Mortain were alive, uninjured and on their way to captivity in England. Old Stuteville, Edgar Aetheling, Crispin and Ferrers had been ransomed and released. William Clito had been spared and released into the care of one of Robert's most loyal supporters. Before Duke Robert took his last voyage to England, in a final act of subjection to his brother, he ordered all the castellans of Normandy to yield their fortresses and swear fealty to Henry. It was the last act of a man who had lost everything. Or perhaps it is better to say, a man who was surrendering everything.

By the end of the year a ship brought him to England where he was conveyed into the custody of Bishop Roger of Salisbury, one of the king's appointed co-regents during Henry's absence. While the Count of Mortain was sent to the Tower of London, Robert discovered he was to be imprisoned in a not unpleasant spot in Wiltshire, the Castle of Devizes. Since Duke Robert and Mortain were blood relatives of Henry it is assumed that they were not treated harshly. Not only because chroniclers were writing in defence of Henry's treatment of them, but because both men lived such remarkably long lives. The Count of Mortain lived for a further thirty-six years, dying in 1140 as a Cluniac monk of Bermondsey Abbey.

Duke Robert, who was allowed to keep the title of duke for the term of his life, lived until 1134, partly at Devizes and partly at Bristol, Wareham and Cardiff Castle. As we have seen in an earlier chapter, the last and greatest misfortune of his unfortunate life was to occur in 1128 when his only son, William Clito, was wounded in an insignificant battle and died a few days later. But Robert went on living, a further six years of solitude. It is most likely that he turned in these final years to study and reflection, to the pursuits of reading and prayer, becoming more and more monk-like in his habits, renouncing the world that had already renounced him. And so he went on, a man without a family, without heirs, without a duchy, without a following, a lonely prisoner who went on stoutly living in the quiet faith of Christian retirement a life that might, just might, have suited him all along.

Chapter Ten
The Obscure Life and Death of Edgar Aetheling

At the very beginning of his life, two facts about Edgar Aetheling clash. First, he came from a long line of old English kings; second, he was born in Hungary. As a possible heir to the throne of England, to have been born in Hungary was indeed to begin life obscurely. Worse, he was born in exile. His father, Edward, had been banished in 1016, many years before Edgar's birth. A more or less stateless figure, in danger of attempts on his life, Edward *père* settled far away from England, living on handouts and the goodwill of his wife's relatives. Perhaps all these factors were de-stabilising to the young Edgar, who, ever afterwards, in all the undertakings of his life, would have trouble in framing certainties. He was thrown into a volatile flux of political fortunes almost from his first days. He never worked out where to set his feet down without feeling the ground tremble beneath them.

For someone who lived a long and adventurous life and was well connected, he leaves very little trace in the records. Great portions of his life disappear from view; he is like a traveller voyaging in a distant vessel; we catch the merest glimpse of him from time to time as he manifests briefly on the horizon of this or that zone then passes on. The chroniclers Orderic Vitalis and William of Malmesbury supply these glimpses, as does the Anglo-Saxon Chronicle, along with a passing reference in the Domesday Book. But even when we have assembled all the sources, although we might establish a narrative of sorts, we find little insight into this fascinating, perplexing and obscure figure who had a walk-on part in so many of the great events of his age but never shone in the foreground of any of them, even though he had once been destined to inherit the throne of England.

As noted, Edgar Aetheling was the son of Edward the Exile and grandson of Edmund Ironside, who was King of England for eight months in 1016. When Ironside was murdered in November of that year, the young Edward was sent into exile, along with his brother Edmund, by the new Danish King Cnut. At some point thereafter he married a lady called Agatha, a daughter of the Hungarian royal house and a relative of the German Emperor, Henry III. The couple went to live in Hungary and had two daughters. Some time, around 1050, while the exiled family was living in Hungary, Edgar was born. He was the last child and only son of an ancient lineage, last of the House of Wessex, a descendant from that most famous of English kings, Alfred the Great. He was never to reap any benefit from these distinctions.

However, there was a moment when things looked really good for the refugee family. In 1057 King Edward the Confessor sent an embassy to Edward the Exile, summoning him back to England with his household. This looked like a welcome turn in their fortunes, proof that they had not been forgotten. A summons to England could mean only one thing: the promise of a throne. Finally, a rightful inheritance would be conferred on this unfortunate family. It is thought the Confessor had a plan to make the Exile his heir. Had that been the case, presumably Edgar Aetheling would have followed in succession and become king in due course. Their astonishment must have been great, however, when they realised that the person assigned to carry out the embassy to bring them home was none other than Harold Godwinson, himself a pretender to the throne of England. This was rather like sending a fox to invite a chicken to take over the barnyard. We do not know how the transport was managed or whether the family travelled overland or by ship. If by ship, as seems likely, did they return in the same vessel with Harold? If so, dare one even speculate about the amount of tension brewing in this scenario? In the light of subsequent events, suspicions cannot fail to be aroused, and sides taken. One almost feels the tension of that return voyage, uncertainty in the salt winds, danger in the grinding swells. Feet slipping on wet decks, perilously angled. As they ploughed back through the waves towards the English coast, did the returning exiles have any misgivings about what might be facing them, or were they full of rejoicing to be going home at last?

Edward the Confessor, who reigned from 1042 until 1066, was Edgar's uncle and may very well have been intent on reinstating his family at the heart of the court. Both Edgar and his father, Edward, bore the title Aetheling which was a traditional proclamation of destiny. 'Aetheling' was an old English word meaning 'princely' or 'throneworthy'. It was a designation rather than a name; it proclaimed a heritage and promised a future. But for someone whose life passed in obscurity this title was to become something of an irony, fortune's jest, a cruel deception.

One almost despairs that a life so long, so full of incident, so crammed with long journeys, a life that touched the powerful and famous all over Europe, should be so impenetrable to historians. Posterity has suffered a loss by not being able to reconstruct in more detail the life of this man. But there is a fascination with obscurity. A figure glimpsed in the mist is inherently mysterious. Why, for example, did this English princeling come to be born in Hungary? The obvious answer seems to be that when his father, Edward, married a daughter of a Hungarian king, he chose to settle in that kingdom. But he might have found patronage in many other Christian states nearer to home. In fact, the Kingdom of Hungary had only recently come into being, emerging as a Christian kingdom around 1000 with the coronation of Stephen I. After conversion to Christianity, despite some lapses into heathenism, it established itself as a political entity, opening up to trade with other Christian realms. An influx of artisans and merchants from the Italian kingdoms and the Germanic states, as well as craftsmen and peasants, helped revive the economy and develop an urban lifestyle in this feudal monarchy. Thus Hungary entered the Christian family of kingdoms where Christian marriages could be made. Even when considering the difficulties of travel and the huge risks involved, intermarriage among the princely families of far-flung kingdoms was distinctly not prohibited by distance. When we read in the chronicles about these marriages or about felons who 'fled into exile' often to distant places, we are talking about a huge undertaking, an arduous and very dangerous journey, subject to a thousand risks of shipwreck, robbery, and murder. Yet it is sometimes forgotten that during the medieval period, and before, many people made long journeys. Most were of upper social ranks, courtiers and ministers travelling on royal business, but long journeys were also made by soldiers, monks and pilgrims. King Alfred travelled to Rome twice in his life, overland, the first time when he was only a boy of five. The route to Rome was so well-used that there was an established system of hostelries for overnight stops, mostly maintained and run by the church. All journeying was risky and none of it was comfortable. Nevertheless, it happened rather more frequently than we might imagine.

Even so, the scope of Edgar's travels is remarkable, totalling some thousands of miles. From Hungary to England, then to Scotland, later to Apulia in the south of Italy which was dominated by Norman forces. He is recorded as travelling to the Holy Land on two occasions and perhaps even stayed there for a number of years. What was he doing? We don't know. Slight indications have him returning to England by way of the Byzantine and German courts where he is said to have been treated well. These imperial courts were far more powerful and opulent than the cash-strapped English court, but we do not know the impression they made on Edgar. We do know that, over a lifetime, Edgar clocked up a significant mileage. This must have furnished him with something of an experiential education; he was an observer of places and customs; he must have known many languages and been able to mix with a diverse range of people. But what he had by way of formal education remains a mystery.

Unusually, we know more about his sisters, Christina and Margaret, than about Edgar himself. In January 1066, at the time the Confessor died, Margaret was about twenty years old and had spent many years in the convent at Wilton.

It is said that she was reluctant to marry Malcolm Bane, King of Scotland, being more inclined to take the veil and dedicate herself to a life of prayer. Her later reputation as a lady of extreme piety, so marked that some even called her a saint, suggest that she may well have had a genuine vocation. But her religious inclinations did not prevent her from producing many children, one of whom, as already noted, was Edith, later Queen Matilda, wife of Henry I. As an uncle of Matilda, Edgar was therefore related to King Henry I. Royal intermarriage gave him international horizons and a complex web of personal connections. Through his mother, Agatha, Edgar was related to the Hungarian and German royal houses. Through his father, Edward the Exile, he was descended from the royal house of Wessex. He was the nephew of Edward the Confessor, at whose court he resided; he knew Harold, who became king in 1066; he knew William, Duke of Normandy who seized the throne later that year. In fact, Edgar became his hostage for a time. It is interesting to note that, of the many occasions when Edgar was captured, imprisoned, detained or otherwise disempowered, he was invariably released, turning up a free man again, even though in that capacity he may have represented some danger. Or was he freed precisely because something in him seemed distinctly *un*threatening?

    In those rare moments when Edgar steps clearly into the light of the records, as at Tinchebrai in 1106, it is on the losing side. Unfortunately, with a few brave exceptions, that is where he spent most of his life.

***

It was all meant to be so different. When the family of Edward the Exile arrived back in England at the summons of Edward the Confessor, it was with great confidence in the future. Surely it must mean that Edward the Confessor intended to nominate Edward as his heir. There was no candidate with more right of lineage, no-one more popular with the common people, certainly none more deserving. But, just days after their return, on April 19th, 1057, to the utter dismay of his family, Edward the Exile died. Was he ailing? Had he fallen sick on the long and dangerous journey which had only just safely ended? Or was there something more malevolent at work? Naturally, there are suspicions that this was a murder, a political killing, perhaps by Harold Godwinson who did not want any rival English claimants to the throne. Harold's family now established themselves as Earls of Wessex and the dominant force at the Confessor's court. Harold himself was a proven warrior and had a loyal following among the anti-Norman faction. Moreover, Harold probably knew he would have to go head-to-head with William, Duke of Normandy, for the throne of England when the Confessor died, so cutting down the number of rivals would be an astute, if ruthless, move. Again, all we have here is speculation. Edgar was a child at this time, a fatherless boy now in need of protection. For the next nine years the bereaved family found it at the Confessor's court. It may be surprising to some that, essentially, this was a Norman court. The Confessor had spent his early life in Normandy, surrounded by Norman relatives and when he assumed the throne of England at the age of 38, he was thoroughly Nomanised. During the course of his twenty-four-year reign Norman French became the dominant speech among the nobles and at court. So,

Edgar and his sisters were thoroughly grounded in the language and customs of Nomandy and spoke its language as a matter of course. But the more formal elements of Edgar's education are not recorded.

Around this time, the sisters, Christina and Margaret, were sent to the royal convent at Wilton which would supply them with a first-rate education. We know more about their formal education than about Edgar's because we can pinpoint both his sisters to the nunnery at Wilton in Wiltshire. The reputation of this house had not reached its full zenith, but it was already prestigious. After 1066, with the influx of English noblewomen escaping from Norman land seizures or massacres of their menfolk, it became a centre of asylum where women could find safety and perhaps a vocation. Educational standards were already good and later on, during the next ten or twenty years, would reach a par with the most outstanding religious houses in Normandy. Here, the sisters would have learned to read and write in Latin and Norman French and would probably have learned English well enough to read some of the ancient texts, including the religious translations of their illustrious ancestor, Alfred the Great. As an educational innovator, Alfred had done all he could to encourage scholarship and literacy in his kingdom among all classes. But the education of Margaret and Christina came to an abrupt end in the New Year of 1066.

When Edward the Confessor, the family protector, died on the day before Epiphany 1066 (Jan 5th), Margaret was nineteen years old. She had spent most of her life in a nunnery and showed every sign of wishing to continue in the holy life, perhaps with a view to taking the veil. Christina, as far as we know, was also devout and did eventually take the veil, becoming a nun at Wilton and later Abbess of Romsey. The Confessor's death was most unfortunate for Edgar. He was still too young to be seriously considered for high office. He was then anything between ten and fourteen years old, no age in which to engage in a deadly fight for a throne. He might be the most legitimate candidate, but legitimacy did not matter unless you had strong military backing and some political capital. Since Harold Godwinson had both, he seized the moment and had himself crowned. An act that found some favour among the English generally who gave him support as the most battle-tested English candidate.

While Harold's shield wall was drawn up on Senlac Hill during the battle that was destined to bear the name of Hastings and while the thegns of the Godwins stood on the heights, clattering their shields and roaring defiance at their enemies below, Edgar's family must have been wondering deeply about the outcome. Would it be better for them if Harold won? And if he failed, what should the Aetheling do? Get himself proclaimed in his place - an English King for the English people? If William won, should he still make the claim, staking everything on his lineage and legitimacy? Evidently, he had some support because the monks of Ely, in the process of selecting a new Abbot, sent to Edgar for confirmation of their choice soon after Harold's death. The Anglo-Saxon Chronicle tells us that: 'the local people expected he would be king, and the Aetheling gladly gave consent to it.'

It is interesting to consider that, amidst all the propaganda around William's victory at Hastings, and the justificatory story of the events leading up to it, given powerful visual articulation in the Bayeux Tapestry, there is no depiction anywhere of Edgar or his family. No representation at all. Some historians have drawn attention to this omission. Whether he should be there or not is a moot point, and irresolvable. What is perhaps more interesting is the symbolism of his absence. Again, as so often, you look for Edgar and he is not there. Fleeing before the unfolding of his destiny, just a step ahead, never seen clearly, like some particle that passes through space and leaves only a trace.

A faint trace appears on the skyline of London in 1066. When Harold was killed at the Battle of Hastings in October 1066, Edgar Aetheling was proclaimed king by some of his supporters. This was a risky and ill-thought out move since Edgar had no real backing and no army with which to oppose the fierce onslaught of the Conqueror's progress towards London. Over a period of six weeks sweeping in an arc through the countryside so as to approach London from the west, burning crops and villages as they went, the Normans progressed towards the capital. When they arrived in London and crowned the new king on Christmas Day 1066, Edgar Aetheling had no alternative but to come to terms with the Conqueror. Going out from the gates of the city with Archbishop Aldred, the Bishops of Worcester and Hereford, the Earls Morcar and Edwin, along with many aldermen and burghers, Edgar made his submission to William. He had just witnessed his inheritance taken from him in the most uncompromising terms and must have known, even though a great part of the English population would have supported him, that any kind of opposition was out of the question. Once the Conqueror had seized London and forced the recognition of the church, once he had been crowned, he was practically unassailable. It did little good to gloat that the coronation was botched, that a riot broke out, that part of the chancel was burnt, that the whole ceremony lacked dignity and gravitas. Once the Conqueror was installed in the kingdom, only God could put him out. Perhaps it is an indication that William the Conqueror rather feared the inflammation of nationalist sentiments when, several months after his coronation in the spring of 1067, Edgar found himself one of a number of leading Englishmen taken into custody and shipped off to Normandy. Whatever Edgar said or did to reassure the jumpy William, it must have worked because he was back in England by December the same year.

***

Our next glimpse of Edgar finds him fleeing over the border to Scotland two years later, taking his mother and sisters with him. Again, if you reflect on the magnitude of that little word 'fleeing', implying a journey of some four hundred miles if the starting point was London, on bad roads, through countryside riven by faction and the de-stabilization of war, open to roving bands of starving dispossessed people, robbers, deserters, and the flotsam of unsettled times, this was an undertaking of great risk and hardship. In mitigation, we are told by the Anglo-Saxon Chronicle that this journey was undertaken in summer, that the fugitives were accompanied by one, 'Maerleswein, and many good men with them' and that they had already received the protection of King Malcolm of Scotland who evidently recognised the young Edgar's potential for fomenting discontent in England.

Malcolm was determined to oppose the Conqueror and over the next thirty or so years he did so in a constant round of battles, truces, treaties and more battles.

This King Malcolm, known as Canmore, was the man who killed Macbeth, taking the throne from him at the Battle of Lumphanan in 1057. By the time Edgar and his family arrived in Scotland, nearly ten years later, Malcolm was firmly established as king and had two sons, Duncan and Donald, by a wife, Ingebiorg, who soon disappears from the chronicles. Presumably she had died, perhaps in childbirth, as so many women did. This was the situation into which Edgar brought his sisters and, within a year of their arrival, a marriage deal had been done. Margaret, the highly educated, devout young girl who had wanted to be a nun, would become Queen of Scotland. The Anglo-Saxon Chronicle suggests some pressure was put on Edgar to persuade his sister to this marriage, claiming it was 'against her will' but the chroniclers argue that it was manifestly the will of God that such a pious and saintly consort should have come Malcolm's way. In the Worcester Manuscript they write: 'The foreknowing Creator knew beforehand what he wanted to have done by her because she would increase the glory of God in that land…' Which is more or less to say that this was a marriage made in heaven.

By her elevation through this marriage, Margaret becomes an important figure both in the development of Roman Christianity in the Scottish church and in the sophistication of the court. Having grown up, like Edgar, on the Continent, she was familiar with some of the royal courts of Europe and some of their leading churchmen. Indeed, when she later founded Dumfermline Abbey it was to the Italian

Lanfranc, now Archbishop of Canterbury, that she turned when she wanted monks for the original community there. She was considered worthy of a 'Life', a work commissioned by her daughter Edith-Matilda whom we have encountered as Queen of England in an earlier chapter. The title of this work: 'The Life of Saint Margaret' is already proclaiming as fact what it is in reality proposing. Unreliable as to fact, it is rather a statement of piety and pious intentions, but the commissioning of such a work indicates a serious intention to establish an afterlife of devotion. The spirituality of Margaret's 'saintliness' contrasts strongly with her obstetric history. Here we can find more substantial details. Saint or not, Margaret was the mother of a large brood, six sons and two daughters, Matilda and Mary. Thus Edgar was uncle to several future kings and queens of Scotland and England. However, in sharp contrast to his sister's career of public esteem and private fertility, Edgar was never the subject of a hagiography, never married, never, as far as is known, had any children.

***

While his sister settled into her new regal role, Edgar was entering a new phase of life as a rebel. We next glimpse him participating in the great northern rebellion of 1069 when he is at the head of Northumbrian rebels who enter York. Later that year he is sighted amongst northern nobles raiding into Lincolnshire by ship. This rebellion, like all the rebellions that were to follow in the next few years, was ruthlessly put down. William lived up to his title, Conqueror. It was not a grace and favour title; he did not get it because he won a battle at Hastings. William got it because he carried out the most relentless and thorough subjection of the kingdom. Conquest through complete suppression; Conquest as total victory and supreme control. And in the north of England, where rebellion was most fiercely entrenched, Conquest by fire and slaughter on a devastating scale.

Probably in pursuit of rebels, the Conqueror came north in 1072 and put pressure on Scotland which resulted in Edgar being expelled from Malcolm's court, despite his sister being queen. He is glimpsed in Flanders in 1074, then again in Scotland the same year. Frenetically looking for a post and a purpose, he hurries hither and thither, belonging nowhere, dragging around with him his lineage and title which have actually become irrelevant in the new Norman age. Finally, he concedes to the new reality, makes peace with the Conqueror, and spends the next few years at his court. William of Malmesbury, a chronicler writing many years after these events, criticises Edgar for these indolent years, but one can imagine that he was still trying to find his way. He was now about twenty-five years of age. He had lost a patrimony and had not yet found a role. He had a place at two courts, neither of which was satisfactory to a young man of ambition and a sense of destiny. William kept him at court without employment, without honour, without lands, save for two estates in Herefordshire at Barkway and Hormead which he had acquired by 1086 for they are mentioned in the Domesday Book. It may be during these years that he struck up a friendship with Robert Curthose, the king's eldest son. As we have seen in an earlier chapter, Robert was often subject to his father's indifference or outright mockery. His brothers, Henry and William, were contemptuous of him and he was in dire need of friendship. It may be that he found it with Edgar. These two young men were of an age, they felt marginalised, they were not given the honour and trust befitting their rank, they both felt resentful of the tricks fate had played them, they both had grounds for dissatisfaction with their lot. Perhaps Edgar and Robert spoke of these things together, being drawn by their thwarted expectations to share something of their hopes for the future, perhaps in the course of these conversations they spoke of the 'great deeds' of knight errantry, where young men of mettle slay foreign dragons, or plunge into the dreamt glory of faraway battles.

The next time we glimpse Edgar he is on the high seas with two hundred knights in tow, heading off to Apulia in the south of the Italian peninsula in pursuit of adventure. Apulia was then under Norman rule, having been conquered over the last several decades. By 1080 Robert Guiscard, one of the Hauteville family, was able to call himself Duke of Apulia and Calabria. He controlled great swathes of the territory by pressing down hard on the people and was in the process of consolidating his territory by building castles and fortified towers. Presumably Edgar sought him out at one of these strongholds and offered his services. But we can only guess. There is no record of what he did in Apulia. No story survives of his time there, no rumour of his deeds, his presence goes unnoticed, he is not even a shadow on a wall cast by the blinding Italian light.

In 1087 he is back in Normandy, at the court of his friend Robert Curthose who has, in the meantime, become Duke in succession to his father, the Conqueror, who died that year. At last, in Normandy, Edgar is given land and favour by his old comrade and becomes one of his principal advisers. Finally, he feels he has been granted work worthy of his abilities.

Robert needs friends. His brother William, his childhood antagonist, has laid claim to the throne of England. The Conqueror's reign is over, now it is the time of King William Rufus. But Duke Robert feels that he, as eldest son, should succeed to his father's throne, not William. And so a war, or rather a series of battles, is waged between them in the years 1087 and 1091. These sporadic, indecisive encounters ended in defeat for the unfortunate Robert and the obscure Edgar, two soulmates in failure. King William Rufus not only asserted his right to the English throne but began to cast envious eyes at Normandy and the next few years were filled with crises, aggressive diplomacy and outright battles. Many times, defeat in these battles did not consist of military failure but of failure in the negotiations afterwards. These were often no more than one-sided truces where too much was given away. Discontent followed and led to renewed struggle. The Anglo-Saxon chronicle reports on these events in some detail, many times with the comment that though the protagonists 'parted in great reconciliation, it did not last long.' At one point, negotiations between Edgar and Robert on one side and King William Rufus on the other went so badly wrong that Edgar was ejected from his Norman territories.

At another time, Edgar was banished from Scotland. No matter how many times he was imprisoned or how many times he was banished, Edgar always found a way back. He must have been infinitely flexible in his approach to events and people; he surely had some kind of charm or social suppleness, a quality of pleasing or placating. Maybe he was just likeable in some indefinable way. A pliant, forgiving nature may have been his chief strength. However, many times he turned up on the wrong side, or supported this or that lost cause, he always seemed to stage a comeback.

Edgar is sighted again in 1097 in just such a role. Having been pardoned by William Rufus, he is spotted leading an army into Scotland where he is charged with putting his nephew Edgar on the throne of Scotland after the demise of his brother-in-law, Malcolm. This he seems to have done with some success, but what reward he gained from William Rufus the Anglo-Saxon Chronicle does not tell us, nor how long he spent in Scotland. Perhaps he took the time to visit the Abbey of Dumfermline which his sister, Queen Margaret, had founded years before. There he might have said prayers for the repose of her soul. She had died in 1093, three days after her husband and eldest son had been killed in the battle of Alnwick. Her early death, some said from a broken heart, did much to enhance her reputation which had been consolidated by many holy works over the years. She was buried before the high altar at Dumfermline Abbey. It would have been fitting if Edgar had taken the time to kneel there and reflect on the fleetingness of life and the unaccountable turns of fortune that the Creator sends to mortals. In a penitent mood he may have asked for forgiveness, although the chroniclers fail to give us any details on specific transgressions. Again, he is no more than a shadow in the records, a shade without substance, without even that most defining of all moral substances, sin.

The next glimpse we have of Edgar, at an uncertain date sometime between 1098 and 1100, finds him hurrying off to take part in a pilgrimage to Jerusalem. Orderic Vitalis places him in the Mediterranean fleet on the way to participate in the holy war to liberate the city from the heathen. These facts are unstable but, since we know that Edgar's friend, Robert Curthose, was among the soldier-pilgrims who responded to Pope Urban's preachings in 1095 and took up arms to liberate the Holy Sepulchre, it is at least possible that Edgar fought under his banner.

William of Malmesbury suggests that Edgar made a pilgrimage to Jerusalem in 1102 but this is without much evidence. Some modern historians have suggested that Edgar served in the Varangian Guard of the Byzantine Empire around this time, which, if true, would lend Edgar the kind of cachet that a member of special forces might carry today. The Varangian Guard was the elite bodyguard of the Byzantine Emperors, largely composed of warriors from Northern Europe: Norsemen, Danes and Scandinavians as well as English and Normans, who were outside the tribal loyalties and intense rivalries of Byzantine politics. They were used to suppress revolts, manage discontent, protect the Emperor, maintain the security of the palaces and sometimes fight in battles. Organised along the lines of the Roman Praetorian Guard, the unit cultivated a reputation for fierceness and incorruptibility.

Knowing what we know of Edgar, it seems highly unlikely that he ever became a member of this body of fighters, although he may have taken part in the pilgrim's war and received gifts from the Emperor alongside his friend and fellow-pilgrim, Robert Curthose. It is most likely that it is in the context of the Holy War that we find him journeying to Jerusalem in 1102. But if that is so, then Robert and Edgar had gone their separate ways because, by the summer of 1102, Robert is back in England laying claim to the throne.

As we have seen in an earlier chapter, William Rufus was killed in August 1100. With lightning speed, his brother, Henry, immediately seized the throne. Many theories have been advanced about this 'accidental killing.' It looks so much like murder that it is easy to draw erroneous conclusions. In answer to the question 'cui bono?' the culprit was surely Henry. But whether Henry arranged for the deed to be done or merely benefitted when it had been done by someone else, or whether he organised and paid that someone else, or whether he had nothing to do with the death at all and was merely the innocent recipient of divine beneficence, we do not know. There was no inquiry into the circumstances of the death at the time. At best, the events of the day can be pieced out from a variety of sources and given coherence, as attempted in Chapter Four.

Whether Robert suspected one of his brothers of murdering the other is not known but the situation makes for interesting speculation. What is striking about the events of that day, August 2nd, 1100, is the speed with which Henry put in motion his bid for the crown. It was late afternoon when the king was killed. By dawn the following day Henry had got himself proclaimed king by the senior barons on the scene in Winchester. He had taken the castle, seized the treasury and secured consent from the bishop. A mere three days later, on 5th August, he is in London being crowned by the Bishops of Hereford and London. These events are rapid, well-executed and effective. Whether they are long planned, plotted or carefully thought out, or merely the reaction to chance happenings, we will never know. But, in whatever way Henry came by the throne, Robert Curthose did not agree with his occupation of it.

We have seen how, even though successfully landing a fleet in an English port and disembarking an army, Robert's campaign against Henry faltered and failed. Within a very short time he had entered into one of those unsatisfactory, poorly negotiated treaties which had the effect of giving away the greater part of his gains. It is a feature of this period that, whereas a decisive battle might settle things for many years, negotiations which end in unsatisfactory resolutions quickly drift into renewed dispute and disaccord. The cause of this phenomenon can be found in looking at the protagonists. In an astonishingly high number of cases where simmering disputes erupt into outright violence, the leading men on both sides are related by family ties. This acts as an inbuilt brake on escalation. Family ties, often entrammelling religious connections through marriage, baptismal sponsorship or binding oaths, has the effect of fostering compromise with a view to limiting damage to property, reducing expenditure and sparing lives, and, even better, avoiding war altogether by negotiation. But this practice simply granted a peaceful interval without resolving the underlying problem that had caused the violence in the first place. This was the state of affairs that occurred in Normandy during the years after Henry took over the throne from William Rufus. Henry was not content with control of England; he wanted Normandy as well. Robert Curthose, feeling himself already cheated of the rightful succession to the English throne, was determined to hang on to the duchy at all costs. But he was fatally weak in allies and forces. As we have seen in the previous chapter, in the years between 1102-1106 the situation in Normandy degenerated into lawlessness and chaos. Robert's rule was constantly challenged by powerful noblemen such as Robert de Bellême who were fighting their own private wars, respecting neither the duke's authority nor the sanctity of the church. In response to this, setting himself up as the solution to the woes of Normandy, Henry determined to take control. And so, we come to Tinchebrai. Our last clear sighting of Edgar Aetheling.

Tinchebrai was an extremely short battle. Some said it lasted little more than an hour. The conditions were poor, constant rain and storms having mired the fighting ground, making the use of heavy cavalry impossible. Nevertheless, it was decisive. It settled things once and for all between the battling brothers. There would be no more skirmishes, no more failed treaties, no more broken bonds. Henry won outright on the battlefield on September 28th, 1106. Normandy came indisputably into his overlordship while many opponents were taken prisoner. Among them, not only his brother, Robert, but several of Robert's allies, named in the Anglo-Saxon Chronicle as the Earl of Mortain, William Crispin, Robert d'Estouteville and, of course, Edgar Aetheling.

It seems somehow fitting that Robert and Edgar suffered a similar fate at that battle: defeat and capture. These two had known each other for many years, they had shared a similar story of marginalisation, a failure to accede to the expectations of their inheritance; they had both sought glory in the Holy Land, they had both found brief fame and riches there and they were both taken into captivity at Tinchebrai when the battle was lost. While a great deal is known about what subsequently happened to Robert, only a few scant facts remain about Edgar. The Anglo-Saxon Chronicle tells us that he was 'seized' after the battle but was among those 'whom the king afterwards let go unmolested.' This is not surprising. Edgar was the uncle of Henry's wife. He had spent years at Henry's court. He was family. Also, and perhaps most crushingly, Henry had discovered that he was, essentially, harmless.

And now darkness really does fall. After his release Edgar more or less disappears, surrounded by a fog of rumours. He is believed to have travelled to Scotland late in life, perhaps as late as 1120 by which time he must have been around seventy. William of Malmesbury suggests he was still alive in 1125, writing of that year that Edgar: "now grows old in the country in privacy and quiet." In whatever way he spent his last years, Edgar's strange obscure life was crowned by a fittingly obscure death. The place, the date, even the location of his grave, are unknown.

We know nothing about his final resting place, but we can hope that, wherever it is, he does, finally, rest. As noted, before there was an unfixedness about his life, as if he lacked the ability or opportunity to settle anywhere, as if he could not work out where to set his feet. His life was a fugue composed of interminable journeys to somewhere else. Unusually for a medieval figure of his standing, he is not associated with any*where*, a place, a region, inherited land. He is not 'of' anywhere. This is a striking absence. What he has instead is the appellation, 'Aetheling' which is not associated with any physical location. Instead, it has distinction, it is full of possibility and potential. But it is a wish for the future without substance or attachment to any place. It proclaims lineage and predicts inheritance, but it confers nothing. In the end it turns out to be nothing more than a lifelong unfulfilled promise.

At his birth and at his christening the blaze of his lineage might have projected a life in the forefront of power as the King of England. Specifically, as the king who prevented a Norman Conquest. Given a slight adjustment of circumstances or the odd stroke of luck, the obscure figure of Edgar Aetheling might have been thrust into the historical narrative as the pivotal changer of history. Had his father, Edward, lived to inherit from the Confessor, and had Edgar succeeded in due time, extending the legitimate line of English kings beyond Duke William's active years, then the Conquest might never have happened, and all would have been different. William would have been deprived of the justification of removing a dubious pretender, Harold, and would almost certainly have failed to gain the vital backing of the pope. Edgar would have legitimately blocked the path to the Conquest. Indeed, perhaps it is not too much to say that Edgar's life, obscure though it was, held for a moment the promise, perhaps even the possibility, of an alternative national destiny.

Chapter Eleven
William Warelwast: A Double Destiny

The career of William Warelwast is one of the least well known and most fascinating of the early Norman period. His life was both extraordinary and obscure. Although we know tantalisingly little about his personal details, including where and when he was born, his public career is fairly well-documented. What we do know reveals a man of genuine ability in many areas of endeavour, supremely negotiation and diplomacy. His career spanned the great transformative years of Norman rule as he gave service to his royal masters in various branches of administration. He travelled widely on missions both secret and open, covering many thousands of miles in his active years. He was trusted by two kings whom he served diligently in tasks that varied from the difficult and distasteful to the downright unpleasant. He could be both a conciliator and a provocator, able to cajole, persuade, flatter and, when necessary, bribe and browbeat. He understood the intricacies of secular power and the arcane workings of church government and could handle sensitive issues sensitively. The success of the king's business was his purpose, whoever the king, whatever the task.

William Warelwast has every right to be considered the first professional civil servant in our history. "He was equipped to forward the interests of the government," writes the scholar R W Southern, "not by main force but by negotiation amidst the intricate issues of law and theology." There is no earlier instance in England's history of this type of official. The fact that he is not famous is a testimony in part to his success as a functionary. He is a pale figure when compared with Ranulf Flambard who, although conducting similar work for the same kings, progressed through his career like a comet visible to all, whereas William Warelwast remains unseen just below the horizon. The best civil servants avoid personal scandal and, though they may have their detractors, never embroil themselves in conflict. They have an eye to subtle shifts in trends, they keep ahead of policy, they manipulate situations.

William Warelwast was the embodiment of all this. He was what might be called 'a slick operator,' but even the slickest operator must, from time to time, tread on toes. Yet one of the more remarkable things about him is that, even his most serious detractors, the people he severely offended, were often mollified in the long term. Even Eadmer, who with some justification formed a low opinion of Warelwast, later veered in his opinion and seems to have revised his views. Or perhaps it was Warelwast who softened his approach as he aged. It is tempting to think of William Warelwast, the career administrator, the hard-headed negotiator and the first professional civil servant, as a thoroughly secular individual. However, it was usual for such men, at the end of their professional lives, to be rewarded with high ecclesiastical office. The ease with which they pass into the church hierarchy without any sign of penitence, conscience or embarrassment, and then turn out to be surprisingly effective churchmen, is a speciality of the times. William Warelwast's second career was as successful as the first and he continued to enjoy the respect of the church hierarchy and to remain close to the king. This remarkable figure touches the lives of many of the personalities in this book, sometimes with dramatic results, producing tense scenes and excruciating encounters. So it is intriguing to know that, while inevitably attracting hostility from his contemporaries, he seems to have escaped damaging censure in the long term. What was the secret of his success? Insofar as it can be told, his story is worth the telling.

***

Before the reign of William II, we have only the merest glimpse of William Warelwast. His unforgettable name probably derives from the area of Normandy in which his family originated: Ver-à-Val, near Yvetot in the Seine-Maritime, which lay about twenty-three miles north-west of the Norman capital of Rouen. It is not impossible that the young Warelwast gravitated towards Rouen, for cities always draw young men in search of employment or education. One of the greatest attractions in Rouen was the Romanesque cathedral which had been consecrated in the presence of William the Conqueror in October 1063, three years before his attempt on England when he was looking for all the help he could get from God and his representatives. Since Rouen was the seat of government and the cathedral was the primary see of Normandy, the attraction of this city to a young man eager to go places in the world was great, especially one in need of an education. It is possible that the young William found his way there and became attached to a monastery or a house of canons where groups of priests lived together under a certain 'rule.' Although often attached to a cathedral, the priests of the 'canon houses' were not necessarily monks but were usually educated and conducted their lives according to the rules of the church.

Some disparaging chroniclers refer to Warelwast as "illiterate" but this is unsubstantiated. It is also unlikely because no-one could have pursued the career he did without a high degree of education. Diplomacy conducted at a superior level throughout Europe, both in the ecclesiastical and secular spheres, called for a high standard of competence in rhetoric, law and theology. Public speaking would have been a necessity, as would an ability to prepare speeches or arguments and to deliver them at short notice. And it should not be forgotten that other sorts of knowledge were called for.

Royal diplomacy involved extensive travel to and from the continental courts and to St Peter's in Rome. These were long and gruelling journeys. From Rouen or London to Rome could take anything from three weeks to several months. Travelling required planning and organisation, especially when large amounts of money were to be carried on the journey. All these things had to be put in place and a diplomat had to recruit staff to do it. In addition, a traveller had to have a certain level of social *savoir-faire*: how to address the clergy and nobility en route, how to avoid falling into the hands of bandits, how to get the best from associates, workmen, villagers and horses. And, above all, how to be discreet among strangers.

Everything about William Warelwast's subsequent career suggests that he must have possessed some or all of these talents. He would also have required a formal education, both in Latin and in canon law, perhaps in rhetoric as well because he became an accomplished speaker, eloquent and daring, not to say belligerent at times. He was extensively involved with written documents: attesting writs, witnessing charters, carrying top secret letters between courts and, on at least one occasion, ensuring that illegal messages were not being smuggled out of the country.

We have no real evidence that Warelwast served William the Conqueror although it is possible that he came to notice as a chaplain or clerk in his household at some time before 1087. The king had an eye for spotting talent in his secretariat and often gave advancement to able men of undistinguished birth. Ranulf Flambard was one, William Warelwast may have been another. But the first reliable references in the documents appear early in the reign of William II, that is, after 1087. He was by now a royal clerk. Between 1087 and 1095 he established a reputation for professional reliability sufficient for the king to send him abroad on a particularly delicate mission in 1095. At this date William Warelwast steps into full view as an accomplished negotiator in a complicated high-stakes case involving a king, an archbishop and a pope. Here we can follow his first known mission. The background can be sketched as part of the ongoing power struggle between the church and the king.

Ever since William Rufus had nominated him to the see of Canterbury in 1093, Archbishop Anselm had been making trouble. Not overtly, not aggressively, but simply by being Anselm, a man of conscience, a man who owed obedience to Pope Urban and would not come to a compromise with the king because the king did not recognise Urban as Pope. This complication lay in the fact that there were at that time two contesting papal candidates in Rome: Urban and Clement. Anselm, who until 1093 had been Abbot of Bec in

Normandy, had in accordance with Norman practice recognised Urban. But the king of England refused to be pushed into recognising a pope. He would not do so until he was ready, until he had got the greatest benefit out of his present course of keeping everybody guessing. One of the benefits of not recognising a pope was that there were, as a result, no papal legates in England. Like his father before him, William II resented the presence of papal legates. They were the pope's agents and informers, and they interfered in the governance of the realms to which they were dispatched. William had no desire to share his power with papal representatives and knew that the longer he delayed recognition of a pope, the longer he could keep them at bay.

At the same time, this situation was complicated by the fact that, to confirm him in the office of Archbishop, Anselm needed to receive a very important object from the pope. This was known as the *pallium*. An unremarkable object of almost wholly symbolic significance, the *pallium* was a piece of material worn around the neck by bishops and archbishops, denoting the pope's recognition of their appointment and their participation in papal authority. This little garment, of obscure historical origin, was of immense significance to Anselm, who considered that the *pallium* would convey the sanction and blessing of the pope. He believed it would give him spiritual authority and legitimacy in a role to which he had been appointed by the king. He was tormented by the illegitimacy of that appointment and still felt himself completely unsuited to the role. Anselm made it clear that, until he received the *pallium*, there would be no acceptable compromise between himself and the king. On the contrary, he would go on insisting that the king should recognise Pope

Urban, thus posing a challenge to William's sovereign right to exercise a choice. And William would go on refusing to do so, in defence of his inherited right. To William it was an important part of his sovereignty as a monarch. He would not consent to be advised by churchmen. Now, here was Anselm trying to force on him a disadvantageous course of action. It was a situation from which William Rufus could not see a clear way out. But Anselm's position, too, was complicated. He was being accused by the king's ministers of being a traitorous subject because he would not abjure his allegiance to Urban. Eadmer records that in a fraught meeting early in 1095 at Rockingham, the king threatened to exile Anselm who was forced to defend himself against accusations of disloyalty. Eadmer records his words on this occasion: "No-one can prove me false to the oath and allegiance I owe my earthly king because I refuse to abjure allegiance to the Pope. To anyone who tries, I will answer in the name of the Lord."

These issues may seem unimportant to us now, but they were of extreme significance at the time. Such controversies might cause a breakdown in relations between churchmen and princes, rifts between nations, even wars. The ramifications of this dispute could have the most serious consequences. But in spite of the bitter exchanges and angry accusations a compromise was reached at the last moment. Long discussions between the bishops and barons and representatives of the king and archbishop reached a finale when a peace package was hammered out, resulting in a truce between the two sides. The truce would run from the end of February to May 20th. Its terms were that, if no final resolution had been reached by then, Anselm would leave the kingdom with a safe conduct granted by the king and would be able to go to Rome himself in search of his *pallium*. The king implied that, if Anselm did so, he would not be welcome back in England and would, in effect, be going into exile.

***

Such was the complicated state of affairs, in effect a stalemate, that had been reached towards the end of February 1095, when someone, possibly Warelwast, came up with a creative idea. Why not, while the truce was in operation and Anselm had quietly taken refuge among his monks, why not send someone to Rome to get the *pallium*, bring it back to England and deliver it to the king before the date on which the truce expired? The king could then confer it on Anselm and bring the controversy to a happy conclusion. Or he could use it as a means to get rid of Anselm by immediately conferring it on someone else. This plan survived preliminary discussion by the counsellors and was put to the king who agreed. Anselm, having no idea about the arrangement and thinking that the king might be ready to make compromises by May, agreed to retire to his diocesan estates and await a reconciliation.

If it was William Warelwast who came up with the idea, it is likely that he also volunteered for the mission. In that event it is more than possible that he chose to take with him another canny operator with whom he worked in the king's household, a wily and capable clerk called Gerard Chancellor. We don't know how these men were selected, whether by the king himself or by his chief counsellors, but they must have attained a certain level of recognition for their smooth and subtle qualities, so necessary in any dealings with the papal court which was among the most corrupt in Christendom. Their object was to go to Rome, bribe and smooth-talk the Curia, secure the *pallium* and return with it before the expiry of the truce. But securing the *pallium* from a pope whom their own sovereign had not yet recognised was no easy matter. It would involve them in moral compromises, hypocrisy, false promises, or worse. How far would they be prepared to go?

Rome lies about one thousand two hundred miles from London. The road system was badly decayed since the days of the Roman Empire when a royal official could send mail from Britannia to Rome in as little as ten days. In 1095, even with favourable conditions, it would take at least three weeks to get to Rome. A further three weeks would be spent in negotiation, for the *curia* worked at snail's pace, and a further three to return, making nine weeks in all. March, April and the first two weeks in May. Could the king's two agents get to Rome, secure the *pallium* and return to England before the truce ran out?

Eadmer, as a loyal acolyte of Anselm, claims that Warelwast and Chancellor had secret orders from the king to offer the royal recognition of Urban as Pope in return for Anselm's deposition. This is unlikely. This view is partisan and therefore suspect, as also is the claim that the king wanted his agents to convey the *pallium* to him so that he could oust Anselm and appoint another archbishop. This, too, sounds questionable. Not because it would involve bribery, for that was almost certainly employed; not even because William would not have removed Anselm, but because that was not necessarily the outcome that would settle the issue.

What William really wanted was some sort of compromise with Urban so that he himself could have control of his kingdom and Anselm could properly function as an archbishop. So the ruse was not so much a conspiracy against Anselm, as Eadmer suspected and alleged, but rather a plan to move things forward in a direction favourable to the king. Eadmer's account of what happened is full of his suspicion and annoyance, no doubt the result of justifiable anger that such an important piece of diplomacy between the king and the pope had been conducted in an underhand manner without the knowledge of Anselm and his household.

What we know for certain is that the king's agents acted speedily. Leaving England, some time after February 28th, 1095, they completed the journey to Rome, conducted the business with the Pope and made the return journey in astonishingly quick time. Even today, negotiations at the papal court, notoriously rule-choked and ritualistic, can drag out for weeks. Yet by 13th May they were back in England reporting to the king.

How successful were they?

From Warelwast's point of view the mission must count as entirely successful. A journey of over two thousand miles had been accomplished within the strict time limit. Not only did he achieve an interview with Urban, with a partial settlement of some issues, but he also succeeded in getting the *pallium* and bringing it back safely to England. On the downside, it must be said that there was a rather unfortunate condition attached to the *pallium*. That is to say, actually attached to it. It came in the shape of Walter of Albano, a papal legate, who was assigned the safekeeping of the *pallium* until such time as it was delivered into the hands of

Anselm. He kept it at all times close by him and would not let it out of his sight. That this unlikely group, Walter of Albano, Gerard Chancellor and William Warelwast, made such good time on the journey back to England is truly astonishing. Landing clandestinely in Dover, the trio hurried across country to the court, avoiding Canterbury so that the monks would not be alerted to the disturbing news that a papal legate had entered the realm when the king had explicitly forbidden their presence.

By sending Walter of Albano as official guardian of the *pallium*, Urban prevented the king from using it as a means of ousting Anselm and installing another in his place. It underscored Urban's support of Anselm. On the other hand, it risked alienating the king who would be furious as soon as he saw a papal legate in England. Walter of Albano, however, was quite able to defend his master's interests and was a skilled diplomat who proceeded to mollify William with strong reassurances. The upshot was that Walter showed such persuasive politeness and made so many confident promises that he gave the impression that William merely had to express a wish and Urban would grant it. Thus reassured, William was soon ready to abandon his previous position on papal recognition. In the belief that he had received cast iron assurances from Urban that he would be granted freedom from papal interference in all matters if he did so, William recognised Urban's claim to the pontificate.

Then, during the days of discussion after May 20th, King William was delighted to discover that Walter's promises were indeed backed by firm assurances from Urban. All the royal customs and rights that had been in dispute would be granted for life. Moreover, Urban was ready to promise that no papal legate should be sent henceforth to England without the king's express command. Even more importantly, it was agreed that no archbishop, bishop, monk or clerk in England should receive or send papal letters without the king's authority. William now had control of the flow of information to and from Rome. This was an immense advantage. It meant that no cleric, at any level of the church hierarchy, could undermine his rule with complaints, appeals or allegations. It was the position his father had enjoyed. In return for the recognition of Urban as Pope and Anselm as archbishop, William had got the thing dearest to his heart – never to reduce by one jot the full enjoyment of his inheritance. And William Warelwast had been instrumental in bringing this about.

If we can see clear gains for William II and Pope Urban, can we see any for Anselm? Eadmer thinks not, but Eadmer was susceptible to the belief that the king was plotting to oust his master from office and would use the *pallium* to effect his ejection. That this was not the case was revealed later when it became clear that Urban had made the granting of royal privileges to William dependent on the continuation of Anselm as Archbishop of Canterbury. So, in a sense, everyone made gains but none of the gains was as satisfying as could be wished. No-one got everything, but everyone got something. But this has always been how the best diplomacy proceeds.

Undoubtedly Warelwast's part in all this was noted by the king. His first important mission abroad had not only been efficiently and effectively carried out, but the king had gained exceptional and unprecedented advantages. William Warelwast was establishing himself as a man who could be employed on the most difficult and delicate tasks. The spectacular success of the Rome mission allowed him to build upon his growing reputation as 'the wiliest clerk in England.'

***

There is one little coda to this story about the *pallium*. Eadmer gives us an account of what happened next and recognises the efforts of the king who: "…casting behind him the cause of their past dispute…restored his favour to Anselm and allowed him……to exercise everywhere throughout England the authority that belonged to his office." So far so good, but when Anselm was asked if he was now ready to receive the *pallium* from the hand of the king, he astounded everyone by saying 'No'. He bluntly refused. He resisted all persuasions. In spite of the reconciliation, he still could not, in all conscience, receive an object so deeply imbued with religious significance from a mere layman, even if that layman was the king. Anselm's blank refusal might have led to a further break-down in relations, but William was eager to exploit a favourable image by presenting the affair of the *pallium* as a diplomatic success. Keeping his temper and placating Anselm, the king devised a plan.

How far Walter of Albano played a part in what happened next is not clearly recorded, even by Eadmer, our chief reporter for this affair. Eadmer was no more fond of papal legates than the king, but the upshot was that an agreement was made whereby Walter undertook to go to Canterbury and place the *pallium* on the high altar of the cathedral, from where Anselm would retrieve it. A week later, on Sunday

27th May, a magnificent ceremony was staged at Canterbury Cathedral. Bare-foot, suitably mitred and wearing his episcopal robes, Anselm walked down the nave between massed ranks of monks and prelates and retrieved the *pallium* from the High Altar. At that moment it appeared to all the onlookers that he was taking it not from the king, not from the Pope but, as it were, from God himself.

Not all the disputes between the king and Anselm were to have this sort of perfectly scripted ending. When they next fell out, in 1097, it was over the issue of lands and fiefs and the quality of the knights Anselm had sent for William's war in Normandy. William pressed for money. In turn, Anselm pressed for permission to hold Church Councils, which was part of his plan to hasten moral reform in the church. The king took this as criticism of his rule. They were on separate and colliding paths; a final rift was inevitable.

It came in October 1097. The king sent for Anselm to come to Windsor urgently to discuss their differences. By this time, Anselm's position was again perilously close to treason. Refused permission to hold Church Councils, Anselm was now pressing to be allowed to go to Rome and was even threatening to go without the king's permission. In doing so he was putting a higher value on his allegiance to the Pope than to the king. This was not an impermissible stance for a churchman, if only he would be discreet about it. But Anselm was trumpeting his discontent up and down the country and, by playing the martyr to the king's oppression, was within a hair's breadth of treason. This was too much for King William. He would be better off without an Archbishop of Canterbury. Let him go into exile. Besides, when out of the country, William would seize his lands. The Windsor meeting was to be their last. Failing to reach agreement, Anselm was given eleven days to quit England and granted a safe conduct to the sea. He was then told that one of the king's officials would meet him at Dover and inform him of what he was, and was not, allowed to take out of the country. The appointed official was, of course, William Warelwast.

Anselm got to Dover on the day before the expiry of the deadline and there waited for the weather and tides to turn favourable. Several days went by but winds and lashing storms kept the boats inshore. When the weather improved, the winds were not favourable for a further few days. Anselm and his household hung about Dover in low spirits. At last, on November 8th, came the signal from the sailors that they were to embark. All the luggage was brought to the shore, bags and crates full of the personal belongings of his household which included his secretary, Baldwin, Eadmer, a few monks, minor officials and his servant, Adam. It was bitterly cold, and a strong wind was blowing. It was then that William Warelwast appeared and demanded to search the archbishop's baggage. Eadmer gives us a dramatic account of the incident: "So the bags and chests were brought before him and opened up and all Anselm's household chattels were overturned and ransacked in the hope of finding money, while a huge crowd of people standing round watched this disgraceful work, astonished at its novelty…" It is most unlikely that the search happened in this way and what Eadmer is really describing is his own outrage. This is the high point of Eadmer's anger against Warelwast. By contrast, some of his later accounts are considerably softer in tone. The incident was certainly alarming and perhaps, as Eadmer claims, unprecedented. But, as a professional diplomat with an eye to the future, William Warelwast would be unlikely to heap gratuitous insults on the departing archbishop who might, in after years, be recalled. Besides, with his own ambitious gaze set on a bishopric at some time in the future, it would be foolish to inflict so grotesque a humiliation on the 'Primate of all Britain.' It is more likely that he carried out the king's orders without needless offence, although there was no easy way to do it. He was looking for papers and illicit letters from discontented prelates, gifts for the pope, Canterbury plate and perhaps the king's coin. Since nothing of this sort was found, Anselm was allowed to depart for Normandy and William Warelwast returned to court. They would meet again.

***

William Warelwast's service to King William Rufus came to an abrupt end on August 2nd, 1100, when the king was shot dead in Brockenhust Forest while out hunting. Like many of his fellow servants, Warelwast immediately transferred allegiance to his brother, Henry, and was among his earliest supporters, most of whom ditched Robert Curthose, Duke of Normandy, whose claim to the throne, as eldest brother, was undoubtedly superior. Henry most probably recognised in Warelwast a man of shrewd and subtle intelligence who had served his brother well and should be encouraged to do the same for him. It was a trait shared by William Rufus and Henry that they were able to spot good servants, use them well, keep them loyal and reward them handsomely. Within a few days of Henry's coronation on August 5th, 1100, Warelwast was attesting a letter written by Henry to Anselm, asking the archbishop to return. Being called on to attest or witness a royal document was a sign of favour and probably meant that Warelwast was no longer simply a clerk in the royal household. This was the first of many tasks William Warelwast was to perform for King Henry while serving him loyally for the whole of his reign.

In 1101 Warelwast was again dispatched to the papal court where a great change had taken place. Pope Urban had died and had been succeeded by Pope Paschal II. But the old arguments rumbled on as the church still struggled to take away from laymen the control of investiture and homage. The granting of episcopal appointments by laymen was increasingly viewed as a scandal. Ecclesiastical offices were *spiritual* offices which only the church had the right to confer. Kings and princes might confer *temporal* power but only the church could appoint pastors to the people. Such was the church's reasoning. But kings and princes were perfectly aware of the immense wealth and power of the church and were not willing to give up that part of it over which they had some control. So the arguments went on, neither side wishing to concede. In 1103 William Warelwast was again in Rome confronting Pope Paschal in a case concerning investitures. In the intervening years he had grown in confidence and audacity. He was the king's representative. He did not mince words. He firmly declared that all present at the papal court must understand that King Henry would never relinquish the investiture rights which had been conferred on him by Urban. In response, Paschal swore equally firmly that he would never allow King Henry to keep them. These things were declared openly in public announcements. But then, as now, different deals went on behind closed doors and, for the moment, things were not pushed to a breach. But this controversy was to go on for decades in one form or another, occasionally reaching crisis point, then dying down until the next eruption. This ongoing and unresolvable controversy was behind one of Warelwast's rare failures.

In 1103 Warelwast and Anselm were sent on a joint mission to Rome to resolve another dispute between Henry and the pope, this time over the king's investiture of bishops. Anselm, of course, supported the pope's position. Whether the two emissaries travelled together, in whatever degree of harmony, on the long journey to Rome is not clear but Eadmer gives no account of it. He does report, however, that the king gave secret instructions to Warelwast. If the mission were to fail Warelwast was to instruct Anselm that unless he changed his mind and agreed with the King's position, he would not be welcome back in England. In other words, his lands, his *temporalities*, would be seized by the king and he would be exiled. Perhaps there was a certain inevitability in the fact that Warelwast, the bag-searcher of Dover beach, should be assigned to deliver this crushing ultimatum. But Warelwast, it appears, did not relish the task and showed none of the brazenness that might be expected. Instead, he seems to have quailed at the enormity of the charge as if he couldn't quite bring himself to deliver it, delaying until the last moment, putting it off as long as possible. Even the disapproving Eadmer can't quite keep that impression out of his account.

"When we left Rome," he writes, "William [Warelwast] stayed on there, giving out that he was bound by a vow to visit St Nicholas of Bari." (The saint's relics were kept in the Basilica di San Nicola in Bari.) Eadmer goes on to allege that Warelwast secretly aimed to stay in Rome and persuade the pope to alter his decision. If so, this failed, but he did obtain from the pope a conciliatory letter to the king, so as not to return empty-handed. Eadmer then notes that when Anselm and his party arrived in Piacenza on their journey back to England, they found William Warelwast already there "and were not a little surprised at the speed with which he travelled from St Nicholas." The tone of this terse remark suggests Eadmer suspected that Warelwast had not been completely honest with them and had never been to Bari. The two parties fell in and travelled together until they arrived at Lyon. It was late evening, too late to enter the city gates, so they took lodgings at a way station outside the walls. It was only then that Warelwast disclosed the reason for his presence.

Eadmer makes a point of recording his words: "I had hoped our case in Rome would turn out differently,' he said, 'and I have refrained until now from revealing the true state of affairs between you and the king. But, since we must part here, I have to tell you, the king will not welcome you in England unless you accept all those matters which you have so far refused to accept." That is how Eadmer records the scene which has, in spite of Eadmer's disapproval of the man, a certain sense that Warelwast did not relish this task, in fact found it embarrassing, even distasteful and had been putting it off for as long as possible.

The following morning, while Warelwast left for England, Anselm passed through the gates of Lyon into the walled city. He was entering exile. It would last for three years.

***

Long before a final reconciliation between King Henry and Anselm took place, that is to say, before Anselm could be recalled from exile, negotiations were going on and the same old questions were coming up. But by the summer of 1105 both king and archbishop seem to have been anxious for an agreement which would satisfy the pope. In July they met at a place called Laigle in southeastern Normandy and made what they called a 'settlement' although in their letters to the pope neither explained the terms of this 'settlement.' Other sources suggest that Henry was willing to shift his ground on investitures, at least sufficiently to satisfy Anselm and thereby present a united front to the pope. On the issue of homage, he was less amenable but since Paschal had been gradually dropping the issue of homage from his list of demands, the prospect that the pope would ratify the agreement seemed good. William Warelwast was almost certainly among the king's entourage of officials and ministers at this meeting, but what part he played in the negotiations is not known. The central issue was still there, irreducible and stark, how could a layman possibly confer spiritual office on a man of God? Anselm often said, "Christ alone is the door of the sheepfold." By this he meant that a layman confers only the emblems of office, the spirituality of office derives from God's grace alone. There is no doubt that Anselm firmly agreed with the Pope's stance on this issue, but he was uncomfortable being on bad terms with Henry and, in particular, with the queen.

Queen Matilda wrote frequent letters lamenting the quarrel and begging him to come home. The monks at Canterbury did the same. He was urged on every side to make a compromise, but he could never compromise his conscience on a profound spiritual issue. After the Laigle meeting Anselm went back to his monastery at Bec, the only place he ever really felt at home.

With the Laigle protocol threatening to stall, Henry and Anselm next agreed to send emissaries to Rome. Anselm was represented by his right-hand man, his long-serving secretary and head of household, Baldwin of Tournai. Henry was represented, as might be expected, by William Warelwast. This mission was more successful than the last and the Pope's ratification of the agreement of Laigle was given. Warelwast was able to report positively on the venture and to hand over a conciliatory letter from the pope. Meanwhile Anselm had returned to the monastery at Bec to await an outcome.

Although Henry had every faith in Warelwast to bring back a ratification of the Laigle compromise, he began to fear that he might already have delayed too long. At Laigle he had noticed how aged and frail the seventy-year-old Anselm had become. If Anselm died in exile, Henry's carefully constructed self-image of a monarch who could work with the church would be harmed. Having been promoting himself as a tough negotiator but a fair and principled monarch, he was intending to invade Normandy and seize it from his brother Robert Curthose. At a time when he was contemplating an outrageously aggressive act, it would be of immense value to have a calm and docile Archbishop of Canterbury back in England. But Anselm's health was precarious. There may not be much time left to bring him home.

In late May 1106, William Warelwast found himself again on an urgent mission. This time to Bec, under instructions to do everything in his power to persuade Anselm to return to England. He carried a letter from the king, pleading with the venerable prelate to accept his terms and come home. But when he went to present it to Anselm in person, he found himself detained at the doorway by Baldwin, his reluctant colleague from the trip to Rome, who told him that Anselm was ill. Baldwin would never really know whether Anselm's illness was physical or feigned. Sometimes he thought it was a genuine illness, but not of the body. Sometimes he suspected that it was an affliction brought on by the suppressed, unrecognised fear of being uprooted from Bec.

Bec was the only home he had known, having spent thirty years as monk and Abbot in its precincts and cloisters. There he had grown into Benedictine discipline. There he had presided in the chapterhouse, sung in the quire and prayed in the chapel. There he had written some of his great works. There, over three decades he had meditated, studied and developed his theology. He had spent his mature years instructing young monks and sending them out to take up the leadership of surrounding priories and abbeys. Bec was the place to which he had attracted a generation of scholars avid to read his treatises. It was the place where he was known and loved by many, his one secure home. It is possible that the thought of leaving Bec for good caused his spirit to fail and his body to fall ill. The scholar R. W. Southern, made the astute point that Bec monks always continued to be Bec monks, wherever they went or whatever their new status.

Frustrated by Anselm's delay and anxious to get on with his conquest of Normandy, Henry crossed the channel with his army. Leaving his force encamped, and accompanied only by a small escort, he then made a dash to Bec and arrived on August 15th, the Feast of the Assumption of the Blessed Virgin. Whatever the nature of his indisposition, within days of Henry's arrival Anselm was up and walking, eating with some appetite and ready to conduct a mass in the abbey church. This done, Henry and Anselm formally met, embraced and declared themselves ready to be reconciled. William Warelwast, a probable witness to this momentous occasion which he had done so much to bring about, might have felt a degree of relief when Anselm gave the king his sacred promise of an immediate departure for England. A joyful letter was despatched immediately to the Canterbury monks, alerting them to the imminent arrival of their pastor after three years of exile. While the king went off to rejoin the army that would, in September that year, 1106, conquer Normandy and take Robert Curthose captive, William Warelwast, having another successful mission to his credit, slipped back into England.

***

The year 1106 was a significant one for the Anglo-Norman world. It was the year in which Henry lost and won. He lost out on Investiture but won Normandy. Several things fell into place for him. Firstly, the pope held off from issuing an excommunication which would have seriously damaged his public image. He then met successfully with Anselm at

Bec who gave him a formal blessing and a solemn promise to go home. With good luck still clinging to his royal person, Henry went on to make war against his brother, Robert Curthose, and seized control of Normandy. He had been working towards this end for some time and everything came together after Bec. The publicity around the Archbishop's benediction had played into Henry's carefully-wrought fiction of setting himself up as 'the saviour of the Norman Churches,' thus making his grab for the duchy a matter of Christian duty. In these circumstances, the fact that he had sworn away his right of investiture hardly mattered. There is a difference between the right of a thing and the practice of it. As far as kings were concerned, the practice of investiture was bound up with the amount of power they had, and Henry had just hugely increased his power by taking Normandy from his brother. In reality, he had not given up the power of investiture in any meaningful way.

In the end, after years of discontent, of endless channel-crossings, of talks and meetings and compromises, the fate of Normandy was settled by an obscure battle fought on September 28th, 1106. As chance would have it, this was exactly forty years to the day since William the Conqueror had landed at Pevensey. The Battle of Tinchebrai has been distinctly unmemorable over the centuries. What happened on that rain-washed afternoon barely gets a footnote in the pages of military history. But it was at Tinchebrai, the Earl of Mortain's fortress sixty miles south of Caen, that the realms of England and Normandy were once again brought under the sway of one ruler as they had been in the days of the Conqueror.

Henry was now more satisfied, more powerful and more likely to be generous to his chief servants than ever before and William Warelwast knew that he was in the running for a reward. He had already been given the archdeaconry of Exeter and more or less promised the bishopric after the death of the incumbent, Bishop Osbern, in 1103. With the settlement of the investiture quarrel, the way was clear for Henry to keep his promises to all those loyal servants who had helped to bring it about. That Henry had sworn to renounce the right to invest candidates to ecclesiastical office was barely an inconvenience, for reasons we have noted. Moreover, his sudden increase in power gave him some protection against papal fury and the threats of Pascal, who was now unlikely to issue an excommunication. And so, in the following year, 1107, William Warelwast was created Bishop of Exeter. This was an undoubted reward for diplomatic service, the conferment of a lucrative and prestigious post for life.

His consecration took place on August 11th, 1107, at Winchester. The city was packed with a backlog of nominees waiting to be consecrated by Anselm, many of them well-known to him. Some were genuinely spiritual men like the scholar William Giffard of Winchester and Roger of Salisbury, the king's chief administrator and custodian of the imprisoned Robert Curthose. Less well suited to the religious vocation was Queen Matilda's former chancellor, Reinhelm of Hereford and the overly young Welshman, Urban of Llandaff. They had all been prevented from being consecrated by the intervening years of dissension over investiture. Now they were eager to take up their appointed offices. Whatever his private thoughts about the quality of some of the candidates, Anselm set to work, righting some of wrongs that had occurred during the long-drawn out controversy which had for so long held back from the church men of talent.

What Anselm might have been thinking as he consecrated in a solemn ceremony his long-standing antagonist, William Warelwast, we can only imagine. The sole indication we have of any reaction in Anselm's household to Warelwast's promotion is the slight softening of tone in Eadmer's account. William Warelwast was known as a worldly diplomat, an astute and wily royal fixer, a man without any experience of monastic life who only held an archdeaconry on the gift of the king. He had never been a friend to Anselm, but he had never acted or spoken against him either. He had never shown personal antagonism. As a servant of the king, a justice and envoy, a representative and diplomat, William Warelwast had taken an oath of service. And as a constant, loyal and devoted servant, he had fulfilled that oath. Eadmer's softened tone suggests that these things did not go unrecognised in the archbishop's household. Oath-taking was a sacred undertaking. Breaking an oath was a kind of sacrilege. On these terms, William Warelwast's conduct was not without merits to those whose whole way of life was based on sacred vows. Anselm would have appreciated that. There is, however, a touch of the tragi-comic in the spectacle of the bag-searcher of Dover Beach being made a bishop by the consecrating hands of his former victim.

After his elevation, William Warelwast continued to serve the king, as the frequent appearance of his name in the documents of the period attests. In 1108 he was again sent as a messenger to Anselm. This may have been their last meeting. At Easter the following year, Anselm died. What part the Bishop took in the ceremonies and masses conducted by the clergy all over England for the repose of Anselm's soul we do not know. But great and solemn mourning would have attended the departure of the illustrious Archbishop of Canterbury, Primate of the English Church, a scholar renowned throughout Europe, a man of outstanding intellect and high principles and a controversial figure to the end. Unfortunately for us, Eadmer's valuable insights dry up after 1109 and we get no more intimate glimpses of his master or of Bishop William of Exeter.

Warelwast continued to serve the king. We know that, as a royal judge, he heard a case in Tamworth in 1114. We have evidence that he was with the king in Normandy in 1111, 1113 and 1118 and may have been there more frequently. In Henry's reign, he witnessed twenty of the king's charters. In 1115 he was again sent to Rome to negotiate with Paschal who was angry that the king was still forbidding the presence of papal legates in England and was refusing to allow clerics to appeal to the papal court. These were prickly, longstanding issues and Warelwast was unable to resolve them, although he did manage to forestall any punitive sanctions against the king.

Like his contemporary and fellow royal servant Ranulf Flambard, William Warelwast pursued a second career as the bishop of an important diocese. For many years he conducted the affairs of the chapterhouse, introduced reforms, added to the buildings and represented the bishopric at Church Councils in Reims and in Rouen. He founded a house of canons in Bodmin, re-founded Plympton Priory as a house of Augustinian canons and made adjustments to the staffing of other religious foundations. Then, some time before his death, he fades from the records. Some chroniclers say that he went blind in his later years, that he resigned his office retired to Plympton and became a simple canon. There may have been certain things that lay heavy on his conscience for which he was seeking redemption. A lifetime of service in the higher realms of the state as diplomat, negotiator, envoy and advocate would certainly have involved moral compromises. He was adept at bribery, as indeed any envoy to the papal court had to be. In the rivalrous, cut-throat world of Curial politics, he had to be both sharp and subtle.

Perhaps it is fitting that the first professional civil servant in our history, who inhabited the shadowy world of court diplomacy and dealt frequently with a papal court mired in bribery and corruption, should be absent from the records at the time of his death. We do not have reliable facts about either his birth or his death. Some chroniclers record his death as taking place on 27th September 1137 and claim that he was buried in the chapterhouse of the Priory there. This date is plausible since his nephew, Robert Warelwast, succeeded him as Bishop of Exeter in 1138 and the *Annales Plymtoniensis* record that a certain Robert of Bath gave Warelwast the last rites on 26th September 1137.

William Warelwast outlived his master King Henry by two years, serving him faithfully to the end. His career foreshadows the development of what would later become a professional civil service. He presented the example of a recognisable type: proficient, loyal, resourceful, hard-working, morally flexible, pragmatic. For most of his working years he was close to the sources of power with all that implies by way of moral contaminations and compromises of conscience. During the last two years, fading from the records in the cloisters of Plymptom Priory as the country declined into anarchy, he might well have been reflecting on the purpose and cost of it all. By that time, Anselm, the victim of so much of his diplomacy, had been dead for twenty-eight years. Although many difficulties dogged their relationship for more than a decade, neither Anselm nor Eadmer, it seems, bore William Warelwast a lasting grudge. And so, perhaps we can hope that the bag-searcher of Dover Beach earned forgiveness at the last and died gently, with a good conscience.

Chapter Twelve
The Connecting Life – Anselm

The twelfth life of this series belongs, of course, to Anselm. His place is guaranteed by his overarching importance in this period. It is not by chance that he has already appeared in many of the previous chapters. His presence weaves itself into the lives of the other characters in this book and connects them. Without him, their portraits lack an important dimension. In a sense, Anselm has been a constant presence in these pages in innumerable references, in various ways, on numerous occasions. He strides through all the great episodes of English and Papal diplomacy in the years 1093 to 1109, travelling all over France and Italy in the course of his long and controversial life. He touched other lives for good or ill, in small ways or large. It was a life recognised by many as a holy life, a saint's life. Others saw him as a shrewd and canny negotiator, others as a man of unshakeable conscience, others as a devoted upholder of canon law and an obedient servant of the Pope. Still others saw him as a dogmatist and many English monks saw him as a sore disappointment to the English church, a *fainéant* archbishop who consistently failed to defend its distinctive rites and character. He was by no means faultless, nor universally popular. But ephemeral fame was never his goal. He was cosmopolitan in outlook, perhaps caused by his frequent periods of exile and extensive travel; a writer, a scholar, a theologian, a man who struggled against kings to defend the interests of the church but who maintained to the end of his life that he had never wanted to be anything more than a simple monk.

Over the course of the previous eleven chapters much of his story has been told. We see him intervening in the great love story of Gunhild and Count Alan, battling with William Rufus for four years before being exiled, crushing Eadmer's writing ambitions because of his overscrupulous modesty, unknowingly causing heartbreak to his greatest admirer. We see him as the dogged opponent of Ranulf Flambard in many royal disputes, as a spiritual adviser to Gunhild and frequent correspondent with Edith/Matilda. We see his battles and eventual reconcilement with King Henry, for he was always fearless in opposition but ready to concede when necessary.

Eadmer, his closest observer, has left us a memorable picture of Anselm in the 'Life of Saint Anselm' (*Vita Sancti Anselmi*) and the 'Recent Events in England' (*Historia Novorum in Anglia*.) With his alert, steady gaze, Eadmer was both his nearest critic and greatest admirer. He has left us vivid glimpses of the man at work, permitted us to catch the tone of his speech and revealed some of his characteristics. There are hints, too, of his insecurities and admiration of his intellectual prowess. Robert Curthose, William Rufus, King Henry - Anselm knew them all, the sons of the Conqueror and the Conqueror himself. From the highest in the land to the lowliest monk to whom he spoke words of sympathetic wisdom, Anselm touched innumerable lives. Argumentative, principled, always in denial of his own personal ambitions, Anselm was infuriating to work with, as Ranulf Flambard found on many occasions. His zeal to save both Gunhild and Edith/Matilda from losing their souls certainly caused pain and distress, but he would not flinch from hard truths on the path to eternal life.

Eadmer lived and travelled with Anselm for thirteen years. It was a journey that took him from blinkered devotion to wide-eyed disappointment. He knew Anselm better than most and never ceased in loyal service. It is from Eadmer that we derive the most intimate glimpses of Anselm's household, his private views and confidences, his memories and confessions. Intimate details are rare, but Eadmer seizes on them. We know that Eadmer did not lightly report information which he did not himself believe and Anselm was notoriously unforthcoming about his past. What we can piece together is a mere patchwork which makes this chapter the shortest in the book. Yet the man the monk and the prelate must necessarily rise to dominate not only this book but Eadmer's book as well as the lives of his contemporaries and the times in which he lived.

Anselm was born in Aosta, an Alpine town on the southern boundary of what was then the kingdom of Burgundy. When he was born, in 1033, Emperor Conrad II had recently added Burgundy to his empire so technically this moved Aosta into the Holy Roman Empire. His father, Gandulf and his mother, Ermenberger were, according to Eadmer, "both of noble birth, so far as worldly dignity goes, and living spaciously in the city of Aosta." Eadmer recounts that Gandulf had a reputation for "good-hearted generosity" and "as a prodigal and spendthrift," whereas his mother, was "blameless and upright". Eadmer suggests that at one stage "Anselm gave himself up to youthful amusements" and forgot about his studies or his desire for the religious life. These are hints merely, and nothing very detailed ever comes out in the account which rather suggests that Anselm did not want to talk about his early life. A few nuggets can be found but the style is such that we can barely distinguish allegory or parable from vision or dream. One 'dream' is recounted in some detail by Eadmer which may have come from Anselm's early life in Aosta. As a boy raised in mountainous country, Eadmer tells us, Anselm "imagined that heaven rested on the mountains, that the court of God was there and that the approach to it was through mountains." One night, Eadmer tells us, Anselm had a dream in which he saw himself climb the mountain and come to the royal court where he found God alone with his steward. God called him in, and he sat himself at the feet of God who asked him "in a pleasant and friendly way" who he was, where he had come from and what he wanted. When he had replied as best he could, God summoned the steward to bring food. In the dream fresh bread was brought, not just any bread but the "whitest of white bread", and not just white bread but the most glistening, shining (*nitidissimus*), heavenly bread which he shared with God in the radiant halls of heaven. Eadmer records the dream, but the style is such that we can barely distinguish it from parable or allegory. Anselm may have had such a dream as a boy, or it may be simply the sort of dream that the subject of a holy biography was *expected* to have. Whatever the case, it remains one of the few references to Anselm's early life.

The scholar, RW Southern, thinks the family was heading into 'decayed nobility' at about this time. Perhaps the father, Gandulf, was of the merchant class and was losing money, not helped by a spendthrift son. There are tantalising hints that the young Anselm fell out with his father and ran away, but details are scant because they were almost certainly deliberately suppressed. At some point Anselm went off to the monastery at Montecassino, having developed an urge to knuckle down and study. But then he left suddenly. He seems to have been directionless at this time, unsure what path in life to take. A serious vocation to become a monk would have surely taken him to Cluny where Odilo was Abbot. This foundation was about to become a major monastic centre of the region. Cluny Abbots became leaders in international affairs and the monastery would become one of the most powerful and prestigious religious houses in the Roman West. But it seems that Anselm was not sure about his career path and, like many young people today, spent two or three years testing different courses in life and travelling around Burgundy and France. In the end it wasn't Cluny that called to him and revealed his vocation, it was Bec.

The Abbey of Our Lady of Bec in Normandy was gaining a reputation for Benedictine leadership largely due to the presence of one man, Lanfranc of Pavia. This Lombard scholar, famous for his attractive personality and powers of organisation, was drawing recruits to the monastery. Eadmer calls him "a truly good man" (*virum videlicet valde bonum*) and one of "real nobility in the excellence of his religious life and wisdom" which had "drawn to him the best clerks from all parts of the world." Though by no means one of 'the best clerks' by any measure, Anselm was drawn and, on the advice of Lanfranc, some time around 1060, became a monk. Under the guidance of Lanfranc who became prior and master of the monastic school, Anselm seems to have settled down. For the first time since childhood, he rooted himself in a place and a routine, in a way of life, in a spiritual community and a society of scholars. Everything about Bec seems to have satisfied a need. He was to spend the next thirty-three years of his life there. When Lanfranc left in 1062 to become Abbot of St Stephen's Abbey in Caen, Anselm stayed on and eventually became prior himself. The chronology for these early years is murky and disputed but we know that Anselm spent the next decade, studying, writing, contributing to the community, championing young scholars and generally earning himself a reputation. On the strength of this he was unanimously elected Abbot of Bec in 1078.

In the meantime, Lanfranc, continuing on the upward path to high office, became Archbishop of Canterbury in 1070, appointed by William the Conqueror whose trusted adviser he then was. It is generally agreed that Lanfranc maintained excellent relations between church and state during his years of office; he worked well with William and steered the English church away from confrontations. Although he disappointed many Canterbury monks by failing to defend the old liturgy and rites of the English church or to protect its innumerable saints from obscurity, he did not on the other hand unleash a wholesale Normanisation of English practices. The distinctiveness of the English church was a matter of concern to Eadmer who registers a great deal of disappointment in the changes brought about by the Norman Conquest.

When Anselm followed his old mentor, Lanfranc, to Canterbury, becoming Archbishop in 1093, it was not to step smoothly into the succession. In the first place the seat of Canterbury had been vacant for four years. In addition, as we saw in earlier chapters, relations between the new archbishop and the young king, William Rufus, degenerated almost at once to the great disappointment of the Canterbury monks who were looking to him to defend the English church. The damage of the four-year vacancy could not easily be rectified. Lanfranc had been an able administrator, an organiser who grasped the needs and possibilities of the times. Anselm, by contrast, as RW Southern points out: "spent half his life in positions requiring business ability [but] never learned to love business."

From his beginnings in an Alpine town to the episcopal seat at Canterbury, Anselm travelled the real and figurative highways of a Europe undergoing great changes: intellectual, devotional, political and economic. During his long life of seventy-six years, he touched on all these areas, contributing theological works of great significance, living in accordance with Benedictine teaching, actively involved in political affairs, in synods and councils. Although much younger than his powerful contemporaries, he became a giant of the times, the equal of the great towering figures of William the Conqueror and Pope Gregory VII. R W Southern concludes his monumental *St Anselm and His Biographer* by saying: "He touched the thought, piety and the politics of the time at every important point; and whatever he touched looked different afterwards."

Perhaps we should let Eadmer have the last word about Anselm because without him we would know so much less. Towards the end of the *Vita Sancti Anselmi*, Eadmer gathers together some stories of the miracles that were said to have occurred after his death. Such tales were the necessary part of the afterlife of a candidate for sainthood, but Anselm had always shown himself indifferent to such ambitions.

Eadmer himself sounds affectionate but unimpassioned on the point of sainthood, perhaps content with having observed in Anselm a principled and righteous life, the life of a good man. That, in any age, is a rare and wonderful thing. At the end, addressing himself to his dead master, he writes: "I have written these things as best I could, O reverend father Anselm, to show the quality of your life." In the final lines of the manuscript, we hear Eadmer talking to him directly, "Farewell, therefore, my dearest father and advocate." He is addressing a ghost. When he wrote those words, Anselm had been dead for many years and he himself had become an old man. In spite of all the disappointments of his writing career, Eadmer is still bearing witness to Anselm's remarkable life even while his own is nearing its close. And he is still defending the integrity of his writing. "If anyone after my death shall add to what I have written," he warns, "let it be ascribed to him who wrote it, not to me. I for my part have here made an end."

CONCLUSION

It is ironic and tragic that the reign of King Henry I which kept the peace in England for nearly three decades should have been followed by a period of violent bloodshed called 'the anarchy.' On the other hand, it was entirely predictable. Could it have been avoided? Perhaps. The main contributing element was that Henry left no adult son to inherit. As we saw in the case of the Conqueror, it is risky to leave doubts about the succession because it will likely lead to war. Wise kings want a smooth transition, preferably when their eldest legitimate son follows in natural progression, surrounded by a loyal and capable administration. Henry was most unfortunate that his only legitimate son died in the White Ship catastrophe and again unfortunate that he failed to produce an heir with his second wife, Adeliza. Unfortunate again that his daughter, Maud, could not conceive a son with her first husband, Emperor Henry V, which might have given him an adult grandson at the time of his death. Unfortunate that, at the time of his death, both his grandsons from Maud's second marriage were no more than toddlers. The clear line of succession was muddied. Maud wanted to succeed her father but was up against gigantic prejudice against female rulers. Besides, medieval kings needed to lead in battle and, although not entirely unknown, this was very rare for a woman. Female warriors were looked at askance, always suspected of witchery or perversion, an abomination. A strong Queen might rule but she needed a strong man to take to the field. Such a man could always decide he wanted power for himself and so loyalty was always a problem. As might be expected, Maud's claim to the throne was resisted. Her cousin, Stephen, son of Henry's sister Adela of Blois, was the man who staked his claim. Thus began the Anarchy when these two cousins battled for the throne of England for almost two decades, creating such havoc that the monks called it a time when 'God and his Angels slept.'

Perhaps this is when the decline into oblivion began. Perhaps the horror of the next few decades radically denied Henry 1st a place among the premier monarchs. Today he is barely known at all among the wider public. There is no resonating story told about his reign. He is one of the least well-known monarchs of our history; an overlooked king, unfairly neglected, especially when you bear in mind the length of his reign. Thirty-five years on the throne is a remarkable achievement at any period of history but in the uncertain, precarious early Middle Ages it is almost astounding. Yet, Henry is an unknown figure, we don't learn about him, he does not appear on the school curriculum, he is absent from the national memory; no-one makes TV series about his reign and almost no non-specialist would be able to name a single prominent person from it. Years ago, in the 1962 Raleigh Lecture on English History, R.W. Southern put it like this:

"No English king in a reign of comparable length has left so faint an imprint on the popular imagination or even on the minds of students of history as Henry 1st."

In this respect, nothing has changed since 1962. Henry 1st is still absent from the popular version of royal history and from the cultural imagination. Hence this book which is, in some small way, an attempt to draw attention to the injustice of that situation. Without making undue claims, what happened in his reign is not only remarkable but also well recorded. There is a greater abundance and variety of documents for this reign than for any previous period and the story they tell is the essential one of beginnings. In fact, the origins of some of the most important English institutions, as well as modes and customs of English life, date from this reign. It is a period charged with significant inceptions, notable innovations and striking personalities.

In his lecture, RW Southern goes on to list an impressive catalogue of the achievements of the reign of Henry 1st:

"It is the first, and one of the greatest ages of historical scholarship […] we have the beginnings of the only purely English religious order; the beginnings of the University of Oxford; the earliest English scholastic writers; the rebirth of English science after a long decline. We have our first Charter of Liberties, which became the immediate inspiration of Magna Carta; the first foreign treaty in our history […] the first victory of foot soldiers over mounted knights, foreshadowing the victories of Crécy and Agincourt. We have the first treatise on English law; the first royal financial accounts; the first documents of manorial administration. For the first time it is possible to grasp in some detail the complexity of English government and society."

These are quite remarkable claims made several decades ago by a prominent historian of the period, yet still there is a massive vacuity in the national memory about King Henry 1st and his thirty-five years on the throne of England. Although his reign began in the bloodshed of his brother and ended in the darkening prospect of civil war as relatives fought for the crown, it was remarkably peaceful. England was largely cleared of factional infighting and the clash of war lords. Battles were fought in Normandy, but these were usually small affairs numbering a few thousand men on each side and of limited duration. Henry 1st deserves some credit for this. In an age of warriors, dominated by a war-like ethos and a predisposition to eliminate enemies on the battlefield, Henry's long reign stands out as one of considerable peace and prosperity. Few would claim him as a great king, but his long and steady reign established the roots of an increasingly civilised nation.

europe books